Fundam...

Fundamentals of Therapy

An Extension of the Art of Healing through Spiritual-Scientific Knowledge

Rudolf Steiner, Ph.D.
and
Ita Wegman, M.D.

MERCURY PRESS
Spring Valley, New York

This edition of *Fundamentals of Therapy* by
Rudolf Steiner and Ita Wegman is a translation
by Christa van Tellingen MD of the original German
*Grundlegendes für eine Erweiterung der Heilkunst
nach geisteswissenschaftlichen Erkenntnissen*,
Nr. 27 in the complete edition of Rudolf Steiner's works.

Editorial assistance provided by Susan Goodale,
Hendrik van Heek, Gerald F. Karnow MD, Dorit Winter.

Financial assistance, provided by the Foundation
for Rudolf Steiner Books and Pharma Natura, South Africa,
is gratefully acknowledged.

ISBN 0-929979-75-3

Copyright © 1999
By MERCURY PRESS
Fellowship Community
241 Hungry Hollow Road
Chestnut Ridge, NY 10977
USA

Dr. Rudolf Steiner
Dr. Ita Wegman

Grundlegendes für eine Erweiterung der Heilkunst
nach geisteswissenschaftlichen Erkenntnissen

MERCURY PRESS
Spring Valley, New York

1. Auflage Dornach 1925
Ungekürzte Ausgabe nach dem gleichnamigen Band
der Rudolf Steiner Gesamtausgabe
(Bibliographie-Nr. 27)

CONTENTS

Foreword 5

Translator's note 6

Chapter I
True Insight into the Nature of the Human Being
as a Foundation for the Art of Medicine 7

Chapter II
Why Does the Human Being Become Ill? 18

Chapter III
The Phenomena of Life 22

Chapter IV
On the Nature of the Sentient Organism 26

Chapter V
Plant, Animal, Human Being 30

Chapter VI
Blood and Nerve 34

Chapter VII
The Nature of Healing Functions 38

Chapter VIII
Activities in the Human Organism.
Diabetes Mellitus 42

Chapter IX
The Role of Protein in the Human Body
and Albuminuria 46

Chapter X
The Role of Fat in the Human Organism and
the Deceptive Local Complexes of Symptoms 49

Chapter XI
The Form of the Human Body and Gout 52

Chapter XII
Upbuilding and Secretion in the Human Organism 56

Chapter XIII
On the Essential Nature of Being Ill and of Healing 60

Chapter XIV
On the Therapeutic Way of Thinking 64

Chapter XV
The Method of Healing 68

Chapter XVI
Insight into Medications 72

Chapter XVII
Insight into Substance as Basis for
Insight into Medicines 76

Chapter XVIII
Curative Eurythmy 80

Chapter XIX
Characteristic Case Histories 83

Chapter XX
Typical Medications 106

Preface to the First Edition 113

Postscript 114

Appendix:
How did the Medical Book Arise?
    By M.P van Deventer 115
A New Mystery Book
    By W. Holtzapfel 117

Notes 121

INHALT

Begleitwort 4
I. Wahre Menschenwesen-Erkenntnis als
   Grundlage medizinischer Kunst 7
II. Warum erkrankt der Mensch? 19
III. Die Erscheinungen des Lebens 22
IV. Von dem Wesen des empfindenden Organismus 26
V. Pflanze, Tier, Mensch 30
VI. Blut und Nerv 34
VII. Das Wesen der Heilwirkungen 38
VIII. Tätigkeiten im menschlichen Organismus.
   Diabetes mellitus 42
IX. Die Rolle des Eiweißes im Menschenkörper und
   die Albuminurie 46
X. Die Rolle des Fettes im menschlichen Organismus
   und die trügerischen lokalen Symptomenkomplexe ... 49
XI. Die Gestaltung des menschlichen Körpers
   und die Gicht 52
XII. Aufbau und Absonderung des
   menschlichen Organismus 56
XIII. Vom Wesen des Krankseins und der Heilung 60
XIV. Von der therapeutischen Denkweise 64
XV. Das Heilverfahren 68
XVI. Heilmittel-Erkenntnis 72
XVII. Substanz-Erkenntnis als Grundlage der
   Heilmittel-Erkenntnis 76
XVIII. Heil-Eurythmie 80
XIX. Charakteristische Krankheitsfälle 83
XX. Typische Heilmittel 106
Vorwort zur ersten Auflage 1925 113
Nachwort zur ersten Auflage 1925 114

FOREWORD

When the present book appeared in 1925 anthroposophical medicine was still in its first beginnings. Today – 74 years later – this medical orientation is practiced not only in Europe, but also in the countries of North and South America as well as When the present book appeared in 1925 anthroposophical Australia, Africa and New Zealand. In the meantime it is practiced in more than 40 countries. Thus it is to be welcomed that the present American edition supplements the already existing English version and that the publishers have decided to print the German text side by side with the English text. The virtue of this will soon be evident to whoever works through this book. In reading it, it is not merely a matter of comprehending the content, but it is written so that ever deeper dimensions of medical knowledge are disclosed if the content is not merely worked through word by word, but attention is also directed – like in a work of art – to the placement of a word, an idea, a sentence, a chapter, in the context of the whole book.

This book contains all essential ideas basic to anthoposophical medical science and practice. The aim of this medical orientation is to complement and extend the prevailing natural-scientific medicine with the methods and content of Rudolf Steiner's spiritual-scientific investigations (called "anthroposophy"), so that a true human-centered medicine can arise to do justice to the spiritual existence of the human being as well as the psychological and bodily needs.

In the Appendix two articles are included which provide a helpful orientation regarding the history and the place in history of this unique book.

Michaela Gloeckler, M.D.
Medical Section at the Goetheanum
September 1999

BEGLEITWORT

Als das vorliegende Buch im Jahre 1925 erschien, stand die anthroposophische Medizin noch in ihren ersten Anfängen. Heute – 72 Jahre später – hat sich diese medizinische Richtung nicht nur in Europa, sonder auch in den Ländern Nord- und Südamerikas sowie Australien, Afrika und Neuseeland ausgebreitet und ist inzwischen in mehr als 40 Ländern zu finden. So ist es sehr zu begrüssen, dass mit der vorliegenden Ausgabe jetzt nicht nur eine die bisherige englische Ausgabe ergänzende Übersetzung ins Amerikanische vorliegt, sondern dass die Herausgeber sich auch entschlossen haben, den deutschen Urtext mitzupublizieren. Denn wer das Buch bearbeitet, wird bald bemerken, dass es hier beim Lesen nicht nur um das Verstehen bestimmter Aussagen und Inhalte geht, sondern dass es so geschrieben ist, dass sich immer tiefergehende Erkenntnisdimensionen erschliessen, wenn nicht nur Wort für Wort bearbeitet wird, sondern auch – wie bei einem Kunstwerk – darauf geachtet wird, wo ein bestimmtes Wort in einem Satz, in einem Kapitel, ja im Kontext des ganzen Buches zu stehen kommt.

Dieses Buch enthält alle wesentlichen Gesichtspunkte und Forschungsansätze, die der anthroposophischen Medizin zugrundeliegen. Diese will die gegenwärtig herrschende naturwissenschaftliche Medizin durch die Methoden und Inhalte der geisteswissenschaftlichen Forschung Rudolf Steiners (genannt Anthroposophie) ergänzen, so dass eine wirkliche Humanmedizin entstehen kann, die der geistigen Existenz des Menschen ebenso gerecht wird wie seinen seelischen und körperlichen Bedürfnissen.

Dr. med. Michaela Glöckler
Medizinische Sektion am Goetheanum
September 1999

Translator's Note

At the end of Chapter 12, in the third to the last paragraph, mention is made of the relationship between form and function of an organ. "Bone comes into being in the sphere of the ego organization. When its formation has been concluded then bone serves this ego organization, which from now on no longer forms it, but uses it for voluntary movements." The same organic relationship between form and function can be experienced in *Fundamentals of Therapy*. The more one studies it the more one finds out that the content of the book has determined its form to the finest detail. A study of the form of this book therefore will give important clues about the content, in addition to the text itself.

With this in mind, the attempt has been made to preserve as much of the original form in the translation as possible, as well as having the German text printed next to the English. Wherever possible, paragraphs and sentences were kept intact and the punctuation maintained. The German text is especially rich in verbs. Many of these verbs could be translated with the same English word since the differences in meaning are so subtle. For instance, in Chapter 5 mention is made of "*absondern*", "*ausscheiden*" and "*abscheiden*". These all point to an excretory activity. If they would be translated with the same word, however, chapter 5 would lose its meaning. Another example is "*wandeln,*" "*umwandeln,*" "*verwandeln,*" and "*ändern.*" They all point to change. Of these it is interesting to see that in certain chapters certain verbs are used more, even if they mean almost the same. then there are places in the German text where the subject is plural, and the verb would be plural in German and English, but in fact is singular in the text. These grammatical peculiarities have mostly not been corrected.

Some grammatical questions could not be solved, also not in the German text. Most of these are indicated with a note.

For future editions, improvements, corrections and emendations from interested readers are welcomed.

I would like to thank my patients and coworkers at Raphael House, Fair Oaks, California, who made it possible for me to do this translation. Special thanks to Hendrick van Heek, Gerald Karnow and Dorit Winter for assistance in the many tasks connected with getting this book ready for publication.

Christa van Tellingen, MD

I
WAHRE MENSCHENWESEN-ERKENNTNIS ALS GRUNDLAGE MEDIZINISCHER KUNST

In dieser Schrift wird auf neue Möglichkeiten für das ärztliche Wissen und Können hingewiesen. Richtig beurteilen wird man das Vorgebrachte nur, wenn man sich auf die Gesichtspunkte einlassen kann, die leitend waren, als die medizinischen Anschauungen zustande kamen, von denen hier gesprochen wird.

Nicht um eine Opposition gegen die mit den anerkannten wissenschaftlichen Methoden der Gegenwart arbeitende Medizin handelt es sich. Diese wird von uns in ihren Prinzipien voll anerkannt. Und wir haben die Meinung, daß das von uns Gegebene nur derjenige in der ärztlichen Kunst verwenden soll, der im Sinne dieser Prinzipien vollgültig Arzt sein kann.

Allein wir fügen zu dem, was man mit den heute anerkannten wissenschaftlichen Methoden über den Menschen wissen kann, noch weitere Erkenntnisse hinzu, die durch andere Methoden gefunden werden, und sehen uns daher gezwungen, aus dieser *erweiterten* Welt- und Menschenerkenntnis auch für eine Erweiterung der ärztlichen Kunst zu arbeiten.

Eine Einwendung der anerkannten Medizin kann im Grunde gegen das, was wir vorbringen, nicht gemacht werden, da wir diese nicht verneinen. Nur derjenige, der nicht nur verlangt, man müsse sein Wissen bejahen, sondern der dazu noch den Anspruch erhebt, man dürfe keine Erkenntnis vorbringen, die über die seinige hinausgeht, kann unseren Versuch von vorneherein ablehnen.

Die Erweiterung der Welt- und Menschenerkenntnis sehen wir in der von Rudolf Steiner begründeten Anthroposophie. Sie fügt zu der Erkenntnis des *physischen* Menschen, die allein durch die naturwissenschaftlichen Methoden der Gegenwart gewonnen werden kann, diejenige vom *geistigen* Menschen. Sie geht nicht durch ein bloßes Nachdenken von Erkenntnissen des Physischen zu solchen des Geistigen über. Auf diesem Wege

CHAPTER I

True Insight into the Nature of the Human Being as a Foundation for the Art of Medicine

In this book new possibilities for medical knowledge and skills are outlined. To evaluate properly what is presented it is necessary to enter into the points of view that prevailed when the medical approach outlined here came into being.

It is not a matter of opposition to contemporary medicine, which works with the scientific principles and methods accepted today; we fully recognize its principles. And we are of the opinion that what we are offering should be used only by those in medical practice, who can work as fully licensed physicians in accordance with those principles.

However, we add further insights, gained through other methods, to what can be known about the human being through today's recognized scientific methods, and out of this *extended* insight into the world and the human being we find ourselves impelled to work also for an extension of the art of medicine.

Fundamentally speaking, contemporary medicine can offer no objection to what we have to say, since we do not negate it. Only someone who not only demands that one affirm his knowledge, but also, in addition, insists that no insight be proposed going beyond the limits of his insight can reject our efforts a priori.

We find the extension of insight into the world and the human being in anthroposophy, which was founded by Rudolf Steiner. To the insight into the *physical* human being which can be gained alone by today's natural-scientific methods, anthroposophy adds that of the *spiritual* human being. It does not turn, through mere reflection, from insights into the

sieht man sich doch nur vor mehr oder weniger gut gedachte Hypothesen gestellt, von denen niemand beweisen kann, daß ihnen in der Wirklichkeit etwas entspricht.

Die Anthroposophie bildet, bevor sie über das Geistige Aussagen macht, die Methoden aus, die sie berechtigen, solche Aussagen zu machen. Um einen Einblick in diese Methoden zu bekommen, bedenke man das Folgende: Alle Ergebnisse der gegenwärtig anerkannten Naturwissenschaft sind im Grunde aus den Eindrücken der menschlichen Sinne gewonnen. Denn wenn auch der Mensch im Experiment oder in der Beobachtung mit Werkzeugen das erweitert, was die Sinne ihm geben können, so kommt dadurch nichts *wesentlich* Neues zu den Erfahrungen über *die* Welt hinzu, in der der Mensch durch seine Sinne lebt.

Aber auch durch das Denken, insofern dieses bei der Erforschung der physischen Welt tätig ist, kommt nichts Neues zu dem sinnenfällig Gegebenen hinzu. Das Denken kombiniert, analysiert usw. die Sinneseindrücke, um zu Gesetzen (Naturgesetzen) zu gelangen; aber es muß sich der Erforscher der Sinneswelt sagen: dieses Denken, das da aus mir hervorquillt, fügt etwas Wirkliches zu dem Wirklichen der Sinneswelt nicht hinzu.

Das aber wird sogleich anders, wenn man nicht bei dem Denken stehen bleibt, zu dem es der Mensch zunächst durch Leben und Erziehung bringt. Man kann dieses Denken in sich verstärken, erkraften. Man kann einfache, leicht überschaubare Gedanken in den Mittelpunkt des Bewußtseins stellen, und dann, mit Ausschluß aller anderen Gedanken, alle Kraft der Seele auf solchen Vorstellungen halten. Wie ein Muskel erstarkt, wenn er immer wieder in der Richtung der gleichen Kraft angespannt wird, so erstarkt die seelische Kraft mit Bezug auf dasjenige Gebiet, das sonst im Denken waltet, wenn sie in der angegebenen Art Übungen macht. Man muß betonen, daß diesen Übungen einfache, leicht überschaubare Gedanken zugrunde liegen müssen. Denn die Seele darf, während sie solche Übungen macht, keinerlei Einflüssen eines halb oder ganz Unbewußten

physical to insights into the spiritual. On such a path one just finds oneself confronted with more or less well-conceived hypotheses, which no one can prove to correspond to anything in reality.

Before making statements about the spiritual, anthroposophy develops the methods which entitle it to make such statements. To gain an insight into these methods consider the following: all results of today's recognized science are fundamentally derived from human sense impressions. For even though the human being may enlarge upon that which is given through the senses in experiments or in observation with the help of instruments, nothing *essentially* new is added by these means to the experience of *that* world in which the human being lives through his senses.

But also through thinking nothing new is added to what is given by the senses, to the extent that it is active in investigating the physical world. Thinking combines, analyzes, etc. the sense impressions to discover laws (the laws of nature); yet, the researcher of the sensory world must admit: the thinking that wells up from within me does not add anything real to the reality of the sense world.

However, that immediately becomes different if one no longer stops short at the thinking which the human being initially acquires through life-experience and education. One can augment and strengthen this thinking in itself.[1] One can place simple, easily encompassed thoughts in the center of consciousness and, with exclusion of all other thoughts, concentrate all the force of soul on such ideas. As a muscle grows strong when exerted again and again in the direction of the same force, so the force of soul grows strong with respect to the region which usually governs thinking, when it is exercised in the above-mentioned way. It must be emphasized that these exercises have to be based on simple, easily encom-

ausgesetzt sein. (Wir können hier nur das Prinzip solcher Übungen angeben; eine ausführliche Darstellung und Anleitung, wie solche Übungen im Einzelnen zu machen sind, findet man in Rudolf Steiners «Wie erlangt man Erkentnisse der Höheren Welten?», in dessen «Geheimwissenschaft» und in anderen anthroposophischen Schriften.)

Es liegt nahe, den Einwand zu erheben, daß jemand, der sich so mit aller Kraft bestimmten, in den Mittelpunkt des Bewußtseins gerückten Gedanken hingibt, allerlei Autosuggestionen und dergleichen ausgesetzt ist, und daß er einfach in das Gebiet der Einbildung hineinkommt. Allein Anthroposophie zeigt zugleich, wie die Übungen verlaufen müssen, damit dieser Einwand völlig unberechtigt ist. Sie zeigt, wie man innerhalb des Bewußtseins in vollbesonnener Art während des Übens so fortschreitet wie beim Lösen eines arithmetischen oder geometri-schen Problems. Wie da das Bewußtsein nirgends ins Unbe-wußte ausgleiten kann, so auch nicht während des angedeuteten Übens, wenn die anthroposophischen Anleitungen richtig befolgt werden.

Im Verfolge dieses Übens kommt man zu einer Verstärkung der *Denkkraft,* von der man vorher keine Ahnung hatte. Man fühlt die waltende Denkkraft in sich wie einen neuen Inhalt seines Menschenwesens. Und zugleich mit diesem Inhalt des eigenen Menschenwesens offenbart sich ein Weltinhalt, den man vorher vielleicht geahnt, aber nicht durch Erfahrung gekannt hat. Sieht man einmal in Augenblicken der Selbstbeobachtung auf das gewöhnliche Denken hin, so findet man die Gedanken schattenhaft, blaß gegenüber den Eindrücken, die die Sinne geben.

Was man jetzt in der verstärkten Denkkraft wahrnimmt, ist durchaus nicht blaß und schattenhaft; es ist vollinhaltlich, konkret-bildhaft; es ist von einer viel intensiveren Wirklichkeit als der Inhalt der Sinneseindrücke. Es geht dem Menschen eine neue Welt auf, indem er auf die angegebene Art die Kraft seiner Wahrnehmungsfähigkeit erweitert hat.

passed thoughts. For in doing the exercises the soul must not be exposed to any kind of influences that are semiconscious or unconscious. (We can but indicate the principle of such exercises here; a detailed description and instructions on how in particular such exercises should be done can be found in Rudolf Steiner's books *Knowledge of the Higher Worlds*, *Occult Science*,[2] and other anthroposophical works.)

It lies near-at-hand to object that if someone thus gives himself up with all his strength to certain thoughts placed in the center of consciousness, he will thereby expose himself to all manner of autosuggestion and the like, and that he will simply enter the region of fantasy. But anthroposophy shows at the same time how the exercises should be done, so that this objection loses its validity altogether. It shows how to proceed in full consciousness and wide-awake while doing the exercises, as in the solving of an arithmetical or geometrical problem. As consciousness can at no point veer off into unconscious regions in doing the latter, so also not in doing the indicated exercises, provided the instructions of anthroposophy are well observed.

In the course of such practice an increase of the *power of thought* is attained, of which one had not the remotest idea before. The exercising of the power of thought is felt within oneself as a new content of one's being. And along with this new content of one's being, a world-content is revealed which was not known by actual experience before, though one may perhaps have divined its existence. If one has taken the occasion, in moments of introspection, to observe everyday thinking, one finds the thoughts shadowlike, pale compared to the impressions given by the senses.

What is now perceived in the strengthened force of thinking is not pale or shadowlike at all; it is full of inner content, vividly real and graphic; it is, indeed, of a reality far more

Indem der Mensch in dieser Welt wahrnehmen lernt, wie er früher nur innerhalb der sinnlichen Welt wahrnehmen konnte, wird ihm klar, daß alle Naturgesetze, die er vorher gekannt hatte, *nur* in der physischen Welt gelten; und daß das Wesen der Welt, die er jetzt betreten hat, darin besteht, daß ihre Gesetze andere, ja die entgegengesetzten gegenüber denen der physischen Welt sind. In dieser Welt gilt nicht das Gesetz der Anziehungskraft der Erde, sondern im Gegenteil, es tritt eine Kraft auf, die nicht von dem Mittelpunkt der Erde nach auswärts wirkt, sondern umgekehrt so, daß ihre Richtung von dem Umkreis des Weltalls her nach dem Mittelpunkt der Erde geht. Und entsprechend ist es mit den andern Kräften der physischen Welt.

In der Anthroposophie wird die durch Übung erlangte Fähigkeit des Menschen, diese Welt zu schauen, die imaginative Erkenntnis-Kraft genannt. Imaginativ nicht aus dem Grunde, weil man es mit «Einbildungen» zu tun habe, sondern weil der Inhalt des Bewußtseins nicht mit Gedankenschatten, sondern mit Bildern erfüllt ist. Und wie man sich durch die Sinneswahrnehmung im unmittelbaren Erleben in einer Wirklichkeit fühlt, so auch in der Seelentätigkeit des imaginativen Erkennens. Die Welt, auf die sich diese Erkenntnis bezieht, wird von der Anthroposophie die ätherische Welt genannt. Es handelt sich dabei nicht um den hypothetischen Äther der gegenwärtigen Physik, sondern um ein wirklich geistig Geschautes. Der Name wird im Einklange mit älteren instinktiven Ahnungen dieser Welt gegeben. Diese haben gegenüber dem, was gegenwärtig klar erkannt werden kann, keinen Erkenntniswert mehr; aber will man etwas bezeichnen, so braucht man Namen.

Innerhalb dieser Ätherwelt ist eine neben der physischen Leiblichkeit des Menschen bestehende ätherische Leiblichkeit wahrnehmbar.

intense than the content of sense impressions. A new world begins to dawn for the human being as he has thus expanded the strength of his faculty of perception.

Learning to perceive in this world where before one was only able to perceive in the world of the senses, we become aware that all the laws of nature known to us before are valid *only* in the physical world; the intrinsic nature of the world he has now entered is that its laws are different, in fact the very opposite of those of the physical world. In this world the law of gravity of the earth does not apply; on the contrary, a force appears, working not from the center of the earth outwards but in reverse direction, from the circumference of the universe towards the center of the earth. And the situation is similar for the other forces of the physical world.

In anthroposophy, the faculty attained by exercise of perceiving this world is called the capacity for imaginative knowledge. Imaginative not for the reason that one is dealing with "fantasies," but because the content of consciousness is filled, not with thought shadows, but with pictures. And as one has the immediate experience of being in a real world through sense perception, so also in the activity of soul called imaginative knowledge. The world to which this knowledge relates is called in anthroposophy the etheric world. This is not to suggest the hypothetical ether of modern physics; it is something actually beheld in spirit. The name is used in keeping with older, instinctive presentiments about that world. In the face of what can now be known with full clarity, these old presentiments no longer have a scientific value, but to designate something one needs a name.

Within this ether world an etheric bodily nature of the human being is perceptible that exists besides the physical bodily nature.

Diese ätherische Leiblichkeit ist etwas, das sich ihrem Wesen nach auch in der Pflanzenwelt findet. Die Pflanzen haben ihren Ätherleib. Die physischen Gesetze gelten tatsächlich nur für die Welt des leblosen Mineralischen.

Die Pflanzenwelt ist auf der Erde dadurch möglich, daß es Substanzen im Irdischen gibt, die nicht innerhalb der physischen Gesetze beschlossen bleiben, sondern die alle physische Gesetzmäßigkeit ablegen und eine solche annehmen können, die dieser entgegengesetzt ist. Die physischen Gesetze wirken wie ausströmend von der Erde; die ätherischen wirken wie von allen Seiten des Weltumfanges auf die Erde zuströmend. Man begreift das Werden der Pflanzenwelt nur, wenn man in ihr das Zusammenwirken des Irdisch-Physischen und des Kosmisch-Ätherischen sieht.

Und so ist es mit Bezug auf den Ätherleib des Menschen. Durch ihn geschieht im Menschen etwas, das nicht in der Fortsetzung des gesetzmäßigen Wirkens der Kräfte des physischen Leibes liegt, sondern das zur Grundlage hat, daß die physischen Stoffe, indem sie in das Ätherische einströmen, sich zuerst ihrer physischen Kräfte entledigen.

Diese im Ätherleibe wirksamen Kräfte betätigen sich im Beginne des menschlichen Erdenlebens – am deutlichsten während der Embryonalzeit – als Gestaltungs- und Wachstumskräfte. Im Verlaufe des Erdenlebens emanzipiert sich ein Teil dieser Kräfte von der Betätigung in Gestaltung und Wachstum und wird Denkkräfte, eben jene Kräfte, die für das gewöhnliche Bewußtsein die schattenhafte Gedankenwelt hervorbringen.

Es ist von der allergrößten Bedeutung zu wissen, daß die gewöhnlichen Denkkräfte des Menschen die verfeinerten Gestaltungs- und Wachstumskräfte sind. Im Gestalten und Wachsen des menschlichen Organismus offenbart sich ein Geistiges. Denn dieses Geistige erscheint dann im Lebensverlaufe als die geistige Denkkraft.

This etheric bodily nature is also to be found in its essence in the plant world. Plants have their ether body. The physical laws are indeed only valid for the world of lifeless minerals.

The plant world is possible on earth because there are substances in the earthly element which do not remain within the sphere of physical laws, but which can lay aside the whole complex of physical law and take on one which is opposite to it. Physical laws work as though streaming out from the earth; the etheric laws work as though streaming to the earth from all sides of the universe. It is only possible for the human being to comprehend how the plant world comes into being when he sees in it the working together of the earthly-physical with the cosmic-etheric.

And so it is with regard to the ether body of the human being. Through it something happens in the human being which is not a continuation of the lawful working of the forces of the physical body, but is founded on the principle that physical substances, as they stream into the etheric element, initially divest themselves of their physical forces.

These forces functioning in the ether body are active at the beginning of the human being's life on earth—most distinctly during the embryonal period—as the forces of formation and growth. During the course of earthly life a portion of these forces emancipates itself from this occupation with formation and growth and becomes forces of thinking, just those forces which, for the ordinary consciousness bring forth the shadowlike world of thoughts.

It is of the utmost importance to know that the human being's ordinary forces of thinking are refined form and growth forces. A spiritual element reveals itself in the forming and growing of the human organism. And this spiritual element then appears during the course of later life as the spiritual power of thought.

Und diese Denkkraft ist nur ein Teil der im ätherischen webenden menschlichen Gestaltungs- und Wachstumskraft. Der andere Teil bleibt seiner im menschlichen Lebensbeginne innegehabten Aufgabe getreu. Nur weil der Mensch, wenn seine Gestaltung und sein Wachstum vorgerückt, das ist, bis zu einem gewissen Grade abgeschlossen sind, sich noch weiter entwickelt, kann das Ätherisch-Geistige, das im Organismus webt und lebt, im weiteren Leben als Denkkraft auftreten.

So offenbart sich der imaginativen geistigen Anschauung die bildsame (plastische) Kraft als ein Ätherisch-Geistiges von der einen Seite, das von der andern Seite als der Seelen-Inhalt des Denkens auftritt.

Verfolgt man nun das Substantielle der Erdenstoffe in die Ätherbildung hinein, so muß man sagen: diese Stoffe nehmen überall da, wo sie in diese Bildung eintreten, ein Wesen an, durch das sie sich der physischen Natur entfremden. In dieser Entfremdung treten sie in eine Welt ein, in der ihnen das Geistige entgegenkommt und sie in sein eigenes Wesen verwandelt.

So aufsteigen zu der ätherisch-lebendigen Wesenheit des Menschen, wie es hier geschildert wird, ist etwas wesentlich anderes als das unwissenschaftliche Behaupten einer «Lebenskraft» bis zur Mitte des neunzehnten Jahrhunderts üblich war, um die lebendigen Körper zu erklären. Hier handelt es sich um das wirkliche Anschauen – um das geistige Wahrnehmen – eines Wesenhaften, das im Menschen wie in allem Lebendigen ebenso vorhanden ist wie der physische Leib. Und um dieses Anschauen zu bewirken, wird nicht etwa in unbestimmter Art mit dem gewöhnlichen Denken weitergedacht; es wird auch nicht durch die Einbildungskraft eine andere Welt ersonnen; es wird vielmehr das menschliche Erkennen in ganz exakter Art erweitert, und diese Erweiterung ergibt auch die Erfahrung über eine erweiterte Welt.

Die Übungen, die ein höheres Wahrnehmen herbeiführen, können fortgesetzt werden. Man kann, wie man eine erhöhte

This power of thought is only one part of the human capacity for form and growth that weaves in the etheric. The other part remains true to the purpose it fulfilled in the beginning of the human being's life. Only because the human being continues to evolve even when his form and his growth are advanced, that is, when they are to a certain degree completed, does the etheric spiritual force, which lives and works in the organism, appear in later life as the power of thought.

To imaginative spiritual vision the sculptural[3] (plastic) force from one aspect thus reveals itself as an etheric spiritual element, and from another aspect it appears as the soul content of our thinking.

If one now pursues the substantiality of earthly matter into the ether formation one must say: wherever substances enter into this formation they assume a mode of being which alienates them from physical nature. In this state of alienation they enter into a world where the spiritual comes to meet them, converting them into its own being.

To rise to the etherically living nature of the human being in the way described here is essentially different from the unscientific postulation of a "vital force" which was customary even up to the middle of the nineteenth century in order to explain living corporealities. Here it is a matter of actually beholding—of spiritually perceiving—a reality which exists in the human being and in everything that is alive, just as the physical body exists. To bring about this perception, the ordinary way of thinking is not carried on in some indefinite manner, nor is another world invented through fantasy; rather, human cognition is extended in a very exact way, and this extension then yields the experience of an extended world.

The exercises leading to higher perception can be carried further. Just as one exerts an enhanced force in concentrating

Kraft anwendet, sich auf Gedanken, die man in den Mittelpunkt des Bewußtseins gerückt hat, zu konzentrieren, auch darauf wieder eine solch erhöhte Kraft anwenden, die erlangten Imaginationen (Bilder einer geistig-ätherischen Wirklichkeit) zu unterdrücken. Dann erlangt man den Zustand des völlig leeren Bewußtseins. Man ist bloß wach, ohne daß zunächst das Wachsein einen Inhalt hat. (Das Genauere findet man in den oben erwähnten Büchern.) Aber dieses Wachsein ohne Inhalt bleibt nicht. Das von allen physisch- und auch ätherisch-bildhaften Eindrücken leer gewordene Bewußtsein erfüllt sich mit einem Inhalt, der ihm aus einer realen geistigen Welt zuströmt, wie den physischen Sinnen die Eindrücke aus der physischen Welt zuströmen.

Man hat durch die imaginative Erkenntnis ein zweites Glied der menschlichen Wesenheit kennengelernt; man lernt durch die Erfüllung des leeren Bewußtseins mit geistigem Inhalt ein drittes Glied kennen. Die Anthroposophie nennt das Erkennen, das auf diese Art zustande kommt, dasjenige durch Inspiration. (Man soll sich durch diese Ausdrücke nicht beirren lassen; sie sind einer primitiven Zeiten angehörigen instinktiven Art, in geistige Welten zu sehen, entnommen; aber, was hier mit ihnen gemeint ist, wird ja exakt gesagt.) Und die Welt, in die man durch die Inspiration Eintritt gewinnt, bezeichnet sie als die astralische Welt. – Spricht man, wie hier auseinandergesetzt, von «ätherischer Welt» so meint man die Wirkungen, die vom Weltumfange nach der Erde zu wirken. Spricht man aber von «astralischer Welt», so geht man in Gemäßheit dessen, was das inspirierte Bewusstsein beobachtet, von den Wirkungen aus dem Weltumfang zu bestimmten Geist-Wesenheiten über, die in diesen Wirkungen sich offenbaren, wie in den von der Erde ausgehenden Kräften sich die Erdenstoffe offenbaren. Man spricht von aus den Weltenfernen wirkenden konkreten Geist-Wesenheiten, wie man beim sinnlichen Anblick des nächtlichen Himmels von Sternen und Sternbildern spricht. Daher der Ausdruck

on thoughts placed deliberately in the center of consciousness, so one can now also apply such an enhanced force to suppress the attained imaginations (pictures of a spiritual-etheric reality). One then reaches a state of completely empty consciousness. One is awake and aware, but the wakefulness has, to begin with, no content. (Further details are to be found in the above-mentioned books.) But this wakefulness without content does not remain. The consciousness that is emptied of any physical or etheric pictorial impressions becomes filled with a content that pours into it from a real world of spirit, even as the impressions from the physical world pour into the physical senses.

Through imaginative knowledge one has come to know a second member of the human being; through the emptied consciousness that becomes filled with spiritual content one learns to know a third. Anthroposophy calls the insight that comes about in this way knowledge by inspiration. (One should not be confused by these terms; they are borrowed from the instinctive way of looking into spiritual worlds which belonged to primitive ages, but the sense in which they are used here is stated exactly.) And the world to which the human being gains entry by inspiration is called the astral world.— When one speaks in the way explained here of an "etheric world," the forces working actively from the circumference of the universe towards the earth are meant. When one speaks of the "astral world," though, one proceeds in accordance with the perception of inspired consciousness from the active working of the cosmos towards certain spiritual beings which reveal themselves in this working, just as earthly substances reveal themselves in the forces that radiate out from the earth. One speaks of actual spiritual beings actively working from the distant universe just as one speaks of the stars and constellations when one gazes to the sky at nighttime with the senses. Hence the expression "astral world." In this astral

«astralische Welt». In dieser astralischen Welt trägt der Mensch das dritte Glied seiner Wesenheit: seinen astralischen Leib.

Auch in diesen astralischen Leib muß die Erdenstofflichkeit einströmen. Sie entfremdet sich damit weiter ihrer physischen Wesenheit. – Wie der Mensch seinen ätherischen Leib mit der Pflanzenwelt, so hat er seinen astralischen Leib mit der Tierwelt gemeinsam.

Die den Menschen über die Tierwelt hinaushebende, eigentlich menschliche Wesenheit wird durch eine noch höhere Erkenntnisart als die Inspiration erkannt. Die Anthroposophie spricht da von Intuition. In der Inspiration offenbart sich eine Welt geistiger Wesenheiten; in der Intuition wird das Verhältnis des erkennenden Menschen zu dieser Welt ein näheres. Man bringt das zum Vollbewußtsein in sich, was rein geistig ist, wovon man im bewußten Erleben unmittelbar erfährt, daß es mit dem Erleben durch die Körperlichkeit nichts zu tun hat. Dadurch versetzt man sich in ein Leben, das ein solches als Menschengeist unter anderen geistigen Wesenheiten ist. In der Inspiration *offenbaren* sich die geistigen Wesenheiten der Welt; durch die Intuition *lebt* man mit diesen Wesenheiten.

Man gelangt dadurch zur Anerkennung des vierten Gliedes der menschlichen Wesenheit, zum eigentlichen «Ich». Wieder wird man gewahr, wie die Erdenstofflichkeit, indem sie sich dem Weben und Wesen des «Ich» einfügt, sich noch weiter ihrem physischen Wesen entfremdet. Die Wesenheit, welche diese Stofflichkeit als «Ich-Organisation» annimmt, ist zunächst die Form des Erdenstoffes, in der sich dieser am meisten seiner irdisch-physischen Art entfremdet.

Was man in dieser Art als «astralischen Leib» und «Ich» kennen lernt, ist nicht in gleicher Art an den physischen Leib in der Menschenorganisation gebunden wie der ätherische Leib. Inspiration und Intuition zeigen, wie im Schlafe sich «astralischer Leib» und «Ich» vom physischen und ätherischen Leib trennen, und wie nur im Wachzustande ein völliges Durchdrin-

world the human being bears the third member of his nature: his astral body.

Earthly materiality must also flow into this astral body. Through this it is further estranged from its physical nature.— Just as the human being has his etheric body in common with the plant world, so he has his astral body in common with the animal world.

The specific human essence, which raises the human being above the animal world, can be recognized through a form of cognition still higher than inspiration. Anthroposophy speaks here of intuition. In inspiration, a world of spiritual beings reveals itself; in intuition, the relationship of the discerning human being to this world grows more intimate. One now brings the purely spiritual to full consciousness within oneself and realizes in ones conscious experience immediately that it has nothing to do with the experience through the body. Through this, one transplants oneself into a life where one is human spirit among other spirit beings. In inspiration, the spiritual beings of the world *reveal* themselves; through intuition, one *lives* with these beings.

Thereby one comes to acknowledge the fourth member of the human being, the true "I." Once again one becomes aware of how earthly substance, in adapting to the weaving and being of the "I," estranges itself yet further from its physical nature. The nature which this substance assumes as "ego organization" is, to begin with, the form of earthly substance which is most estranged from its earthly physical character.

That which one thus learns to know as "astral body" and "I" is not bound to the physical body in the human organization the way the etheric body is. Inspiration and intuition show how in sleep "astral body" and "I" separate from the physical and etheric body, and that only in the waking state is there full

gen der vier Glieder der Menschennatur zur menschlichen Einheitswesenheit vorhanden ist.

Im Schlafe sind in der physischen und ätherischen Welt der physische und ätherische Menschenleib verblieben. Sie sind da aber nicht in der Lage, in der physischer und ätherischer Leib eines Pflanzenwesens sind. Sie tragen in sich die Nachwirkungen der astralischen und der Ich-Wesenheit. Und in dem Augenblicke, in dem sie diese Nachwirkungen nicht mehr in sich tragen würden, muß Erwachen eintreten. Ein menschlicher physischer Leib darf niemals bloßen physischen, ein menschlicher Ätherleib niemals bloßen ätherischen Wirkungen unterliegen. Sie würden dadurch zerfallen.

Nun zeigen aber Inspiration und Intuition noch etwas anderes. Die physische Stofflichkeit erfährt eine Weiterbildung ihres Wesens, indem sie zum Weben und Leben im Ätherischen übergeht. Und *Leben* hängt davon ab, daß der organische Körper dem Wesen des Irdischen entrissen und vom außerirdischen Weltall herein aufgebaut wird. Allein dieser Aufbau führt wohl zum *Leben*, nicht aber zum *Bewußtsein* und nicht zum *Selbstbewußtsein*. Es muß sich der Astralleib seine Organisation innerhalb der physischen und der ätherischen aufbauen; es muß ein Gleiches das Ich in bezug auf die Ich-Organisation tun. Aber in diesem *Aufbau* ergibt sich keine bewußte Entfaltung des Seelenlebens. Es muß, damit ein solches zustande kommt, dem Aufbau ein *Abbau* gegenüberstehen. Der astralische Leib baut sich seine Organe auf; er baut sie wieder ab, indem er die Gefühlstätigkeit im Bewußtsein der Seele entfalten läßt; das Ich baut sich seine «Ich-Organisation» auf; es baut sie wieder ab, indem die Willenstätigkeit im Selbstbewußtsein wirksam wird.

Der Geist entfaltet sich innerhalb der Menschenwesenheit *nicht* auf der Grundlage *aufbauender* Stofftätigkeit, sondern auf derjenigen *abbauender*. Wo im Menschen Geist wirken soll, da muß der Stoff sich von seiner Tätigkeit zurückziehen.

mutual permeation of the four members of human nature to form a unified human entity.

In sleep the physical and etheric human body remain behind in the physical and etheric world. Yet they are not in the same position as the physical and the etheric body of a plantlike being. They bear within them the aftereffects of the essence of the astral and the I. Indeed, in the very moment they would no longer bear these aftereffects within them, the human being must awaken. A human physical body must never be subjected to purely physical, nor a human ether body to purely etheric influences. Through this they would disintegrate.

Now, inspiration and intuition also show something else. Physical substance experiences a further development of its nature in its transition to living and moving in the etheric. And *life* depends on the fact that the organic body is torn out of the earthly state to be built up by the extraterrestrial cosmos. This building up, however, leads to *life*, but not to *consciousness*, and not to *self-consciousness*. The astral body must build up its organization within the physical and the etheric element; the I must do the same with regard to the ego organization. But this *upbuilding* does not result in a conscious development of soul life. For this to occur, a process of breaking down must counter the process of building up. The astral body builds up its organs; it breaks them down again in that it allows the activity of feeling to develop in the conscious soul; the I builds up its "ego organization"; it breaks it down again, in that will activity becomes active in self-consciousness.

The spirit does *not* unfold within the human being on the basis of *upbuilding* of substance, but on the basis of a *breaking-down* of substance. Wherever the spirit is to be active in the human being, substance must withdraw from its activity.

Schon die Entstehung des Denkens innerhalb des ätherischen Leibes beruht nicht auf einer Fortsetzung des ätherischen Wesens, sondern auf einem Abbau desselben. Das *bewußte* Denken geschieht *nicht* in Vorgängen des Gestaltens und Wachstums, sondern in solchen der Entgestaltung und des Welkens, Absterbens, die fortdauernd dem ätherischen Geschehen eingegliedert sind.

In dem bewußten Denken lösen sich aus der leiblichen Gestaltung die Gedanken heraus und werden als seelische Gestaltungen menschliche Erlebnisse.

Sieht man nun auf der Grundlage einer solchen Menschenerkenntnis auf das Menschenwesen hin, so wird man gewahr, wie man sowohl den Gesamtmenschen wie auch ein einzelnes Organ nur durchschauen kann, wenn man weiß, wie in ihm der physische, der ätherische, der astralische Leib und das Ich wirken. Es gibt Organe, in denen vornehmlich das Ich tätig ist; es gibt solche, in denen das Ich nur wenig wirkt, dagegen die physische Organisation überwiegt.

Wie man den gesunden Menschen nur durchschauen kann, wenn man erkennt, wie sich die höheren Glieder der Menschenwesenheit des Erdenstoffes bemächtigen, um ihn in ihren Dienst zu zwingen, und wenn man auch erkennt, wie der Erdenstoff sich wandelt, indem er in den Bereich der Wirksamkeit der höheren Glieder der Menschennatur tritt, so kann man auch den kranken Menschen nur verstehen, wenn man einsieht, in welche Lage der Gesamtorganismus oder ein Organ oder eine Organreihe kommen, wenn die Wirkungsweise der höheren Glieder in Unregelmäßigkeit verfällt. Und an Heilmittel wird man nur denken können, wenn man ein Wissen darüber entwickelt, wie ein Erdenstoff oder Erdenvorgang zum Ätherischen, zum Astralischen, zum Ich sich verhält. Denn nur dann wird man durch Einfügung eines Erdenstoffes in den menschlichen Organismus, oder durch Behandlung mit einer Erdentätigkeit bewirken können, daß die höheren Glieder der Menschenwesenheit sich ungehindert entfalten kön-

Even the development of thinking in the etheric body does not depend on a continuation of etheric essence but, on the contrary, on its breaking down. *Conscious* thinking does *not* happen in processes of formation and growth, but in processes of deformation and of withering away and dying, which are continually interwoven into the etheric events.

In conscious thinking, thoughts liberate themselves from the form of the body, and, as soul forms, become human experiences.

Looking at the human being on the basis of such an insight into his nature, one becomes aware that the human being as a whole, or any single organ, can only be understood with clarity if one knows how the physical, the etheric, the astral body and the I are active in him.[4] There are organs in which mainly the I is active; in others the I works but little, and instead the physical organization is predominant.

Just as healthy man can only be comprehended by recognizing how the higher members of the human being take possession of earthly substance in order to compel it into their service, and also by recognizing how earthly substance changes when it enters the sphere of action of the higher members of the human being, so also can one understand the diseased human being only if one realizes the situation into which the organism as a whole, or a certain organ or series of organs enter when the mode of action of the higher members falls into irregularity. And one will only be able to think of medicines when one develops a knowledge of how an earthly substance or earthly process is related to the etheric, to the astral, to the I. For only then will one know how to enable the higher members of the human being to unfold unhindered, by introducing an earthly substance into the human organism or by treating it with an earthly activity, or also to enable the earth substance to find, in what has been administered, the

nen, oder auch, daß die Erdenstofflichkeit an dem Zugefügten die nötige Unterstützung findet, um auf den Weg zu kommen, auf dem sie Grundlage wird für irdisches Wirken des Geistigen.

Der Mensch ist, was er ist, durch Leib, Ätherleib, Seele (astralischer Leib) und Ich (Geist). Er muß als Gesunder aus diesen Gliedern heraus angeschaut; er muß als Kranker in dem gestörten Gleichgewicht dieser Glieder wahrgenommen; es müssen zu seiner Gesundheit Heilmittel gefunden werden, die das gestörte Gleichgewicht wieder herstellen.

Auf eine medizinische Anschauung, die auf solche Grundlagen baut, wird in dieser Schrift hingedeutet.

necessary support to be on the way to becoming the foundation for the earthly working of the spiritual element.

The human being is what he is by virtue of physical body, ether body, soul (astral body) and I (spirit). He must, in health, be looked at from the viewpoint of these members; in disease he must be perceived in the disturbed equilibrium of these members; for his healing one must find medications that restore the disturbed balance.

A view of medicine built on such foundations is outlined in this book.

II
WARUM ERKRANKT DER MENSCH?

Wer über die Tatsache nachdenkt, daß der Mensch krank sein kann, der kommt, wenn er rein naturwissenschaftlich denken will, in einen Widerspruch hinein, von dem er zunächst annehmen muß, daß er in dem Wesen des Daseins selbst liege. Was im Krankheitsvorgang geschieht, ist, obenhin betrachtet, ein Naturprozeß. Was an seiner Stelle im gesunden Zustand vorgeht, ist aber auch ein Naturprozeß.

Naturprozesse kennt man zunächst nur durch die Beobachtung der außermenschlichen Welt und durch die Beobachtung des Menschen nur insofern, als man diese genau ebenso anstellt wie diejenige der äußeren Natur. Man denkt sich dabei den Menschen als ein Stück der Natur, ein solches, in dem die auch außer ihm zu beobachtenden Vorgänge sehr kompliziert sind, aber doch von derselben Art, wie diese äußeren Naturprozesse.

Es entsteht da aber die von diesem Gesichtspunkte aus unbeantwortbare Frage: wie entstehen innerhalb des Menschen – vom Tiere soll hier nicht gesprochen werden – Naturprozesse, die den gesunden entgegengesetzt sind?

Der gesunde menschliche Organismus scheint als ein Stück der Natur begreiflich zu sein; der kranke nicht. Er muß daher aus sich selbst begreiflich sein durch etwas, das er nicht von der Natur hat.

Man stellt sich wohl vor, daß das Geistige im Menschen zur physischen Grundlage einen komplizierten Naturprozeß wie eine Fortsetzung des außerhalb des Menschen befindlichen Natürlichen habe. Aber man sehe doch, ob jemals die im gesunden menschlichen Organismus begründete Fortsetzung eines Naturprozesses das geistige Erleben als solches hervor-ruft? Das Gegenteil ist der Fall. Das geistige Erleben wird ausgelöscht, wenn

CHAPTER II

Why Does The Human Being Become Ill?

Whoever thinks about the fact that a human being can be ill, becomes involved in a paradox if he wants to think purely along the lines of science in the usual sense. To begin with, he will have to assume that this paradox lies in the nature of existence itself. What happens in the course of illness is, considered superficially, a process of nature. What takes place in its stead in health, though, is also a process of nature.

Processes of nature are known first of all only through observation of the world external to the human being, and through observation of the human being only to the extent that one observes him in exactly the same way as one does outer nature. One conceives of the human being as a part of nature then, specifically one in which the processes, which can also be observed external to him, are very complicated, yet are of the same kind as these outer processes of nature.

However, a question arises here which cannot be answered from this point of view: How do processes of nature originate in the human being—the animal will not be spoken of here—which run counter to healthy processes?

The healthy human organism would seem to be intelligible as a part of nature; the diseased does not. Therefore it must in some way be inherently intelligible, by virtue of something which it does not have from nature.

One may well imagine that the spiritual, nonphysical in the human being has as its physical foundation a complicated process of nature, which is like a continuation of the processes of nature found outside the human being. However, has ever the continuation of a process of nature based in a healthy human organism been seen to evoke conscious, nonphysical experience as such? The opposite is the case. Conscious, nonphysical experience is

der Naturprozeß sich in gerader Linie fortsetzt. Es geschieht dies im Schlafe; es geschieht in der Ohnmacht.

Man sehe dagegen, wie das bewußte Geistesleben verschärft wird, wenn ein Organ erkrankt. Schmerz stellt sich ein oder wenigstens Unlust und Unbehagen. Das Gefühlsleben erhält einen Inhalt, den es sonst nicht hat. Und das Willensleben wird beeinträchtigt. Eine Gliedbewegung, die sich im gesunden Zustande selbstverständlich vollzieht, kann nicht ausgeführt werden, weil sich der Schmerz oder die Unlust hemmend entgegenstellen.

Man beachte den Übergang von der schmerzbegleiteten Bewegung eines Gliedes zu dessen Lähmung. In der schmerzbegleiteten Bewegung liegt der Anfang der gelähmten. Das aktiv Geistige greift in den Organismus ein. Im gesunden Zustande offenbart sich dieses zunächst im Vorstellungs- oder Denkleben. Man aktiviert eine Vorstellung; und eine Gliedbewegung folgt. Man geht mit der Vorstellung nicht bewußt in die organischen Vorgänge ein, die zuletzt zur Gliedbewegung führen. Die Vorstellung taucht in das Unbewußte unter. Zwischen der Vorstellung und der Bewegung tritt im gesunden Zustande ein Fühlen ein, das nur seelisch wirkt. Es lehnt sich nicht deutlich an ein körperlich Organisches an. Im kranken Zustande ist das aber der Fall. Das Fühlen, das im gesunden Zustande als losgelöst von dem physischen Organismus erlebt wird, verbindet sich im kranken Erleben mit diesem.

Die Vorgänge des gesunden Fühlens und des kranken Erlebens erscheinen dadurch in ihrer Verwandtschaft. Es muß etwas da sein, das im gesunden Organismus mit diesem nicht so intensiv verbunden ist als im kranken. Der geistigen Anschauung enthüllt sich dieses als der astralische Leib. Er ist eine übersinnliche Organisation innerhalb der sinnlichen. Er greift entweder lose in ein Organ ein, dann führt er zum seelischen Erleben, das für sich besteht und nicht in Verbindung mit dem Körper empfunden wird. Oder er greift intensiv in ein Organ ein; dann führt er zum Erleben des Krankseins. Man muß sich eine der Formen des Krankseins in

extinguished when the process of nature continues in a direct line. This is what happens in sleep and it happens in fainting.

Consider, on the other hand, how conscious spiritual life becomes intensified when an organ becomes diseased. Pain arises, or at least discomfort and displeasure. The life of feeling acquires a content which it normally does not have. In addition, the life of will is impaired. The movement of a limb, which in health happens as a matter of course, cannot be accomplished, because pain or discomfort counteract and hinder it.

Observe the transition from the painful movement of a limb to its paralysis. Movement accompanied by pain is the initial stage of paralysis. An active spiritual element intervenes in the organism. In health, it reveals itself above all in the life of mental imaging or thinking. A certain mental image is activated, and a limb movement follows. One does not consciously enter with the mental image into the organic processes which culminate in the movement. The mental image dives into the unconscious. In the healthy state a feeling that is active only at the soul level arises between mental image and movement. It does not relate distinctly to any organic bodily process. This is the case, however, in a state of disease. The feeling, experienced in health as released from the physical organism, joins with it in the experience of illness.

Thus the relation between the processes of healthy feeling and pathological experience becomes evident. Something must be present, which, in the healthy organism, is less intensively joined with it than in the diseased organism. To spiritual perception this discloses itself to be the astral body. It is a supersensible organization within the physical-sensory organization. Either it takes hold of an organ loosely and leads to an independent soul experience which is not felt to be connected with the body, or it takes hold of an organ intensively, and

einem Ergreifen des Organismus durch den astralischen Leib vorstellen, die den geistigen Menschen tiefer in seinen Körper untertauchen läßt, als dies im gesunden Zustande der Fall ist.

Aber auch das Denken hat seine physische Grundlage im Organismus. Es ist im gesunden Zustande nur noch mehr von diesem losgelöst als das Fühlen. Die geistige Anschauung findet außer dem astralischen Leib noch eine besondere Ich-Organisation, die sich seelisch frei im Denken darlebt. Taucht mit dieser Ich-Organisation der Mensch intensiv in sein Körperhaftes unter, so tritt ein Zustand ein, der die Beobachtung des eigenen Organismus derjenigen der Außenwelt ähnlich macht. – Beobachtet man ein Ding oder einen Vorgang der Außenwelt, so liegt die Tatsache vor, daß der Gedanke im Menschen und das Beobachtete nicht in lebendiger Wechselwirkung stehen, sondern unabhängig voneinander sind. Das tritt für ein menschliches Glied nur dann ein, wenn es gelähmt wird. Dann wird es Außenwelt. Die Ich-Organisation ist nicht mehr lose wie im gesunden Zustande mit dem Gliede vereinigt, so daß sie sich in der Bewegung mit ihm verbinden und gleich wieder loslösen kann; sie taucht sich dauernd in das Glied ein und kann sich nicht mehr aus ihm zurückziehen.

Wieder stellen sich die Vorgänge des gesunden Bewegens eines Gliedes und die Lähmung in ihrer Verwandtschaft nebeneinander. Ja, man sieht es deutlich: die gesunde Bewegung ist eine angefangene Lähmung, die sogleich in ihrem Anfange wieder aufgehoben wird.

Man muß in dem Wesen des Krankseins eine intensive Verbindung des astralischen Leibes oder der Ich-Organisation mit dem physischen Organismus sehen. Aber diese Verbindung ist doch nur eine Verstärkung derjenigen, die in einer loseren Art im gesunden Zustande vorhanden ist. Auch das normale Eingreifen des astralischen Leibes und der Ich-Organisation in den menschlichen Körper sind eben nicht den gesunden Lebensvorgängen verwandt, sondern den kranken. Wirken Geist und Seele, so heben sie die gewöhnliche Einrichtung des Körpers auf; sie verwandeln sie

leads to the experience of illness. One form of illness must be conceived of as a seizing of the organism by the astral body, which causes the spiritual human being to submerge more deeply into his body than is the case in health.

But thinking, too, has its physical basis in the organism. In the healthy state it is even more loosened from the organism than feeling. Spiritual perception finds, in addition to the astral body, also a special ego organization which expresses itself freely in the soul in thinking. If, with this ego organization, the human being submerges himself intensively into his bodily nature, a condition occurs which makes the observation of his own organism similar to that of the external world.—In observing an object or process of the outer world it is a matter of fact that the thought of the human being and that which is observed are not in living interaction, but are independent of each other. In a human limb this only occurs when it becomes paralyzed. Then it becomes outer world. The ego organization is no longer loosely united with the limb as it is in health, when it can unite with it in the movement and withdraw again at once; it submerges into the limb permanently and is no longer able to withdraw from it.

Here again the processes of healthy limb movement and of paralysis stand side by side in their relatedness. Indeed, one sees it clearly: healthy movement is a beginning paralysis, which at its onset is immediately neutralized again.

One must see the essence of being ill as an intensive union of the astral body or ego organization with the physical organism. Yet this union is only an intensification of what exists more loosely in health. Also the normal intervention of astral body and ego organization in the human body is not related to healthy life processes, but to pathological ones. Wherever the soul and spirit are at work, they suspend the ordinary arrangement of the body; they convert it into its

in eine entgegengesetzte. Aber damit bringen sie den Organismus auf einen Weg, bei dem das Kranksein beginnen will. Er wird im gewöhnlichen Leben sofort nach dem Entstehen durch eine Selbstheilung reguliert.

Eine gewisse Form des Krankseins tritt dann ein, wenn das Geistige oder Seelische zu weit nach dem Organismus vor-stoßen, so daß die Selbstheilung entweder gar nicht oder nur langsam eintreten kann.

In der Geist- und Seelenfähigkeit hat man also die Ursachen des Krankseins zu suchen. Und das Heilen muß in einem Loslösen des Seelischen oder Geistigen von der physischen Organisation bestehen.

Das ist die eine Art des Krankseins. Es gibt noch eine andere. Es können die Ich-Organisation und der astralische Leib abgehalten sein, es zu der losen Verbindung mit dem Körper-lichen zu bringen, die im gewöhnlichen Dasein das selbständige Fühlen, Denken und Wollen bedingen. Dann tritt in den Organen oder Vorgängen, an die Geist und Seele nicht heran können, eine Fortsetzung der gesunden Vorgänge über dasjenige Maß hinaus ein, das dem Organismus angemessen ist. Und der geistigen Anschauung zeigt sich in diesem Falle, daß dann der physische Organismus doch nicht bloß die leblosen Prozesse der äußeren Natur vollbringt. Der physische Organismus ist von einem ätherischen Organismus durchsetzt. Der bloße physische Organismus könnte niemals einen Selbstheilungsvorgang hervorrufen. Ein solcher wird in dem ätherischen Organismus angefacht. Damit aber wird die Gesundheit als der Zustand erkannt, der im ätherischen Organismus seinen Ursprung hat. Heilen muß daher in einer Behandlung des ätherischen Organismus bestehen.*

---

*Durch ein Vergleichen dessen, was im ersten Kapitel gesagt ist, mit dem Inhalte des zweiten wird sich das Verständnis dessen besonders ergeben, was in Betracht kommt.

opposite. In doing so they bring the organism on the way to where illness tends to set in. In normal life this is regulated by a process of self-healing as soon as it is generated.

A certain form of illness occurs when the spirit or the soul presses too far into the organism, so that the self-healing process can either not arise at all or only slowly.

Therefore, one must seek the causes of illness in the activity of soul and spirit. And healing must consist in releasing the soul or spiritual element from the physical organization.

This is one kind of illness. There is another. The ego organization and astral body may be prevented from making the loose connection with bodily nature which is the condition for independent feeling, thinking and willing in ordinary life. Then, a continuation of the healthy processes, beyond the measure appropriate for the organism, occurs in the organs or processes which the soul and spirit are unable to approach. And in such a case it is apparent to spiritual perception that the physical organism does indeed not just carry out the lifeless processes of external nature. The physical organism is permeated by an etheric organism. The physical organism alone could never evoke a process of self-healing. This is kindled in the etheric organism. This then leads to the recognition of health as that condition which has its origin in the etheric organism. Healing must therefore consist in treating the etheric organism.*

---

* By comparing what was said in the first chapter with the content of the second, insight can be gained especially in this respect.

III
DIE ERSCHEINUNGEN DES LEBENS

Man kommt nicht zum Verständnis des gesunden und kranken menschlichen Organismus, wenn man sich vorstellt, daß sich die Wirkungsart irgendeines mit der Nahrung aufgenommenen Stoffes aus der äußeren Natur in das Innere des Organismus einfach fortsetzt. Nicht um eine solche Fortsetzung der Wirkung, die man an dem Stoffe außerhalb des menschlichen Organismus beobachtet, handelt es sich, sondern um deren Überwindung.

Die Täuschung, als ob im Organismus die Stoffe der Außenwelt in ihrer Eigenart fortwirkten, entsteht dadurch, daß vor der gewöhnlichen chemischen Denkungsart das so erscheint. Diese gibt sich nach ihren Untersuchungen dem Glauben hin, der Wasserstoff z. B. sei im Organismus so vorhanden wie in der äußeren Natur, weil er sich in den als Nahrungsmittel eingenommenen Speisen und Getränken, und dann wieder in den Ausscheidungsprodukten: Luft, Schweiß, Urin, Faeces und in den Absonderungen, z. B. Galle, findet.

Man empfindet heute keine Notwendigkeit zu fragen, was mit dem als Wasserstoff vor dem Eintritt in den Organismus und nach dem Austritt Erscheinenden, im Organismus vorgegangen ist.

Man fragt nicht: was macht das als Wasserstoff Erscheinende im Organismus durch?

Man wird sogleich gedrängt, wenn man diese Frage aufwirft, die Aufmerksamkeit auf den Unterschied zwischen dem schlafenden und dem wachenden Organismus zu lenken. Im schlafenden Organismus bildet dessen stoffliche Wesenheit keine Grundlage zur Entfaltung der bewußten und selbstbewußten Erlebnisse. Aber sie bildet doch eine Grundlage zur Entfaltung des Lebens. In dieser Beziehung unterscheidet sich der schlafende von dem toten Organismus. In diesem ist die stoffliche Grundlage nicht mehr eine solche des Lebens. So lange man diesen Unterschied nur in der verschiedenen Zusammensetzung der Stoffe beim toten und

CHAPTER III

The Phenomena Of Life

One does not come to an understanding of the healthy and diseased human organism if one has the idea that the way a substance is active in nature outside simply continues on into the inner organism when it is ingested with food. It is not a matter of continuation of the action observed in the substance outside the human organism, but, on the contrary, of overcoming it.

The illusion that substances of the outer world simply continue their specific way of action inside the organism arises from the fact that to the ordinary chemical way of thinking it appears to be so. In accordance with its investigations the latter believes that hydrogen, for example, is present in the organism in the same way as in external nature, because it appears in nutrients consumed as food and drink, and then again in the excretions: air, sweat, urine, feces, and in secretions such as bile.

No necessity is felt today to ask what happens within the organism to what appears as hydrogen before entering into the organism and after leaving it.

One does not ask: What does the substance which appears as hydrogen undergo inside the organism?

When this question is raised one immediately feels the need to turn one's attention to the contrast between the sleeping and the waking organism. The material essence in the sleeping organism provides no foundation for the unfolding of conscious and selfconscious experiences. Yet it still provides a basis for life to unfold. In this respect the sleeping organism is different from a dead one. In the latter the material basis no longer provides for life. One will not progress any further in understanding so long as one sees the distinction only in the different composition of substances in the dead and the living organism.

lebenden Organismus sieht, wird man mit dem Verständnis nicht weiterkommen.

Es hat vor fast einem halben Jahrhundert der bedeutende Physiologe *Du Bois-Reymond* darauf hingewiesen, daß man aus den Stoffwirkungen nie das Bewußtsein erklären könne. Er hat gesagt, nie und nimmer werde man einsehen, warum es einer bestimmten Anzahl von Kohlenstoff-, Sauerstoff-, Stickstoff- und Wasserstoffatomen nicht sollte gleichgültig sein, wie sie liegen, wie sie lagen und liegen werden, und warum sie durch diese ihre Lageveränderung in dem Menschen die Empfindung hervorbringen: ich sehe rot; ich rieche Rosenduft. Weil das so ist, meinte Du Bois-Reymond, könne die naturwissenschaftliche Denkart den wachenden, von Empfindungen erfüllten Menschen nie erklären, sondern nur den schlafenden.

Er gab sich mit dieser Ansicht einer Illusion hin. Er glaubte, aus der Wirkungsart der Stoffe ergäben sich zwar nicht die Bewußtseins-Erscheinungen, wohl aber die des Lebens. In Wirklichkeit muß man aber ebenso wie Du Bois-Reymond für die Bewußtseins-Erscheinungen für die des Lebens sagen: Warum sollte es einer Anzahl von Kohlenstoff-, Sauerstoff-, Wasserstoff- und Stickstoffatomen beikommen, durch die Art, wie sie lagen, wie sie liegen, wie sie liegen werden, die Erscheinung des Lebens hervorzubringen?

Die Beobachtung zeigt doch, daß die Lebenserscheinungen eine ganz andere Orientierung haben als die im Leblosen verlaufenden. Für die letzteren wird man sagen können: sie zeigen sich von Kräften beherrscht, die vom Wesen des Stoffes ausstrahlen, vom–relativen–Mittelpunkt nach der Peripherie hin. Die Lebenserscheinungen zeigen den Stoff von Kräften beherrscht, die von außen nach innen wirken, gegen den – relativen – Mittelpunkt zu. Beim Übergange ins Leben muß sich der Stoff den ausstrahlenden Kräften entziehen und sich den einstrahlenden fügen.

Nun hat ein jeglicher Erdenstoff und auch Erdenvorgang seine ausstrahlenden Kräfte von der Erde und in Gemeinschaft mit ihr.

Almost half a century ago the eminent physiologist, Du Bois-Reymond,[5] pointed out that consciousness can never be explained from reactions of matter. Never, he declared, shall it be understood why it should not be a matter of indifference to a number of carbon, oxygen, nitrogen and hydrogen atoms, how they were, how they are and how they will be arranged, or why, by altering their position, they should bring about in the human being the sensation: I see red; I smell the scent of roses. Such being the case, Du Bois-Reymond contended, the conventional scientific way of thinking can never explain the waking human being, filled with sensations, but only the sleeping human being.

With this view he was under an illusion. He believed that the phenomena of consciousness indeed would not follow from the reactions of matter, but that those of life would. In reality, however, one must claim the same for the phenomena of life as Du Bois-Reymond claimed for those of consciousness: Why should it occur to a number of carbon, oxygen, hydrogen and nitrogen atoms to evoke the phenomenon of life, through the way they were, are, or will be arranged?

Observation shows, after all, that the phenomena of life have an altogether different orientation from those that run their course within the lifeless element. Of the latter one will be able to say: They show that they are dominated by forces radiating outward from the essence of matter, from the—relative—center towards the periphery. Living phenomena show that matter is dominated by forces working from without inward, toward the—relative—center. In the transition to the sphere of life, substance must withdraw from the forces radiating outward and become subject to those that radiate inward.

Now it is so that every earthly substance and also earthly process derives its outward radiating forces from the earth and has these forces in common with the earth. It is a substance as seen by chemistry only in as much as it is part of the earth body. When it comes to life, then it must cease being a mere part of

Er ist ein solcher Stoff, wie ihn die Chemie betrachtet, nur als ein Bestandteil des Erdenkörpers. Kommt er zum Leben, so muß er aufhören, ein bloßer Erdenteil zu sein. Er tritt aus der Gemeinschaft mit der Erde heraus. Er wird einbezogen in die Kräfte, die vom Außerirdischen nach der Erde von allen Seiten einstrahlen. Sieht man einen Stoff oder Vorgang als Leben sich entfalten, so muß man sich vorstellen, er entziehe sich den Kräften, die wie vom Mittelpunkte der Erde auf ihn wirken, und er komme in den Bereich von anderen, die keinen Mittelpunkt, sondern einen Umkreis haben.

Von allen Seiten wirken sie heran, diese Kräfte, wie nach dem Mittelpunkte der Erde hin strebend. Sie müßten das Stoffliche des Erdenbereichs völlig gestaltlos auflösen, zerreißen, wenn sich nicht in diesen Kräfteraum die Wirkungen der außerirdischen Himmelskörper mischten, die die Auflösung modifizieren. An der Pflanze kann man beobachten, was in Betracht kommt. Die Stoffe der Erde werden in den Pflanzen aus dem Bereich der Erdenwirkungen herausgehoben. Sie streben in das Formlose. Diesen Übergang in das Formlose modifizieren die Sonnenwirkungen und ähnliches aus dem Weltenraume. Wirkt das nicht, oder anders z. B. in der Nacht, dann regen sich in den Stoffen wieder die Kräfte, die sie aus der Erdengemeinschaft haben. Und aus dem Zusammenwirken der irdischen und kosmischen Kräfte entsteht das Pflanzenwesen. Faßt man den Bereich alles dessen, was die Stoffe an Kräftewirkungen unter Erdeneinfluß entfalten, als das Physische zusammen, so wird man die ganz anders gearteten Kräfte, die nicht von der Erde ausstrahlend, sondern in sie einstrahlend sind, mit einem das Andersartige ausdrückenden Namen bezeichnen müssen. Wir finden dasjenige in der menschlichen Organisation hier von einer andern Seite, auf das wir von der einen Seite schon im vorigen Kapitel hingewiesen haben. Im Einklange mit einem älteren Gebrauch, der unter dem Einfluß der neueren, physikalisch orientierten Denkungsart in Verwirrung gekommen ist, haben wir bereits diesen Teil des menschlichen

earth. It leaves its community with the earth. It becomes included in the extraterrestrial forces that radiate inward to the earth from all sides. Whenever one sees a substance or process unfold in forms of life then it must be conceived of as withdrawing from the forces that work upon it as from the center of the earth, and entering the sphere of other forces, which do not have a center, but a periphery.

These forces work from all sides, as if striving towards the center of the earth. They would dissolve the material nature of the earthly into complete formlessness, tear it asunder, were it not for the heavenly bodies beyond the earth which mingle their influences in the field of these forces and modify the dissolving process. In the plant one can observe what happens. The substances of the earth are lifted out of the sphere of earth influences in plants. They strive towards the formless. This transition to the formless is modified by the influences of the sun and similar effects from cosmic space. When these are no longer working, or when they are working differently, for example at night, then the forces which the substances have from their community with the earth begin to stir once more within them. And out of the cooperation of earthly forces and cosmic forces the plant being originates. If one includes in the term 'physical' the sphere of all those functional forces which substances can unfold under the earth's influence, then the entirely different forces which do not radiate outward from the earth, but in toward it, shall have to be designated by a name in which this different character finds expression. Here we come, from another point of view, to that element in the organization of the human being which we had already outlined from one aspect in the previous chapter. In conformity with an older usage, which has become confused under the influence of the modern way of thinking, oriented as it is to physical phenomena, we have already designated this part of the human organism as

Organismus als das Ätherische bezeichnet. Man wird sagen müssen: im Pflanzlichen, das heißt in dem als lebend Erscheinenden, waltet das Ätherische.

Insofern der Mensch ein lebendes Wesen ist, waltet dieses Ätherische auch in ihm. Aber es tritt doch auch in Bezug auf die bloßen Lebenserscheinungen ein bedeutsamer Unterschied gegenüber dem Pflanzlichen auf. Die Pflanze läßt in sich das Physische walten, wenn das Ätherische aus dem Weltenraum seine Wirksamkeit nicht mehr entfaltet, wie das in der Nacht der Fall ist, wo der Sonnenäther aufhört zu wirken. Das Menschen-wesen läßt in seinem Körper das Physische erst im Tode walten. Im Schlafe entschwinden die Bewußtseins- und Selbst-bewußtseins-Erscheinungen; die Lebenserscheinungen aber bleiben bestehen, auch wenn der Sonnenäther im Weltenraum nicht wirkt. Die Pflanze nimmt fortdauernd während ihres Lebens die auf die Erde einstrahlenden Ätherkräfte in sich auf. Der Mensch trägt sie aber schon von seiner Embryonalzeit an individualisiert in sich. Was so die Pflanze aus der Welt erhält, entnimmt der Mensch während seines Lebens *aus sich,* weil er es schon im Leibe der Mutter zur Fortentwicklung erhalten hat. Eine Kraft, die eigentlich ursprünglich kosmisch ist, zur auf die Erde einstrahlenden Wirkung bestimmt, wirkt aus der Lunge oder Leber heraus. Sie hat eine Metamorphose ihrer Richtung vollzogen.

Man wird deshalb sagen müssen, der Mensch trägt das Ätherische in einer individualisierten Art in sich. So wie er das Physische in der individualisierten Gestalt seines physischen Leibes und seiner Leibesorgane an sich trägt, ebenso das ätherische. Er hat seinen besonderen Ätherleib wie seinen besonderen physischen Leib. Im Schlafe bleibt dieser Ätherleib mit dem physischen Leibe verbunden und gibt diesem das Leben; nur im Tode löst er sich von ihm.

the etheric. One shall have to say: in plantlike nature, meaning in that which appears to be living, the etheric is active.

To the extent that the human being is a living being, the same etheric principle is active in him. However, indeed even with respect to the mere phenomena of life, an important difference becomes apparent in comparison to plant nature. The plant allows the physical to hold sway within it when the etheric from cosmic space no longer unfolds its activity, as is the case at night when the sun ether ceases to work. Only at death does the human being let the physical hold sway in his body. In sleep the phenomena of consciousness and self-consciousness vanish, but the phenomena of life remain, even when the sun ether is not working in cosmic space. Throughout its life the plant continually receives into itself the ether forces that ray in toward the earth. The human being, however, from the embryonal period on, carries them within in an individualized form. That which the plant receives in the described way from the universe, he draws *out of himself* during his life, since he received it already in the mother's womb for his further development. A force which originally is cosmic in nature, destined to ray its influences in towards the earth, works out of lung or liver. It has enacted a metamorphosis of its direction.

Thus one shall have to say that the human being bears the etheric within, in an individualized form. As the physical is carried in the individualized form of the physical body and its physical organs, so also the etheric. He has his unique ether body, as he has his unique physical body. In sleep, this ether body remains united with the physical body and gives it life; it only separates from it in death.

IV
VON DEM WESEN DES EMPFINDENDEN ORGANISMUS

Die Pflanzengestalt und Pflanzenorganisation ist ein ausschließliches Ergebnis der beiden Kräftebereiche: des aus der Erde ausstrahlenden und des in sie einstrahlenden; die tierische und menschliche nicht ein ausschließliches. Ein Pflanzenblatt steht unter dem ausschließlichen Einfluß dieser beiden Kräftebereiche; die tierische Lunge steht auch unter deren Einfluß, aber nicht ausschließlich. Für das Blatt liegen alle gestaltenden Kräfte *in* diesen Bereichen; für die Lunge gibt es solche außerhalb derselben. Das gilt sowohl für diejenigen gestaltenden Kräfte, die die Außenform geben, als auch für diejenigen, die die innere Bewegung des Substantiellen regeln, diesem eine gewisse Richtung geben und es verbinden oder trennen.

Man kann sagen, den Stoffen, welche die Pflanze aufnimmt, bleibt es dadurch, daß sie in den Bereich der auf die Erde einstrahlenden Kräfte gelangen, nicht gleichgültig, ob sie leben oder nicht leben. Sie sind innerhalb der Pflanze leblos, wenn die Kräfte des Umkreises nicht auf sie wirken; sie geraten in das Leben, wenn sie unter den Einfluß dieser Kräfte kommen.

Aber es ist der Pflanzensubstanz auch als lebende gleichgültig, wie ihre Glieder lagen, liegen und liegen werden in Bezug auf ihre eigene Betätigung. Sie überlassen sich der Betätigung der aus- und einstrahlenden Außenkräfte. Die tierische Substanz kommt in Wirkungen, die von diesen Kräften unabhängig sind. Sie bewegt sich innerhalb des Organismus, oder sie bewegt sich als ganzer Organismus so, daß diese Bewegungen nicht aus den aus- und einstrahlenden Kräften allein folgen. Es entsteht dadurch die tierische Gestaltung unabhängig von den Bereichen der von der Erde aus- und in sie einstrahlenden Kräfte.

Bei der Pflanze ergibt sich durch das gekennzeichnete Kräftespiel ein Wechsel zwischen einem Eingeschaltetsein in die einstrahlenden Kräfte des Umkreises und einem Ausgeschaltetsein. Das Pflanzenwesen zerfällt dadurch in zwei Glieder. Das eine zielt

CHAPTER IV

On The Nature Of The Sentient Organism

The form and organization of the plant are the exclusive results of both spheres of forces: the one which radiates outwards from the earth and the other which radiates in toward it. This exclusivity is found neither in the animal nor in the human being. The leaf of a plant exists under the exclusive influence of these two spheres of forces; the lung of an animal is also subject to the same influences, but not exclusively. For the leaf, all the form-creating forces lie within these two spheres; for the lung there are others besides these. This applies both to the form-creating forces which give the outer shape, and also to those that regulate the inner movement of substance, giving it a specific direction, combining or separating it.

One can say that for the substances which are taken up by the plant it is not a matter of indifference whether they are alive or not, because they have become part of the sphere of forces radiating in toward the earth. Within the plant they are lifeless if the forces of the circumference do not work upon them; they come to life when they come under the influence of these forces.

But to the plant substance, even when alive, it is a matter of indifference how its parts were arranged, are arranged and will be arranged in relation to its own mode of activity. They give themselves up to the mode of activity of the external forces raying out and in. Animal substance comes under influences that are independent of these forces. It moves within the organism, or moves as a whole organism in such a way that these movements do not follow only the forces radiating outward and inward. Because of this, the form of the animal comes into being independently of the spheres of the forces raying outward from and inward to the earth.

nach dem Leben hin, es steht ganz im Bereich des Umkreises; es sind die sprossenden, Wachstum-, Blüten-tragenden Organe. Das andere zielt nach dem Leblosen, es verbleibt im Bereiche der ausstrahlenden Kräfte, es umfaßt alles, was das Wachstum verhärtet, dem Leben Stütze gibt usw. Zwischen diesen beiden Gliedern entzündet sich und erlöscht das Leben; und das Sterben der Pflanze ist nur das Überhandnehmen der Wirkungen von seiten der ausstrahlenden gegenüber den einstrahlenden Kräften.

Beim Tiere wird etwas von dem Substantiellen ganz aus dem Bereiche der beiden Kräftegebiete herausgezogen. Dadurch entsteht noch eine andere Gliederung als bei der Pflanze. Es entstehen Organbildungen, die im Bereiche der beiden Kräftegebiete verbleiben, und solche, die sich aus ihnen herausheben. Es ergeben sich Wechselwirkungen zwischen den beiden Organbildungen. Und in *diesen* Wechselwirkungen liegt die Ursache, daß die tierische Substanz Träger der Empfindung sein kann. Eine Folge davon ist die Verschiedenheit im Aussehen, in der Beschaffenheit der tierischen Substanz gegenüber der pflanzlichen.

Man hat im tierischen Organismus einen Kräftebereich, der gegenüber dem von der Erde ausstrahlenden und in sie einstrahlenden unabhängig ist. Es ist der astralische Kräftebereich außer dem physischen und ätherischen noch da, von dem, von anderem Gesichtspunkte aus, schon gesprochen ist. Man braucht sich an dem Ausdrucke «astralisch» nicht zu stoßen. Die ausstrahlenden Kräfte sind die irdischen, die einstrahlenden diejenigen des Welt-Umkreises der Erde; in den «astralischen» ist etwas vorhanden, das den beiden Kräftearten übergeordnet ist. Dies macht die Erde selbst erst zum Weltenkörper, zum «Stern» (astrum). Durch die physischen Kräfte sondert sie sich aus dem Weltall heraus, durch die ätherischen läßt sie dieses auf sich wirken; durch die «astralischen» Kräfte wird sie eine selbständige Individualität im Weltall.

Das «Astralische» ist im tierischen Organismus eine selbtändige, in sich abgeschlossene Gliederung wie der ätherische und

In the plant, the play of forces here described results in an alternation between being connected with and disconnected from the forces that ray in from the periphery. The plant being thus falls into two parts. One tends toward life and is fully in the sphere of the circumference; it encompasses the sprouting, the growth- and blossom-bearing organs. The other is oriented toward the lifeless; it remains in the sphere of the forces raying outward; it comprises all that hardens growth, provides support to life, etc. Between these two parts, life is enkindled and extinguished; the dying of the plant is merely the result of the forces raying out gaining the upper hand over the forces raying in.

In the animal, part of the substance is withdrawn completely from the sphere of the two fields of forces. Through this a still different arrangement comes about than in the plant. Organ formations originate which stay within the sphere of the two fields of forces, and others come about which lift themselves out of these. Reciprocal relations between these two organ formations are the result. And in these reciprocal relations lies the reason for animal substance becoming the bearer of sensations. One consequence of this is the difference in appearance and in disposition between animal and plant substance.

In the animal organism there is a sphere of forces independent of those radiating outward from, and radiating inward to, the earth. The astral sphere of forces, already spoken of from another point of view, is there in addition to the physical and etheric. One need not be troubled by the term 'astral.' The forces radiating outward are the earthly, those radiating inward are those of the cosmic circumference about the earth. In the astral, something of a higher order than these two kinds of forces is present. This alone is what makes the earth into a heavenly body, a 'star' (*astrum*). Through the physical forces the earth separates itself from the universe; through the etheric it allows

der physische Organismus. Man kann deshalb von dieser Gliederung als von dem «*astralischen Leib*» sprechen.

Man kann die tierische Organisation nur verstehen, wenn man die Wechselbeziehungen zwischen dem physischen, dem ätherischen und dem astralischen Leib ins Auge faßt. Denn alle drei sind selbständig als Glieder der tierischen Organisation vorhanden; und alle drei sind auch verschieden von dem, was außer ihnen an leblosen (mineralischen) Körpern und an pflanzlich belebten Organismen vorhanden ist.

Der tierische physische Organismus kann zwar als leblos angesprochen werden; aber er unterscheidet sich von dem Mineralisch-Leblosen. Er wird zuerst durch den ätherischen und astralischen Organismus dem Mineralischen entfremdet, und dann wieder, durch Zurückziehen der ätherischen und astralischen Kräfte dem Leblosen zurückgegeben. Er ist ein Gebilde, an dem die im Mineralischen, im bloßen Erdenbereiche, wirksamen Kräfte nur zerstörend sich betätigen können. Er kann dem tierischen Gesamtrganismus nur so lange dienen, als die ätherischen und astralischen Kräfte das Übergewicht haben über das zerstörende Eingreifen der mineralischen.

Der tierische ätherische Organismus lebt wie der pflanzliche, aber nicht in der gleichen Art. Das Leben ist durch die astralischen Kräfte in einen sich selbst fremden Zustand gebracht; es ist aus den auf die Erde einstrahlenden Kräften herausgerissen und dann wieder in deren Bereich versetzt worden. Der ätherische Organismus ist ein Gebilde, in dem die bloß pflanzlichen Kräfte ein für die tierische Organisation zu dumpfes Dasein haben. Er kann dem tierischen Gesamtorganismus nur dadurch dienen, daß die astralischen Kräfte seine Wirkungsweise aufhellen. Gewinnt er die Oberhand im Wirken, so tritt der Schlaf ein; gewinnt der astralische Organismus die Oberhand, so ist das Wachen vorhanden.

Beides, Schlafen und Wachen, darf nicht über eine gewisse Grenze der Wirksamkeit hinausgehen. Geschähe das mit dem Schlafen, so würde in dem Gesamtorganismus das Pflanzliche zum Mineralischen hinneigen; es entstünde als krankhafter Zustand ein

the universe to influence it; through the astral forces it becomes an independent individuality within the universe.

In the animal organism, the astral element is an independent, self-contained part like the physical and the etheric organism. One can therefore speak of it as an "astral body."

The animal organization can only be understood when the reciprocal relations between the physical, the etheric and the astral body are taken into account. For all three are present, independently, as parts of the animal organization; moreover, all three are different from what, beside them, exists by way of lifeless (mineral) bodies or living plantlike bodies.

True, the animal physical organism may be spoken of as lifeless; yet it is different from the lifeless nature of the mineral. At first it is alienated from mineral nature by the etheric and the astral organism, and then, by a withdrawal of etheric and astral forces, it is returned again to lifelessness. Upon this structure the mineral forces that work in the earth sphere exclusively can only act destructively. It can serve the animal organization as a whole only so long as the etheric and astral forces have the upper hand over the destructive intervention of the mineral forces.

The animal etheric organism is alive like that of the plant, but not in the same way. Life has been brought into a condition foreign to itself by the astral forces; it has been pulled away from the forces raying in toward the earth and then has been returned to their sphere. The etheric organism is a structure in which the mere plantlike forces have an existence that is too dull for the animal organization. The etheric organism can only serve the animal organism as a whole through the fact that the astral forces continually lighten up its mode of action. If its working gains the upper hand, sleep ensues; when the astral organism gains the upper hand, waking prevails.

Both sleeping and waking may not go beyond a certain boundary of functioning. If this were to happen in the case of

Überwuchern des Pflanzlichen. Geschähe es mit dem Wachen, so müßte sich das Pflanzliche von dem Mineralischen ganz entfremden; dieses würde in dem Organismus Formen annehmen, die nicht die seinigen, sondern die des außerorganischen Leblosen wären. Es bildete sich ein krankhafter Zustand durch Überwuchern des Mineralischen.

In alle drei Organismen, den physischen, ätherischen, astralischen, dringt die physische Substanz von außen ein. Alle drei müssen in ihrer Weise die Eigenart des Physischen überwinden. Dadurch entsteht eine Dreiheit der Organgliederung. Die physische Organisation bildet Organe, die durch die ätherische und astralische Organisation hindurchgegangen, die aber wieder auf dem Rückwege zu deren Bereich sind. Ganz angekommen in deren Bereich können sie nicht sein; denn das müßte den Tod des Organismus zur Folge haben.

Der ätherische Organismus bildet Organe, die durch die astralische Organisation hindurchgegangen sind, die aber sich dieser immer wieder zu entziehen streben; sie haben in sich die Kraft zur Dumpfheit des Schlafes; sie neigen dazu, das bloß vegetative Leben zu entfalten.

Der astralische Organismus bildet Organe, die das vegetative Leben sich entfremden. Sie können nur bestehen, wenn dieses vegetative Leben sie selbst immer wieder ergreift. Denn da sie keine Verwandtschaft weder mit den von der Erde aus-, noch auf diese einstrahlenden Kräften haben, müßten sie aus dem Bereich des Irdischen ganz herausfallen, wenn sie nicht immer wieder von diesem ergriffen würden. Es muß ein rhythmisches Wechselwirken des tierischen und pflanzlichen in diesen Organen stattfinden. Das bedingt die Wechselzustände von Schlafen und Wachen. Im Schlafen sind auch die Organe der astralischen Kräfte in der Dumpfheit des pflanzlichen Lebens. Sie üben da keine Wirkung auf das ätherische und physische Gebiet. Die sind dann ganz den von der Erde aus- und in sie einstrahlenden Kräftebereichen überlassen.

sleep, plant nature in the whole organism would incline towards the mineral; a hypertrophy of plant nature would be generated as a pathological condition. If it were to happen in the case of waking, plant nature would become entirely alienated from the mineral; the latter would assume forms within the organism not belonging to it, but to the external, inorganic, lifeless sphere. It would be a pathological condition due to hypertrophy of mineral nature.

Into all the three organisms, physical, etheric and astral, physical substance penetrates from outside. All three must in their own way overcome the specific nature of the physical. Through this a threefold organization of the organs comes into being. The physical organization forms organs which have gone through the etheric and astral organizations but which are on the way back again to their sphere. They cannot have arrived there completely, for this would result in the death of the organism.

The etheric organism forms organs which have passed through the astral organization but which are ever and again striving to withdraw from it; in them is a force striving towards the dullness of sleep; they are inclined to develop just vegetative life.

The astral organism forms organs which estrange it from vegetative life. They can only exist if this vegetative life takes hold of them ever and again. Having no relationship either with the forces radiating outward from or with those radiating inward to the earth, they would fall out of the earth sphere altogether if this vegetative life did not again and again take hold of them. A rhythmical interaction between animal nature and plant nature must take place in these organs. This determines the alternating states of sleeping and waking. In sleep, the organs of the astral forces partake also in the dullness of plant life. Then they have no influence on the etheric and physical domain. They are then entirely left to the spheres of forces raying in toward and outward from the earth.

V
PFLANZE, TIER, MENSCH

In dem astralischen Leibe ersteht die tierische Gestaltung nach außen als ganze Gestalt und nach innen als Gestaltung der Organe. Und die empfindende tierische Substanz ist ein Ergebnis dieses gestaltenden astralischen Leibes. Wird diese Gestaltung bis zu ihrem Ende geführt, so bildet sich das Tierische.

Beim Menschen wird sie nicht zu Ende geführt. Sie wird in einem gewissen Punkte ihres Weges aufgehalten, gehemmt.

In der Pflanze ist die Substanz vorhanden, die durch die auf die Erde einstrahlenden Kräfte verwandelt wird. Das ist die lebende Substanz. Sie steht in Wechselwirkung mit der leblosen Substanz. Man hat sich vorzustellen, daß im Pflanzenwesen fortdauernd aus der leblosen Substanz diese lebende herausgesondert wird. In ihr erscheint die Pflanzengestalt als das Ergebnis der auf die Erde einstrahlenden Kräfte. Das ergibt einen Substanzstrom. Lebloses wandelt sich in Lebendes; Lebendiges wandelt sich in Lebloses. In diesem Strom entstehen die pflanzlichen Organe.

Beim Tiere entsteht die empfindende Substanz aus der lebendigen, wie bei der Pflanze die lebendige aus der leblosen. Es ist ein zweifacher Substanzstrom vorhanden. Das Leben wird innerhalb des ätherischen nicht bis zum gestalteten Leben gebracht. Es wird im Flusse erhalten; und die Gestaltung schiebt sich durch die astralische Organisation in das fließende Leben hinein.

Beim Menschen wird auch *dieser* Vorgang im Flusse erhalten. Die empfindende Substanz wird in den Bereich einer weiteren Organisation hineingezogen. Man kann diese die Ich-Organisation nennen. Die empfindende Substanz wandelt sich noch einmal. Es entsteht ein dreifacher Substanzstrom. In diesem ersteht die menschliche innere und äußere Gestalt. Dadurch wird sie zum Träger des selbstbewußten Geisteslebens. Bis in die kleinsten Teile seiner Substanz hinein ist der Mensch in seiner Gestaltung ein Ergebnis dieser Ich-Organisation.

CHAPTER V

Plant, Animal, Human Being

In the astral body, animal form arises outwardly as the whole shape and inwardly as the form of the organs. And sentient animal substance is an outcome of this form-creating astral body. If this form is carried to its conclusion, then the animalic nature develops.

Within the human being it is not carried to its conclusion. At a certain point along its way, it is held up, restrained.

In the plant, substance which is converted by the forces raying in toward the earth is present. This is living substance. It is in interaction with lifeless substance. One must imagine that in plant nature this living substance is continually being separated out from what is lifeless. In it, the plant shape appears as a product of the forces raying in towards the earth. That results in a stream of substance. The lifeless changes into what lives; what is living changes into what is lifeless. In this stream the plant organs come into being.

Within the animal, sentient substance originates from the living, as for the plant living substance originates from lifeless substance. There is a twofold stream of substance. Within the etheric, life does not reach the point of becoming form-creating life. It is kept in flow, and form inserts itself through the astral organization into flowing life.

Within the human being *this* process, too, is kept in flow. Sentient substance is drawn into the realm of a further organization. One may call this the ego organization. Sentient substance changes once again. A threefold stream of substance comes into being. In this the human being's inner and outer shape arises. Thereby it becomes the bearer of self-conscious

Man kann nun diese Gestaltung nach ihrer Substanzseite hin verfolgen. Bei Umwandlung der Substanz von der einen Stufe zur anderen hin erscheint die Substanz als eine Absonderung der oberen Stufe von der unteren und ein Aufbauen der Gestalt aus der abgesonderten Substanz. Bei der Pflanze wird aus der leblosen Substanz die lebendige abgesondert. In dieser abgesonderten Substanz wirken die auf die Erde einstrahlenden, die ätherischen Kräfte, als gestaltbildende. Zunächst findet nicht eine eigentliche Absonderung, sondern eine völlige Umwandlung der physischen Substanz durch die ätherischen Kräfte statt. Das ist aber nur der Fall in der Samenbildung. Bei ihr kann diese völlige Umwandlung stattfinden, weil der Same durch die ihn umhüllende Mutterorganisation vor der Einwirkung der physischen Kräfte geschützt wird. Befreit sich die Samenbildung von der Mutterorganisation, so gliedert sich die Kräftewirkung der Pflanze in eine solche, in der die Substanzbildung nach dem Bereich des Ätherischen hinstrebt und in eine andere, in der sie wieder nach der physischen Bildung hinstrebt. Es entstehen Glieder des Pflanzenwesens, die auf dem Wege des Lebens sind und solche, die dem Absterben zustreben. Diese erscheinen als die Ausscheidungsglieder des Pflanzenorganismus. In der Rindenbildung des Baumes kann man diese Ausscheidung als an einem besonders charakteristischen Beispiele beobachten.

Beim Tier ist eine zweifache Absonderung und auch eine zweifache Ausscheidung im Gange. Zu der pflanzlichen, die nicht zum Abschlusse gebracht wird, sondern im Flusse erhalten wird, tritt die Verwandlung der lebenden Substanz in empfindende hinzu. Diese sondert sich von der bloß lebenden ab. Man hat es mit einer nach dem empfindenden Wesen hinstrebenden und einer von ihm ab-, zum bloßen Leben hinstrebenden Substanz zu tun.

Aber es kommt im Organismus zu einer Wechselwirkung aller seiner Glieder. Deshalb ist auch die Ausscheidung nach dem Leblosen hin, die sich bei der Pflanze sehr stark dem äußerlich Leblosen, dem Mineralischen nähert, noch weit von diesem Min-

spiritual life. The human being is, in his form, a result of this ego organization down to the smallest particles of his substance.

One can now pursue this form from the aspect of substance. In the transformation of substance from one level to the next, substance appears as a separation of the higher level from the lower and a building of shape out of the separated substance. Within the plant, the living is separated out of lifeless substance. The forces raying in toward the earth, the etheric forces, work in this separated substance creating form. To begin with, it is not an actual separation that takes place, but a complete transformation of physical substance by the etheric forces. However, that is only the case in seed formation. Here the complete transformation can take place, because the seed is protected by the surrounding maternal organization from being acted upon by physical forces. When in its development the seed frees itself from the maternal organization, then the forces working in the plant arrange themselves into those, in which the formation of substance strives toward the sphere of the etheric, and into others, in which it strives again toward physical formation. Parts of the being of the plant originate that are on the way toward life and others that tend toward dying. The latter appear as the excreted parts of the plant organism. In the bark formation of the tree one may observe a particularly characteristic example of this process of excretion.

In the animal, a twofold process of separation and also a twofold process of excretion is going on. The plant process of separation is not carried to a conclusion but kept in flow, and added to it is the conversion of living into sentient substance. This is separated from the purely living. One finds substance that is striving toward sentient existence and substance that is striving away from this to the purely living state.

Yet, in the organism a reciprocal relation between all its parts comes about. Therefore, even the excretion toward the lifeless, which in the plant closely approaches the outwardly

eralischen entfernt. Was in der Rindenbildung der Pflanze als Substanzbildung auftritt, die auf dem Wege zum Mineralischen hin ist und sich ablöst, je mehr sie mineralisch wird, das erscheint im Tierischen als Ausscheidungsprodukte der Verdauung. Es ist weiter von dem Mineralischen entfernt als die pflanzliche Abscheidung.

Beim Menschen wird aus der empfindenden Substanz diejenige abgesondert, die dann Träger des selbstbewußten Geistes wird. Aber es wird auch fortwährend eine Abscheidung bewirkt, indem eine Substanz entsteht, die nach der bloßen Empfindungsfähigkeit hinstrebt. Das Tierische ist innerhalb des menschlichen Organismus als eine fortdauernde Ausscheidung vorhanden.

Im wachenden Zustande des tierischen Organismus steht Absonderung und Gestaltung des Abgesonderten, sowie auch Abscheidung der empfindenden Substanz unter dem Einfluß der astralischen Tätigkeit. Beim Menschen kommt dazu noch die Tätigkeit des Ich-Organismus. Im Schlafe sind astralischer und Ich-Organismus nicht unmittelbar tätig. Aber die Substanz ist von dieser Tätigkeit ergriffen und setzt sie wie durch ein Beharrungsstreben fort. Eine Substanz, die einmal innerlich so durchgestaltet ist, wie es von seiten der astralischen und der Ich-Organisation geschieht, die wirkt dann auch während des schlafenden Zustandes im Sinne dieser Organisationen, gewissermaßen im Sinne eines Beharrungsvermögens fort.

Man kann also beim schlafenden Menschen nicht von einer bloß vegetativen Betätigung des Organismus sprechen. Die astralische und die Ich-Organisation wirken in der von ihr gestalteten Substanz auch in diesem Zustande weiter. Der Unterschied zwischen Schlafen und Wachen ist nicht ein solcher, in dem menschlich-animalische und vegetativ-physische Betätigung abwechseln. Der Tatbestand ist ein völlig anderer. Die empfindende Substanz und diejenige, welche den selbstbewußten Geist tragen kann, werden beim Wachen aus dem Gesamtorganismus herausgehoben

lifeless, the mineral world, is still far removed from what is characteristically mineral. What appears in the bark formation of the plant as substance which is already on the way to mineral nature, and which detaches itself the more mineralized it becomes, appears in the animal as the excreted products of digestion. It is farther removed from mineral nature than are the elimination products of the plant.

In the human being, substance, which then becomes the bearer of the self-conscious spirit, is separated out of the sentient substance. But also a continuous elimination is brought about, in that a substance develops which strives toward a merely sentient faculty. Animal nature is thus present within the human organism as a continuous excretion.

In the waking state of the animal organism, separation and giving form to what is separated, as well as elimination of sentient substance, stand under the influence of astral activity. In the human being the activity of the ego organism is added to this. In sleep, astral and ego organism are not directly active. But substance has been taken hold of by this activity and continues it as though by inertia. A substance which has once been formed through and through internally in the way the astral and ego organization do this, will then also go on working in accord with these organizations in the sleeping state, as if it were out of a capacity for inertia.

Thus in the sleeping human being one cannot speak of a purely vegetative mode of activity of the organism. The astral and the ego organization work further in the substance they have formed, even in this state. The difference between sleeping and waking is not such that the human-animalic mode of activity alternates with the vegetative-physical. The reality is altogether different. In waking life sentient substance and that which can act as bearer of the self-conscious spirit are lifted out of the organism as a whole and placed at the disposal of the astral body and the ego organization. The physical and the etheric organism

und in den Dienst des astralischen Leibes und der Ich-Organisation gestellt. Der physische und der ätherische Organismus müssen dann so sich betätigen, daß in ihnen nur die von der Erde ausstrahlenden und in sie einstrahlenden Kräfte wirken. In dieser Wirkungsweise werden sie nur von außen durch den astralischen Leib und die Ich-Organisation ergriffen. Im Schlafe aber werden sie innerlich von den Substanzen ergriffen, die unter dem Einfluß des astralischen Leibes und der Ich-Organisation entstehen; während auf den schlafenden Menschen aus dem Weltall nur die von der Erde ausstrahlenden und auf sie einstrahlenden Kräfte wirken, sind an ihm von innen die Substanzkräfte tätig, die von dem astralischen Leib und der Ich-Organisation bereitet werden.

Wenn man die empfindende Substanz den *Rest* des astralischen Leibes und die unter dem Einfluß der Ich-Organisation entstandene *deren Rest* nennt, so kann man sagen: im wachenden menschlichen Organismus sind der astralische Leib und die Ich-Organisation selbst, im schlafenden sind deren substantielle Reste tätig.

Wachend lebt der Mensch in einer Betätigung, welche ihn mit der Außenwelt durch seinen astralischen Leib und durch eine Ich-Organisation in Verbindung setzt; schlafend leben sein physischer und sein ätherischer Organismus von dem, was die Reste dieser beiden Organisationen substantiell geworden sind. Eine Substanz, die wie der Sauerstoff durch das Atmen sowohl im schlafenden wie im wachenden Zustande aufgenommen wird, muß daher in ihrer Wirksamkeit nach diesen beiden Zuständen hin unterschieden werden. Der von außen aufgenommene Sauerstoff wirkt durch seine Eigenart einschläfernd, nicht aufweckend. Vermehrte Sauerstoffaufnahme schläfert in abnormer Art ein. Der astralische Leib bekämpft fortdauernd im Wachen die einschläfernde Wirkung der Sauerstoffaufnahme. Stellt der astralische Leib seine Wirkung auf den physischen ein, so entfaltet der Sauerstoff seine Eigenart: er schläfert ein.

must then work in such a way that only the forces raying outward from the earth and in toward it are active in them. In this mode of action they are taken hold of by the astral body and the ego organization only from outside. In sleep, however, they are taken hold of inwardly by the substances that come into existence under the influence of astral body and ego organization; while from the universe only the forces radiating outward from the earth and in toward it are working on the sleeping human being, the substance forces which are prepared by the astral body and ego organization act on him from within.

If one calls the sentient substance the *residue* of the astral body, and that which has come into being under the influence of the ego organization *its residue*, then one may say: in the waking human organism the astral body and ego organization themselves are working, in the sleeping human organism their substantial residues are at work.

In waking, the human being lives in a mode of activity which connects him with the outer world through the astral body and through the ego organization; in sleep, the physical and etheric organisms live on what the residues of these two organizations have become in substance form. Therefore, a substance like oxygen, which, through breathing, is taken in both in sleeping and in waking, must be distinguished in its mode of action according to these two conditions. Oxygen absorbed from without has an inherently soporific, not an awakening, effect. Increased intake of oxygen leads to abnormal drowsiness. In waking life the astral body battles continually against the soporific effect of oxygen intake. When the astral body suspends its work upon the physical, oxygen unfolds its inherent nature and sends the human being to sleep.

VI
BLUT UND NERV

In besonders eindrucksvoller Art finden sich die Tätigkeiten der einzelnen menschlichen Organismen in bezug auf den Gesamtorganismus bei der Blut- und Nervenbildung. Indem die Blutbildung in der Fortgestaltung der aufgenommenen Nahrungsstoffe erfolgt, steht der ganze Blutbildungsvorgang unter dem Einfluß der Ich-Organisation. Die Ich-Organisation wirkt von den Vorgängen, die in Begleitung bewußter Empfindung – in der Zunge, im Gaumen – vor sich gehen bis in die unbewußten und unterbewußten Vorgänge hinein – in Pepsin-, Pankreas-, Gallenwirkung usw. – Dann tritt die Wirkung der Ich-Organisation zurück, und es ist bei der weiteren Umwandlung der Nahrungssubstanz in Blutsubstanz vorzüglich der astralische Leib tätig. Das geht so weiter, bis sich das Blut mit der Luft – mit dem Sauerstoff – im Atmungsprozeß begegnet. An dieser Stelle vollzieht der Ätherleib seine Haupttätigkeit. In der im Ausatmen begriffenen Kohlensäure hat man es, bevor sie den Körper verlassen hat, mit vorzugsweise nur lebender – nicht empfindender und nicht toter – Substanz zu tun. (Lebend ist alles, was die Tätigkeit des Ätherleibes in sich trägt.) Von dieser lebenden Kohlensäure geht die Hauptmasse aus dem Organismus fort; ein kleiner Teil aber wirkt noch weiter im Organismus in die Vorgänge hinein, die in der Kopforganisation ihren Mittelpunkt haben. Dieser Teil zeigt eine starke Neigung, ins Leblose, Unorganische überzugehen, obgleich er nicht ganz leblos wird.

Im Nervensystem liegt das Entgegengesetzte vor. Im sympathischen Nervensystem, das die Verdauungsorgane durchsetzt, waltet vornehmlich der ätherische Leib. Die Nervenorgane, die da in Betracht kommen, sind von sich aus vorzüglich nur lebende Organe. Die astralische und die Ich-Organisation wirken auf sie nicht innerlich organisierend, sondern von außen. Daher ist der Einfluß der in diesen Nervenorganen wirksamen Ich- und astralischen Organisation ein starker. Affekte und Leidenschaften

CHAPTER VI

Blood And Nerve

In a particularly striking way, the activities of the single human organisms accommodate themselves in relation to the organism as a whole in the formation of blood and nerves. Insofar as blood formation occurs in the further configuration of ingested nutriments, the whole blood-forming process happens under the influence of the ego organization. The ego organization is at work in processes accompanied by conscious sensation—in the tongue and palate, right into the unconscious and subconscious processes—in the workings of pepsin, pancreatic juice, bile, etc.—Then the working of the ego organization draws back, and the astral body is primarily active in the further transformation of food substance into blood substance. This continues to the point where the blood meets the air—the oxygen—in the breathing process. At this point the ether body performs its main activity. In the carbonic acid that is exhaled, one finds before it has left the body, a substance which is primarily living—neither sentient, nor dead. (Everything that carries in itself the activity of the etheric body is living.) The greater amount of this living carbonic acid leaves the organism; a small portion, however, continues to work in the organism into the processes that have their center in the head organization. This portion shows a strong tendency to become lifeless, inorganic, though it does not become entirely lifeless.

In the nervous system the opposite is the case. In the sympathetic nervous system[6] which permeates the organs of digestion, the etheric body is principally active. The nerve organs which are taken into consideration here are primarily only living organs. The astral and ego organization do not organize them from within but from the outside. Therefore the

haben eine dauernde, bedeutsame Wirkung auf den Sympathikus. Kummer, Sorgen richten dieses Nervensystem allmählich zugrunde.

Das Rückenmarks-Nervensystem mit allen seinen Verzweigungen ist dasjenige, in welches die astralische Organisation vorzüglich eingreift. Es ist daher der Träger dessen, was im Menschen seelisch ist, der Reflexvorgänge, nicht aber dessen, was im Ich, in dem selbstbewußten Geiste vorgeht.

Die eigentlichen Gehirnnerven sind diejenigen, die der Ich-Organisation unterliegen. Bei ihnen treten die Tätigkeiten der ätherischen und astralischen Organisation zurück.

Man sieht, im Bereiche des Gesamtorganismus entstehen dadurch drei Gebiete. In einem unteren wirken die innerlich vorzugsweise vom ätherischen Organismus durchwirkten Nerven mit der Blutsubstanz zusammen, die vornehmlich der Tätigkeit der Ich-Organisation unterliegt. In diesem Gebiete liegt während der embryonalen und nachembryonalen Entwicklungsepoche der Ausgangspunkt für alle Organbildungen, die mit der inneren Belebung des menschlichen Organismus zusammenhängen. Während der Embryonalbildung wird dieses dann noch schwache Gebiet von dem umgebenden Mutterorganismus mit den belebenden und bildenden Einflüssen versorgt. Es kommt dann ein mittleres Gebiet in Betracht, in dem Nervenorgane, die von der astralischen Organisation beeinflußt sind, zusammenwirken mit Blutvorgängen, die ebenfalls von dieser astralischen Organisation und in ihrem oberen Teil von der ätherischen abhängig sind. Hier liegt während der Bildungsperiode des Menschen der Ausgangspunkt für die Entstehung der Organe, welche die äußere und innere Beweglichkeit vermitteln, z. B. für alle Muskelbildung, aber auch für alle Organe, die nicht eigentliche Muskeln sind und die doch die Beweglichkeit verursachen. – Ein oberes Gebiet ist dasjenige, wo die unter dem innerlich-organisierenden Ich stehenden Nerven zusammenwirken mit den Blutvorgängen, die eine starke Neigung dazu haben, ins Leblose, Mineralische überzuge-

influence of the astral and ego organization working in these nerve organs is strong. Emotions and passions have a deep and lasting effect on the sympathetic system. Grief and worries will gradually destroy it.

The spinal nervous system with its many ramifications is where the astral organization primarily intervenes. Thus it is the bearer of that which is of a soul-nature in the human being, of the reflexes, but not of that which takes place in the I, in the self-conscious spirit.

The actual nerves of the brain are the ones which are subject to the ego organization. Here the activities of the etheric and astral organization withdraw.

Thus one can recognize three regions coming into being in the organism as a whole. In a lower region, nerves inwardly permeated mainly by the action of the etheric organism work together with blood substance that is predominantly subject to the activity of the ego organization. In this region, during the embryonal and postembryonal period of development, lies the starting point for all organ formations that are connected with the inner enlivening of the human organism. During embryonal development, this region, being weak as yet, is supplied with forming and enlivening influences by the surrounding maternal organism. Then there is a middle region, where nerve organs influenced by the astral organization work together with blood processes which are likewise dependent on this astral organization and, in their upper component, on the etheric organization. Here, during the period of development of the human being, lies the starting point for the origin of the organs that mediate the processes of outer and inner movement, e.g., for the forming of all muscle, but also for all organs which are not muscles in the proper sense but still bring about mobility.—There is an upper region, where nerves subject to the inner organizing activity of the I, work together with blood processes that have a strong tendency to become lifeless,

hen. Während der Bildungsepoche des Menschen liegt hier der Ausgangspunkt für die Knochenbildung und für alles andere, das dem menschlichen Körper als Stützorgan dient.

Man wird das Gehirn des Menschen nur begreifen, wenn man in ihm die knochenbildende Tendenz sehen kann, die im allerersten Entstehen unterbrochen wird. Und man durchschaut die Knochenbildung nur dann, wenn man in ihr eine völlig zu Ende gekommene Gehirn-Impulswirkung erkennt, die von außen von den Impulsen des mittleren Organismus durchzogen wird, wo astralisch bedingte Nervenorgane mit ätherisch bedingter Blutsubstanz zusammen tätig sind. In der Knochenasche, die mit der ihr eigenen Gestaltung zurückbleibt, wenn man den Knochen durch Verbrennung behandelt, sind die Ergebnisse des obersten Gebietes der Menschenorganisation vorhanden. In der Knorpelsubstanz, die übrig bleibt, wenn man den Knochen der Wirkung verdünnter Salzsäure unterwirft, hat man das Ergebnis der Impulse des mittleren Gebietes.

Das Skelett ist das physische Bild der Ich-Organisation. Die nach dem Leblos-Mineralischen hinstrebende menschlich-organische Substanz unterliegt in der Knochenentstehung ganz der Ich-Organisation. Im Gehirn ist das Ich als geistige Wesenheit tätig. Seine formbildende, ins Physische hinein wirkende Kraft wird aber da ganz vom ätherischen Organisieren, ja von den Eigenkräften des Physischen überwältigt. Dem Gehirn liegt die organisierende Kraft des Ich nur leise zugrunde; sie geht im Lebendigen und in den physischen Eigenwirkungen unter. Gerade das ist der Grund, warum das Gehirn der Träger der geistigen Ich-Wirkung ist, daß die organisch-physische Betätigung da von der Ich-Organisation nicht in Anspruch genommen wird, diese daher als solche völlig frei sich betätigen kann. Das Knochenskelett dagegen ist zwar das vollkommene physische Bild der Ich-Organisation; diese aber erschöpft sich in dem physischen Organisieren, so daß von ihr als geistige Betätigung nichts mehr übrig-

mineral-like. Here lies, during the period of development of the human being, the point of departure for the forming of bones and all else that serves the human body as an organ of support.

One will understand the human brain only if one sees the bone-forming tendency in it, which is interrupted at its very inception. And one will know bone formation only when one recognizes in it the activity of the brain-impulse carried to its final conclusion and permeated from without by the impulses of the middle organism, where astrally determined nerve organs are active together with etherically determined blood substance. In bone ash which remains behind with its own particular form when one subjects bones to combustion, the results of the upper region of the human organization are present. In the cartilaginous substance which remains behind when bones are subjected to dilute hydrochloric acid, one has the result of the impulses of the middle region.

The skeleton is the physical image of the ego organization. Organic human substance which tends toward the lifeless mineral in bone development, is entirely subject to the ego organization. In the brain, the I is active as a spiritual being. Here, however, its capacity to create form down into the physical is overwhelmed entirely by the organizing activity of the etheric, and even by the particular forces of the physical. The organizing force of the I underlies the brain only minimally; this force becomes submerged in the life-processes and in inherent physical activities. That the organic physical activity there is not claimed by the ego organization, is the very reason for the brain being the bearer of the spiritual activity of the I; the latter is therefore able to act as such in full freedom. The bony skeleton, however, may be a perfect physical image of the ego organization; but the latter exhausts itself in physical organizing activity, and nothing is left of it as

bleibt. Die Vorgänge in den Knochen sind daher die am meisten unbewußten.

Die Kohlensäure, die mit dem Atmungsprozeß nach außen gestoßen wird, ist innerhalb des Organismus noch lebende Substanz; sie wird von der in dem mittleren Nervensystem verankerten astralischen Tätigkeit ergriffen und nach außen ausgeschieden. Der Teil der Kohlensäure, der mit dem Stoffwechsel nach dem Kopfe geht, wird da durch die Verbindung mit dem Kalzium geneigt gemacht, in die Wirkungen der Ich-Organisation einzutreten. Es wird dadurch der kohlensaure Kalk unter dem Einfluß der von der Ich-Organisation innerlich impulsierten Kopfnerven auf den Weg zur Knochenbildung getrieben.

Die aus den Nahrungssubstanzen entstehenden Stoffe: Myosin und Myogen haben die Tendenz, sich im Blute abzusetzen; sie sind zunächst astralisch bedingte Substanzen, die mit dem Sympathikus in Wechselwirkung stehen, der innerlich vom ätherischen Leib organisiert ist. Diese beiden Eiweißstoffe werden aber auch zum Teil ergriffen von der Betätigung des mittleren Nervensystems, das unter dem Einfluß des astralischen Leibes steht. Dadurch gehen sie eine Verwandtschaft ein mit Zersetzungsprodukten des Eiweißes, mit Fetten, mit Zucker und zuckerähnlichen Substanzen. Das befähigt sie, unter dem Einfluß des mittleren Nervensystems auf den Weg in die Muskelbildung zu kommen.

spiritual activity. Therefore the processes in the bones are the most unconscious.

The carbonic acid which is expelled in the breathing process is still living substance so long as it is within the organism; it is taken hold of and excreted by the astral activity that has its seat in the middle region of the nervous system. The portion of carbonic acid which is carried up with the metabolism into the head is given the tendency there to come into the sphere of working of the ego organization by combining with calcium. Through this, calcium carbonate is driven toward bone formation under the influence of the cranial nerves, which are inwardly given impulse by the ego organization.

The substances produced out of the nutrients, myosin and myogen, tend to settle in the blood; initially they are astrally determined substances that stand in reciprocal interaction with the sympathetic nervous system, which is inwardly organized by the etheric body. These two proteins are, however, also taken hold of to some extent by the activity of the middle nervous system which stands under the influence of the astral body. They thus come into relationship with breakdown products of protein, with fats, with sugar and substances similar to sugar. This enables them, under the influence of the middle nervous system, to find their way into muscle formation.

VII
DAS WESEN DER HEILWIRKUNGEN

Die menschliche Gesamtorganisation ist nicht ein in sich abgeschlossenes System von ineinandergreifenden Vorgängen. Wäre sie das, sie könnte nicht der Träger des Seelischen und Geistigen sein. Dieses kann den Menschenorganismus nur dadurch zur Grundlage haben, daß er in der Nerven- und Knochensubstanz und in den Vorgängen, in welche diese Substanzen eingegliedert sind, fortwährend zerfällt oder sich auf den Weg der leblosen, mineralischen Tätigkeit begibt.

In dem Nervengewebe zerfällt die Eiweißsubstanz. Aber sie wird in diesem Gewebe nicht wie im Eikeim, oder in anderen Gebilden dadurch wieder aufgebaut, daß sie in den Bereich der auf die Erde einstrahlenden Wirkungen gelangt, sondern sie zerfällt einfach. Dadurch können die Ätherwirkungen, die von den Dingen und Vorgängen der äußeren Umgebung durch die Sinne einstrahlen, und diejenigen, die sich bilden, indem die Bewegungsorgane gebraucht werden, die Nerven als Organe benützen, längs welcher sie sich durch den ganzen Körper fortleiten.

Es gibt in den Nerven zweierlei Vorgänge: das Zerfallen der Eiweißsubstanz und das Durchströmen dieser zerfallenden Substanz mit Äthersubstanz, die zu ihrer Strömung durch Säuren, Salze, Phosphoriges und Schwefeliges angefacht wird. Das Gleichgewicht zwischen den beiden Vorgängen vermitteln die Fette und das Wasser.

Dem Wesen nach angesehen sind diese Vorgänge fortdauernd den Organismus durchsetzende Krankheitsprozesse. Sie müssen durch ebenso fortwirkende Heilungsprozesse ausgeglichen werden.

Dieser Ausgleich wird dadurch bewirkt, daß das Blut nicht nur die Vorgänge enthält, aus denen das Wachstum und die Stoffwechselprozesse bestehen, sondern daß ihm auch eine den krank-

CHAPTER VII

The Nature of Healing Functions

The human organization as a whole is not a self-contained system of interacting processes. If it were, it could not be the bearer of the soul and spirit element. This can only have its basis in the human organism because in nerve and bone substance and in the processes in which these substances are imbedded, this organism is continually disintegrating or moving towards lifeless mineral activity.

Proteinaceous substance disintegrates in nerve tissue. Yet in this tissue, unlike what happens in the egg cell or in other structures, it is not built up again by coming within the sphere of influences radiating in toward the earth, but it simply disintegrates. The ether influences that radiate in through the senses from the objects and processes of the outer environment, as well as those that form themselves when organs of movement are used, are thereby able to utilize the nerves as organs along which they are led throughout the body.

In the nerves there are two kinds of processes: the disintegration of proteinaceous substance, and the flow of ether substance through this disintegrating substance, a flow which is stimulated by acids, salts, and phosphorous and sulfurous elements. The equilibrium between the two processes is mediated by fats and water.

In essence, these are processes of disease which continually permeate the organism. They must be balanced by equally continuous processes of healing.

This balance is brought about by the fact that blood not only contains processes that consist of growth and metabolism, but contains in addition processes to which a continual *healing*

machenden Nervenvorgängen gegenüberstehende, fortdauernde *heilende* Wirkung zukommt.

Das Blut hat in seiner Plasma-Substanz und in dem Faserstoff diejenigen Kräfte, die dem Wachstum und dem Stoffwechsel im engeren Sinne dienen. In dem, was als Eisengehalt bei der Untersuchung der roten Blutkörperchen erscheint, liegen die Ursprünge der *heilenden* Blutwirkung. Es erscheint deshalb das Eisen auch im Magensaft und als Eisenoxyd im Milchsafte. Da werden überall Quellen geschaffen für Vorgänge, die auf die Nervenprozesse ausgleichend wirken.

Das Eisen erscheint bei der Untersuchung des Blutes so, daß es sich als das einzige Metall darstellt, das innerhalb des menschlichen Organismus die Neigung zur Kristallisationsfähigkeit hat. Damit macht es die Kräfte geltend, die äußere, physische, mineralische Naturkräfte sind. Sie bilden innerhalb des menschlichen Organismus ein im Sinne der äußeren, physischen Natur orientiertes Kräftesystem. Dieses aber wird fortdauernd durch die Ich-Organisation überwunden.

Man hat es zu tun mit zwei Kräftesystemen. Das eine hat seinen Ursprung in den Nervenvorgängen; das andere in der Blutbildung. In den Nervenvorgängen entwickeln sich krankmachende Vorgänge, die bis zu dem Grade gehen, daß sie von den ihnen entgegenwirkenden Blutvorgängen fortdauernd geheilt werden können. Die Nervenvorgänge sind solche, die von dem astralischen Leib an der Nervensubstanz und damit im ganzen Organismus bewirkt werden. Die Blutvorgänge sind solche, in denen die Ich-Organisation *im* menschlichen Organismus der äußeren, in ihn fortgesetzten physischen Natur gegenübersteht, die aber in die Gestaltung der Ich-Organisation hineingezwungen wird.

Man kann in diesem Wechselverhältnis die Vorgänge des Erkrankens und der Heilung unmittelbar erfassen. Treten im Organismus Verstärkungen derjenigen Vorgänge auf, die ihren normalen Grad in dem durch den Nervenprozeß Erregten haben, so liegt Erkrankung vor. Ist man imstande, diesen Vorgängen solche

action can be attributed, which counter the illness-inducing nerve processes.

In its plasma substance and in fibrinogen, blood contains those forces which serve growth and metabolism in the narrower sense. In that which appears as iron content when the red blood corpuscles are examined lie the origins of the blood's *healing* function. Accordingly, iron also appears in gastric juice and as iron oxide in chyle. Thus everywhere sources are created for processes that counterbalance the nerve processes.

Upon examination of the blood, iron reveals itself as the only metal which, within the human organism, has the tendency toward crystallization. Thus it maintains forces which are in fact external, physical, mineral forces of nature. Within the human organism they form a system of forces, oriented in terms of outer physical nature. This, however, is continually being overcome by the ego organization.

One is dealing with two systems of forces. One has its origin in nerve processes, the other in blood formation. The pathogenic processes that develop in the nerves do so only to the degree that they can be healed continuously by blood processes which counteract them. Nerve processes are such that they are caused by the astral body in the nerve substance, and thus in the organism as a whole. Blood processes are such that in them the ego organization confronts outer physical nature *within* the human organism. This outer physical nature, which continues on within it, is, however, subjected to the form-giving process of the ego organization.

One can comprehend the processes of becoming ill and of healing directly through this interrelationship. If there is an increase within the organism of such processes as are found to a normal degree in what is stimulated by the nerve process, then there is illness. If one is able to counter these processes with others that represent a reinforcement of functions of outer nature within the organism, then healing can be brought about

gegenüberzustellen, die als Verstärkungen von äußeren Naturwirkungen im Organismus sich darstellen, so kann Heilung bewirkt werden, wenn diese äußeren Naturwirkungen durch den Ich-Organismus bewältigt werden und ausgleichend auf die ihnen entgegengesetzt orientierten Prozesse wirken.

Die Milch hat nur geringe Eisenmengen. Sie ist die Substanz, die als solche in ihren Wirkungen am wenigsten Krankmachendes darstellt; das Blut muß fortdauernd alles Krankmachende über sich ergehen lassen; es braucht daher das organisierte, das heißt das in die Ich-Organisation aufgenommene Eisen – das Häm – als fortdauernd wirkendes Heilmittel.

Beim Heilmittel, das auf einen in der inneren Organisation auftretenden kranken Zustand wirken soll, auch auf einen solchen, der von außen bewirkt ist, aber im Innern des Organismus verläuft, kommt es zunächst darauf an, die Erkenntnis darüber zu gewinnen, inwiefern die astrale Organisation in dem Sinne wirkt, daß ein Zerfall des Eiweißes an irgend einer Stelle des Organismus so eintritt, wie dies durch die Nervenorganisation in normaler Art in die Wege geleitet wird. Man nehme an, man habe es mit Stockungen im Unterleibe zu tun. Man kann dabei in den auftretenden Schmerzen eine überflüssige Tätigkeit des astralischen Leibes bemerken. Dann hat man es mit dem charakterisierten Fall für den Darmorganismus zu tun.

Weiter ist nun wichtig die Frage: wie ist die verstärkte Astralwirkung auszugleichen? Dies kann geschehen, wenn man in das Blut Substanzen bringt, welche gerade von demjenigen Teil der Ich-Organisation ergriffen werden können, der in der Darmorganisation tätig ist. Es sind dies Kalium und Natrium. Führt man diese in irgend einem Präparate, oder in einer Pflanzenorganisation, z. B. Anagallis arvensis dem Organismus zu, so nimmt man dem astralischen Leib seine zu große Nervenwirkung ab und bewirkt den Übergang dessen, was der astralische Leib zu viel tut, auf die von der Ich-Organisation ergriffene Wirkung der genannten Substanzen aus dem Blute heraus.

when these functions of outer nature are mastered by the ego organization, and counterbalance the processes which are oriented in opposition to them.

Milk contains only small quantities of iron. It is the substance which as such is the least pathogenic in its actions. Blood must continually submit itself to all that brings illness; therefore it requires organized iron, the iron taken up into the ego organization—the heme—continually acting as a medication.

For a medication which is to work on a pathological condition appearing in the inner organization, also on one that is due to outer causes but which takes its course within the organism, it is essential first of all to discover to what extent the astral organization is working so that protein disintegration begins at some point in the body in the way this is normally induced by the nerve organization. Assume that one is dealing with stagnations or blockages in the lower abdomen. In the pain that occurs one can note the excessive activity of the astral body. In that case one is dealing with the situation as characterized for the intestinal organism.

The important question is now: how can the intensified astral function be balanced? This can be done by introducing substances into the blood which can be taken hold of by just that part of the ego organization that works in the intestinal system. These substances are potassium and sodium. If one introduces these into the organism in some preparation or in a plant organization, e.g., *anagallis arvensis*, then one takes the excessive nerve function away from the astral body and effects the transition of what the astral body does too much of, to the action of the named substances which has been taken hold of by the ego organization, from out of the blood.

Verwendet man die mineralische Substanz, so wird man dafür sorgen müssen, daß durch Zusatzgaben, oder besser durch die Verbindung des Kaliums oder Natriums im Präparat mit Schwefel diese Metalle richtig in die Blutströmung so gebracht werden, daß die Eiweißmetamorphose vor dem Zerfall aufgehalten wird. Der Schwefel hat nämlich die Eigentümlichkeit, daß er dem Aufhalten des Eiweißzerfalles dient; er hält gewissermaßen die organisierenden Kräfte in der Eiweißsubstanz zusammen. Kommt er so in die Blutströmung, daß er sich mit dem Kalium oder Natrium in Verbindung hält, dann tritt seine Wirkung dort ein, wo das Kalium oder Natrium eine besondere Anziehung zu bestimmten Organen haben. Das ist bei den Darmorganen der Fall.

If mineral substance is used, care must be taken to give additional preparations, or better still to combine the potassium or sodium in the preparation with sulfur, in order that these metals are carried into the blood stream in the right way so that they hold up the metamorphosis of protein before disintegration sets in. Sulfur has the inherent property of preventing protein disintegration; to a certain extent it holds the organizing forces of proteinaceous substance together. When it enters the blood stream in such a way that it maintains its connection with potassium or sodium, then its action will occur where potassium or sodium have a special affinity to particular organs. This is the case with the intestinal organs.

VIII
TÄTIGKEITEN IM MENSCHLICHEN ORGANISMUS. DIABETES MELLITUS

Der menschliche Organismus entfaltet durch alle seine Glieder hindurch Tätigkeiten, die ihre Impulse allein in ihm selber haben können. Was er von außen aufnimmt, muß entweder bloß die Veranlassung dazu sein, daß er eine eigene Tätigkeit entwickeln kann; oder es muß so im Körper wirken, daß die Fremdtätigkeit sich nicht von einer inneren Tätigkeit des Körpers unterscheidet, sobald sie in diesen eingedrungen ist.

Die notwendige Nahrung des Menschen enthält z. B. Kohlehydrate. Diese sind zum Teil Stärke-ähnlich. Als solche sind sie Substanzen, die ihre Tätigkeit in der Pflanze entfalten. In den menschlichen Körper gelangen sie in dem Zustande, den sie in der Pflanze erreichen können. In diesem Zustande ist die Stärke ein Fremdkörper. Der menschliche Organismus entwickelt keine Tätigkeit, die in der Richtung dessen liegt, was Stärke, in dem Zustande, in dem sie in den Körper kommt, als Tätigkeit entfalten kann. Was z. B. in der menschlichen Leber als Stärke-ähnlicher Stoff entwickelt wird (Glykogen), ist etwas anderes als pflanzliche Stärke. Dagegen ist der Traubenzucker eine Substanz, die Tätigkeiten erregt, welche von gleicher Art sind wie Tätigkeiten des menschlichen Organismus selbst. Stärke kann daher in diesem nicht Stärke bleiben. Soll sie eine Wirkung entfalten, die in dem Körper eine Rolle spielt, so muß sie verwandelt werden. Und sie geht, indem sie vom Ptyalin der Mundhöhle durchsetzt wird, in Zucker über.

Eiweiß und Fett werden vom Ptyalin nicht verändert. Sie treten zunächst als Fremdsubstanzen in den Magen ein. In diesem werden die Eiweißstoffe durch das von ihm abgesonderte Pepsin so verwandelt, daß die Abbauprodukte bis zu den Peptonen entstehen. Sie sind Substanzen, deren Tätigkeitsimpulse mit solchen des Körpers zusammenfallen. Dagegen bleibt Fett auch im Magen unverändert. Es wird erst von dem Absonderungsprodukt der Bauchspeichel-

CHAPTER VIII

Activities In The Human Organism.
Diabetes Mellitus

The human organism carries out, in all of its parts, activities which can have their impulses only in the organism itself. What it takes up from outside must either simply provide the opportunity for the organism to carry out its own activity, or, as soon as it has entered into the body, the foreign activity must work in such a way that it does not distinguish itself from an inner activity of the body.

The food required by the human being contains carbohydrates. These are, in part, similar to starch. As such they are substances which unfold their activity in the plant. They arrive in the human body in the state which they are able to attain in the plant. In this state, starch is a foreign body. The human organism does not develop an activity which approximates what starch can unfold as activity while in the state it is in at its entry into the body. For example, what evolves in the human liver as a sub-stance similar to starch (glycogen) is something different from plant starch. On the other hand, grape sugar is a substance which stimulates activities that are of a nature similar to activities of the human organism itself. Starch can therefore not remain starch in it. To develop a function that plays a part in the body, it must be converted. And when it is mixed with ptyalin in the mouth, it is converted to sugar.

Protein and fat are not altered by ptyalin. They enter the stomach initially as foreign substances. There, proteins are converted by the secreted pepsin, so that breakdown products right down to the peptones are generated. In these substances the impulses to activity coincide with those of the body. In contrast, fat remains unaltered even in the stomach. It is first converted

drüse so verwandelt, daß Substanzen entstehen, die sich aus dem toten Organismus als Glycerin und Fettsäuren ergeben.

Nun aber geht die Verwandlung der Stärke in Zucker durch den ganzen Verdauungsvorgang hindurch. Es findet auch eine Umwandlung der Stärke durch den Magensaft statt, wenn diese Umwandlung nicht schon durch das Ptyalin stattgefunden hat.

Wenn die Umwandlung der Stärke durch das Ptyalin stattfindet, so steht der Vorgang an der Grenze dessen, was sich im Menschen im Bereich dessen abspielt, das in dem Kapitel II die Ich-Organisation genannt worden ist. In deren Bereich geht die erste Umwandlung des von außen Aufgenommenen vor sich. Traubenzucker ist eine Substanz, die im Bereich der Ich-Organisation wirken kann. Er ist dem Geschmack des Süßen entsprechend, der in der Ich-Organisation sein Dasein hat.

Entsteht aus dem Stärkemehl durch den Magensaft Zucker, so bedeutet dies, daß die Ich-Organisation in den Bereich des Verdauungssystems eindringt. Für das Bewußtsein ist dann der Geschmack des Süßen nicht da; aber, was im Bewußtsein – im Bereich der Ich-Organisation – vorgeht, während «süß» empfunden wird, das dringt in die unbewußten Regionen des menschlichen Körpers, und die Ich-Organisation wird dort tätig.

In den uns unbewußten Regionen hat man es nun im Sinne von Kapitel II zunächst mit dem astralischen Leib zu tun. Es ist der astralische Leib da in Wirksamkeit, wo im Magen die Stärke in Zucker verwandelt wird.

Bewußt kann der Mensch nur sein durch dasjenige, was in seiner Ich-Organisation so wirkt, daß diese durch nichts übertönt oder gestört wird, so daß sie sich voll entfalten kann. Das ist innerhalb des Bereiches der Fall, in dem die Ptyalinwirkungen liegen. Im Bereich der Pepsinwirkungen übertönt der Astralleib die Ich-Organisation. Die Ich-Tätigkeit taucht unter in die astralische. Man kann also im Bereich des Materiellen die Ich-Organisation an der Anwesenheit des Zuckers verfolgen. Wo Zucker ist, da ist Ich-Organisation; wo Zucker entsteht, da tritt die Ich-Organisation auf,

by the secretions of the pancreatic gland, generating substances which, in the dead organism, appear as glycerin and fatty acids.

Now, however, the conversion of starch into sugar continues throughout the whole digestive process. Transformation of starch also takes place through gastric juice if it has not already happened through ptyalin.

If the transformation of starch happens through ptyalin, the process borders on what takes place in the human being in the sphere of the ego organization as it has been called in Chapter II. In this sphere the first transformation of substance that has been taken in from the outer world takes place. Grape sugar is a substance that is able to work in the sphere of the ego organization. It corresponds to the taste of sweetness, which has its existence in the ego organization.

If sugar is formed from starch by gastric juice, then this means that the ego organization enters into the sphere of the digestive system. For conscious experience the taste of sweetness is then absent. However, what goes on in conscious experience—in the sphere of the ego organization—when "sweetness" is experienced makes its way into unconscious areas of the human body, and the ego organization becomes active there.

In the areas that are unconscious to us, one deals initially, in the sense of Chapter II, with the astral body. The astral body functions where starch is converted into sugar in the stomach.

The human being can only be conscious through that which works in such a way in his ego organization that the latter is not overruled or disturbed by anything, so that it is able to unfold itself to the full extent. This is the case in the sphere where ptyalin functions are located. In the sphere of pepsin functions, the astral body overrules the ego organization. Ego activity immerses in astral activity. So one can pursue the ego organization in the sphere of matter by looking for the presence

um die untermenschliche (vegetative, animalische) Körperlichkeit zum Menschlichen hin zu orientieren.

Nun tritt der Zucker als Ausscheidungsprodukt auf bei Diabetes mellitus. Man hat es dabei mit dem Auftreten der Ich-Organisation an dem menschlichen Organismus in einer solchen Form zu tun, daß diese Organisation zerstörend wirkt. Sieht man auf jede andre Region des Wirkens der Ich-Organisation, so stellt sich heraus, daß diese untertaucht in die astralische Organisation. Zucker unmittelbar genossen ist in der Ich-Organisation. Er wird da zum Veranlasser des Süß-Geschmackes. Stärke genossen und durch das Ptyalin oder den Magensaft in Zucker verwandelt, zeigt an, daß in der Mundhöhle oder im Magen der astralische Leib mit der Ich-Organisation zusammenwirkt und die letztere übertönt.

Zucker ist aber auch im Blute vorhanden. Indem das Blut Zucker enthaltend durch den ganzen Körper zirkuliert, trägt es die Ich-Organisation durch diesen. Überall da aber wird diese Ich-Organisation durch das Wirken des menschlichen Organismus in ihrem Gleichgewicht gehalten. In dem Kapitel II hat sich gezeigt, wie außer der Ich-Organisation und dem astralischen Leib in der menschlichen Wesenheit noch der ätherische und der physische Leib vorhanden sind. Auch diese nehmen die Ich-Organisation auf und halten sie in sich. So lange dies der Fall ist, sondert der Harn keinen Zucker ab. Wie die Ich-Organisation, den Zucker tragend, leben kann, das zeigt sich an den an den Zucker gebundenen Vorgängen im Organismus.

Beim Gesunden kann der Zucker im Harn nur auftreten, wenn er zu reichlich, als Zucker, genossen wird, oder wenn Alkohol, der unmittelbar, mit Übergehung von Verwandlungsprodukten, in die Körpervorgänge sich hineinzieht, zu reichlich aufgenommen wird. In beiden Fällen tritt der Zuckerprozeß als selbständig, neben den sonstigen Vorgängen im Menschen auf.

Bei Diabetes mellitus liegt die Tatsache vor, daß die Ich-Organisation beim Untertauchen in den astralischen und ätherischen Bereich so abgeschwächt wird, daß sie für ihre Tätigkeit an der

of sugar. Where there is sugar, there is ego organization; where sugar is generated, the ego organization appears and orients the corporeality that is sub-human (vegetative, animalic) toward the human.

Now sugar occurs as a product of excretion in diabetes mellitus. In this instance the ego organization appears in a form in which it works destructively for the human organism. In observing every other area of action of the ego organization one becomes aware that it immerses in the astral organization. Sugar, directly consumed, is in the ego organization. There it is the cause of sweet taste. Starch consumed and converted by ptyalin or gastric juice into sugar indicates that in the mouth or in the stomach the astral body works together with the ego organization and overrules the latter.

Sugar is also present in blood, however. Insofar as blood, containing sugar, circulates through the whole body, it carries the ego organization through it. But here the ego organization is everywhere held in balance through the working of the human organism. In Chapter II it became evident how along with the ego organization and the astral body, the etheric and the physical body are also present in the human being. These also take up the ego organization and hold it in themselves. So long as this is the case sugar is not excreted in the urine. How the ego organization can live while carrying sugar is indicated by the sugar-bound processes in the organism.

In a healthy individual, sugar can only appear in the urine if consumed too abundantly in the form of sugar, or if alcohol, which enters directly into the bodily processes skipping intermediate conversion products, is taken in too abundantly. In either case the sugar process occurs independently alongside the other processes in the human being.

It is a fact that in diabetes mellitus the ego organization becomes so weakened by immersion in the astral and etheric sphere that it is no longer effective in acting on the substance of

Zuckersubstanz nicht mehr wirksam sein kann. Es geschieht dann durch die astralischen und ätherischen Regionen mit dem Zucker dasjenige, was mit ihm durch die Ich-Organisation geschehen sollte.

Es befördert alles die Zuckerkrankheit, was die Ich-Organisation aus der in die Körpertätigkeit eingreifenden Wirksamkeit herausreißt: Aufregungen, die nicht vereinzelt, sondern in Wiederholungen auftreten; intellektuelle Überanstrengungen; erbliche Belastung, die eine normale Eingliederung der Ich-Organisation in den Gesamtorganismus verhindert. Das alles ist zugleich damit verbunden, daß in der Kopforganisation solche Vorgänge stattfinden, die eigentlich Parallelvorgänge der geistig-seelischen Tätigkeit sein sollten; die aber, weil diese Tätigkeit zu schnell oder zu langsam verläuft, aus dem Parallelismus herausfallen. Es denkt gewissermaßen das Nervensystem selbständig neben dem denkenden Menschen. Das aber ist eine Tätigkeit, die das Nervensystem nur im Schlafe ausführen sollte. Beim Diabetiker geht eine Art von Schlaf in den Tiefen des Organismus dem Wachzustande parallel. Es findet daher im Verlaufe der Zuckerkrankheit eine Entartung der Nervensubstanz statt. Diese ist die Folge des mangelhaften Eingreifens der Ich-Organisation.

Eine andere Begleiterscheinung sind die Furunkelbildungen bei Diabetikern. Furunkelbildungen entstehen durch ein Übermaß in der Region der ätherischen Tätigkeit. Die Ich-Organisation versagt da, wo sie wirken sollte. Die astralische Tätigkeit kann sich nicht entfalten, weil sie gerade an einem solchen Orte nur im Einklange mit der Ich-Organisation Kraft hat. Die Folge ist das Übermaß der ätherischen Wirksamkeit, die sich in der Furunkelbildung zeigt.

In alle diesem sieht man, wie ein Heilungsvorgang für Diabetes mellitus nur eingeleitet werden kann, wenn man die Ich-Organisation bei dem Diabetiker zu kräftigen imstande ist.

sugar. What should have happened to it through the ego organization then happens to the sugar through the astral and etheric domains.

Diabetes is aggravated by everything that pulls the ego organization away from an engaged functioning in body activity: overexcitement occurring not as a single but as repeated events; intellectual overexertion; a hereditary predisposition which hinders the normal incorporation of the ego organization into the organism as a whole. At the same time all of this is connected with the fact that processes take place in the head organization which should properly be parallel processes to soul and spirit activity; however, because the latter activity takes its course too fast or too slowly, they fall out of the parallelism. It is as though the nervous system were thinking independently alongside the thinking human being. But this is an activity which the nervous system should only carry out during sleep. In the diabetic, a form of sleep in the depths of the organism runs parallel to the waking state. In the further course of diabetes therefore a deterioration of nerve substance takes place. This is the consequence of deficient intervention of the ego organization.

Another concomitant symptom is the formation of boils in diabetics. Boils are generated by an excess in the area of etheric activity. The ego organization fails where it should be active. Astral activity cannot unfold because just at such a place it only has strength in unison with the ego organization. The result is an excess of etheric activity which expresses itself in the formation of boils.

From all this one can see that a healing process for diabetes mellitus can only be initiated if one is able to strengthen the ego organization of the diabetic.

IX
DIE ROLLE DES EIWEISSES IM MENSCHENKÖRPER UND DIE ALBUMINURIE

Das Eiweiß ist diejenige Substanz des lebenden Körpers, die von seinen Bildekräften in der mannigfaltigsten Art umgewandelt werden kann, so daß, was sich aus der umgeformten Eiweißsubstanz ergibt, in den Formen der Organe und des ganzen Organismus erscheint. Um in solcher Art verwendet werden zu können, muß das Eiweiß die Fähigkeit haben, jede Form, die sich aus der Natur seiner materiellen Teile ergibt, in dem Augenblicke zu verlieren, in dem es im Organismus aufgerufen wird, einer von ihm geforderten Form zu dienen.

Man erkennt daraus, daß im Eiweiß die Kräfte, die aus der Natur des Wasserstoffes, Sauerstoffes, Stickstoffes und Kohlenstoffes und deren gegenseitigen Beziehungen folgen, in sich zerfallen. Die unorganischen Stoffbindungen hören auf, und die organischen Bildekräfte beginnen im Eiweißzerfall zu wirken.

Diese Bildekräfte sind an den ätherischen Leib gebunden. Das Eiweiß ist immer auf dem Sprung, entweder in die Tätigkeit des ätherischen Leibes aufgenommen zu werden, oder aus diesem herauszufallen. Eiweiß, das aus dem Organismus, dem es angehört hat, herausgenommen ist, nimmt in sich die Neigung auf, eine zusammengesetzte Substanz zu werden, die sich den unorganischen Kräften des Wasserstoffes, Sauerstoffes, Stickstoffes und Kohlenstoffes fügt. Eiweiß, das ein Bestandteil des lebenden Organismus bleibt, verdrängt in sich diese Neigung, und fügt sich den Bildekräften des ätherischen Leibes ein.

Mit den Nahrungsmitteln nimmt der Mensch das Eiweiß auf. Von dem Pepsin des Magens wird das von außen aufgenommene Eiweiß bis zu den Peptonen, die zunächst lösliche Eiweißsubstanzen sind, verwandelt. Diese Verwandlung wird durch den Pankreassaft fortgesetzt.

Das aufgenommene Eiweiß ist zunächst, wenn es als Nahrungsmittel aufgenommen wird, ein Fremdkörper des menschlichen Or-

CHAPTER IX

The Role of Protein in the Human Body and Albuminuria

Protein is that substance of the living body which can be transformed in the most varied ways by the body's formative forces, so that the forms of the organs and of the whole organism appear as a result of the transformed proteinaceous substance. To be suited for such use, protein must have the ability, the moment it is called upon in the organism to serve a form demanded by it, to lose whatever form may come from the nature of its material constituents.

One recognizes in this that in protein the forces derived from the nature of hydrogen, oxygen, nitrogen, and carbon and from their interrelationships disintegrate within themselves. In protein disintegration, the inorganic substance bonds cease and organic formative forces begin to work.

These formative forces are bound up with the etheric body. Protein is ever on the point of either being taken up into the activity of the etheric body or of falling out of it. Protein that is removed from the organism to which it belonged takes on the tendency to become a composite substance, subject to the inorganic forces of hydrogen, oxygen, nitrogen and carbon. Protein that remains a constituent of the living organism suppresses this tendency in itself and fits into the formative forces of the etheric body.

With his nutrition, the human being ingests protein. Protein which is taken up from outside is converted by the pepsin of the stomach right into peptones which are initially soluble proteinaceous substances. This conversion process is continued by pancreatic juice.

ganismus. Es enthält die Nachwirkungen der Äthervorgänge desjenigen Lebewesens, aus dem es entnommen wird. Diese müssen ganz von ihm entfernt werden. Es muß in die Ätherwirkungen des menschlichen Organismus aufgenommen werden.

Man hat es daher im Verlaufe des menschlichen Verdauungsvorganges mit zweierlei Eiweißsubstanzen zu tun. Im Beginne dieses Vorganges ist das Eiweiß etwas dem menschlichen Organismus Fremdes. Am Ende ist es dem Organismus Eigenes. Dazwischen liegt ein Zustand, in dem das aufgenommene Nahrungseiweiß die vorigen Ätherwirkungen noch nicht ganz abgegeben, die neuen noch nicht ganz aufgenommen hat. Da ist es fast ganz unorganisch geworden. Es ist da allein unter der Einwirkung des menschlichen physischen Leibes. Dieser, der in seiner Form ein Ergebnis der menschlichen Ich-Organisation ist, trägt in sich unorganische Wirkungskräfte. Er wirkt dadurch auf das Lebendige ertötend. Alles, was in den Bereich der Ich-Organisation kommt, erstirbt. Daher gliedert sich die Ich-Organisation im physischen Leib rein unorganische Substanzen ein. Diese wirken im menschlichen physischen Organismus nicht so wie in der leblosen Natur außerhalb des Menschen; aber sie wirken doch eben unorganisch, d. h. ertötend. Diese ertötende Wirkung wird auf das Eiweiß da ausgeübt, wo in der Verdauungsregion das Trypsin tätig ist, ein Bestandteil des Pankreassaftes. -

Daß in der Wirkungsart des Trypsins Unorganisches im Spiele ist, kann auch daraus entnommen werden, daß diese Substanz unter Beihilfe von Alkalischem ihre Tätigkeit entfaltet.

Bis zur Begegnung mit dem Trypsin des Bauchspeichels lebt die Eiweiß-Nahrung auf fremde Art; auf die Art des Organismus, aus dem sie genommen ist. Bei der Begegnung mit dem Trypsin wird das Eiweiß leblos. Man möchte sagen, es wird nur für einen Augenblick im menschlichen Organismus leblos. Da wird es aufgenommen in den physischen Leib gemäß der Ich-Organisation. Diese muß nun die Kraft haben, das, was aus der Eiweißsubstanz geworden ist, in den Bereich des menschlichen Ätherleibes überzuführen.

The protein ingested as food is initially a foreign body within the human organism. It comprises the aftereffects of the ether processes of the living being from which it was derived. These must be entirely removed from it. It has to be taken up into the ether activities of the human organism.

Thus one is dealing with two kinds of protein substances in the course of the human digestive process. At the beginning of this process the protein is foreign to the human organism. At the end it belongs to the organism. In between is a condition where the protein taken up as food has not yet entirely discarded its previous etheric actions, nor yet entirely assumed the new ones. In this in-between state it has become almost completely inorganic. It is only subject to influences of the human physical body there. The latter, which in its form is a product of the human ego organization, bears within itself forces with inorganic action. Therefore it has a deadening effect upon whatever is alive. Everything that enters the sphere of the ego organization dies. Thus the ego organization incorporates purely inorganic substances into the physical body for itself. In the human physical organism these do not work in the same way as in lifeless nature outside the human being; nevertheless they do still work inorganically, i.e. deadening. This deadening effect upon the protein takes place in that part of the digestive tract where trypsin, a constituent of pancreatic juice, is active.

That inorganic forces play a part in the manner of action of trypsin may also be gathered from the fact that it unfolds its activity with the help of alkaline elements.

Until it meets the trypsin in pancreatic fluid, food protein lives in a foreign mode, the mode of the organism from which it was derived. On meeting trypsin, protein becomes lifeless. One would like to say that in the human organism it becomes lifeless just for one moment. Then it is taken up in the physical body in conformity with the ego organization. The latter must now have the force to carry what has become out of the proteinaceous

Das Nahrungs-Eiweiß wird damit Bildestoff für den menschlichen Organismus. Die ätherischen Fremdwirkungen, die ihm vorher anhafteten, treten aus dem Menschen aus.

Es ist nun notwendig, daß der Mensch, um das Nahrungs-Eiweiß gesund zu verdauen, eine so starke Ich-Organisation habe, daß alles für den menschlichen Organismus notwendige Eiweiß in den Bereich des menschlichen Ätherleibes übergehen kann. Ist das nicht der Fall, so entsteht eine überschüssige Tätigkeit dieses Ätherleibes. Der erhält nicht genug von der Ich-Organisation vorbereitete Eiweißsubstanz für seine Tätigkeit. Die Folge davon ist, daß die auf die Belebung des von der Ich-Organisation aufgenommenen Eiweißes orientierte Tätigkeit sich des Eiweißes bemächtigt, das noch fremde Ätherwirkungen enthält. Der Mensch erhält in seinem eigenen Ätherleibe eine Summe von Wirkungen, die nicht hineingehören. Diese müssen auf unregelmäßige Art ausgeschieden werden. Es entsteht eine krankhafte Ausscheidung.

Diese krankhafte Ausscheidung tritt in der *Albuminurie* zu Tage. Es wird da Eiweiß ausgeschieden, das in den Bereich des Ätherleibes aufgenommen werden sollte. Es ist solches Eiweiß, das durch die Schwäche der Ich-Organisation nicht den Durchgangszustand des fast Leblosen hat annehmen können.

Nun sind die Kräfte, die im Menschen die Ausscheidung bewirken, an den Bereich des astralischen Leibes gebunden. Indem dieser bei der Albuminurie gezwungen ist, eine Tätigkeit auszuführen, auf die hin er nicht orientiert ist, verkümmert seine Tätigkeit für diejenigen Stellen des menschlichen Organismus, an denen sie sich entfalten sollte. Das ist in den Nierenepithelien. In der Schädigung der Nierenepithelien ist ein Symptom vorhanden für die Ablenkung der für sie bestimmten Tätigkeit des astralischen Leibes.

Man sieht aus diesem Zusammenhange, wo die Heilung bei der Albuminurie einsetzen muß. Es ist die Kraft der Ich-Organisation in der Pankreasdrüse, die zu schwach ist, zu verstärken.

substance over into the sphere of the human ether body. In this way the protein in food becomes building material for the human organism. The foreign etheric actions formerly belonging to it leave the human being.

Now, it is necessary for a healthy digestion of protein in food that the human being possesses an ego organization that is strong enough to enable all the protein which the human organism needs to make a transition into the sphere of the human ether body. If this does not happen, then a surplus of activity of this ether body results. It receives insufficient protein substance prepared by the ego organization for its activity. The consequence is that activity oriented towards enlivening the protein absorbed by the ego organization takes hold of the protein that still contains foreign ether actions. The human being receives in his own ether body a number of actions that do not belong in it. These must be excreted in an abnormal manner. A pathological excretion comes about.

This pathological excretion becomes noticeable in *albuminuria*. Protein is excreted which should have been taken up into the sphere of the ether body. It is protein which, due to weakness of the ego organization, has not been able to assume the transitional stage of being almost lifeless.

The forces which bring about excretion in the human being are bound up with the sphere of the astral body. Because in albuminuria the astral body is forced to carry out an activity for which it is not prepared, its activity withers away in those areas of the organism where it should have been active. One of these areas is the renal epithelium. In damage of the renal epithelium, a phenomenon is present which shows that the activity of the astral body intended for it has been diverted.

From this connection it is clear where healing must begin in the case of albuminuria. The weakened force of the ego organization in the pancreatic gland must be strengthened.

X
DIE ROLLE DES FETTES IM MENSCHLICHEN ORGANISMUS UND DIE TRÜGERISCHEN LOKALEN SYMPTOMENKOMPLEXE

Das Fett ist diejenige Substanz des Organismus, die sich, indem sie von außen aufgenommen wird, am wenigsten als Fremdstoff erweist. Fett geht am leichtesten aus der Art, die es bei der Nahrungsaufnahme mitbringt, in die Art des menschlichen Organismus über. Die achtzig Prozent Fett, welche z. B. die Butter enthält, gehen durch die Gebiete des Ptyalin und Pepsin unverändert hindurch und werden nur vom Pankreassaft verändert, nämlich in Glycerin und Fettsäuren verwandelt.

Dieses Verhalten des Fettes ist nur dadurch möglich, daß es von der Natur eines fremden Organismus (von dessen ätherischen Kräften usw.) möglichst wenig in den menschlichen hinüberträgt. Dieser kann es leicht seiner eigenen Wirksamkeit einverleiben.

Das rührt davon her, daß das Fett bei der Erzeugung der inneren Wärme seine besondere Rolle spielt. Diese Wärme ist aber dasjenige, in dem, als im physischen Organismus, die Ich-Organisation vorzüglich lebt. Von *jeder* im menschlichen Körper befindlichen Substanz kommt für die IchOrganisation nur soviel in Betracht, als bei deren Wirksamkeit Wärmeentfaltung stattfindet. Fett erweist sich durch sein ganzes Verhalten als eine Substanz, die nur Ausfüllung des Körpers ist, nur von ihm getragen wird und allein durch diejenigen Vorgänge, bei denen sich Wärme entwickelt, für die tätige Organisation in Betracht kommt. Fett, das z. B. als Nahrung aus einem tierischen Organismus genommen ist, nimmt von diesem in den menschlichen Organismus nichts hinüber als allein seine Fähigkeit Wärme zu entwickeln.

Diese Wärme-Entwicklung geschieht aber als eine der spätesten Vorgänge des Stoffwechsels. Es erhält sich daher als Nahrung aufgenommenes Fett durch die ersten und mittleren Vorgänge des Stoffwechsels hindurch und wird erst in dem Bereich der inneren Körpertätigkeit, am frühesten vom Bauchspeichel aufgenommen.

CHAPTER X

The Role of Fat in the Human Organism and Deceptive Local Symptom Complexes

Fat is that substance of the organism which proves itself to be least a foreign body as it is taken in from outside. When taken as a food, fat makes a transition most easily from the mode it brings with it into the mode of the human organism. The eighty percent of fat contained in butter, for instance, pass unaltered through the regions of ptyalin and pepsin and are only altered by pancreatic juice, namely, converted to glycerin and fatty acids.

This way of working of fat is only possible because it carries along as little as possible of the natural essence of a foreign organism (of its etheric forces, etc.) into the human organism. The latter can easily incorporate it into its own functioning.

That is due to the fact that fat plays its special role in the generation of inner warmth. This warmth is again the element in which the ego organization, when in the physical organism, lives especially. For the ego organization only so much of *every* substance found in the body is relevant, as will engender warmth through its functioning. Through its whole way of working, fat proves itself to be a substance which is only a filler for the body, is just carried by it, and for the organization in action fat is relevant only through those processes in which warmth develops. Fat, taken as food (e.g., from an animal organism) will take nothing into the human organism except its ability to develop warmth.

However, this development of warmth happens as one of the last processes of the metabolism. Fat ingested as food therefore remains intact throughout the first and middle processes of metabolism and it is absorbed in the sphere of the

Wenn das Fett in der menschlichen Milch erscheint, so weist dies auf eine sehr bemerkenswerte Tätigkeit des Organismus hin. Der Körper zehrt dies Fett nicht in sich auf; er läßt es in ein Absonderungsprodukt übergehen. Es geht damit aber auch die Ich-Organisation in *dieses* Fett über. Darauf beruht die bildsame Kraft der Muttermilch. Die Mutter überträgt dadurch ihre eigenen bildsamen Kräfte der Ich-Organisation auf das Kind und fügt damit den Gestaltungskräften, die schon durch die Vererbung übertragen worden sind, noch etwas hinzu.

Der gesunde Weg ist dann vorhanden, wenn die menschlich bildsamen Kräfte die im Körper vorhandenen Fettvorräte in der Wärmeentwicklung aufzehren. Ein ungesunder Weg ist derjenige, wenn das Fett nicht von der Ich-Organisation in Wärmeprozessen verbraucht, sondern unverbraucht in den Organismus geführt wird. Solches Fett bildet einen Überschuß an der Möglichkeit, Wärme da und dort im Organismus zu erzeugen. Es ist das Wärme, die beirrend für die anderen Lebensvorgänge da und dort im Organismus eingreift, und die von der Ich-Organisation nicht umfaßt wird. Es entstehen da gewissermaßen parasitäre Wärmeherde. Diese tragen die Neigung zu entzündlichen Zuständen in sich. Die Entstehung solcher Herde muß darin gesucht werden, daß der Körper die Neigung entwickelt, mehr Fett zustande zu bringen, als die Ich-Organisation zu ihrem Leben in der Innenwärme braucht.

Im gesunden Organismus werden die animalischen (astralischen) Kräfte so viel Fett erzeugen oder aufnehmen, als durch die Ich-Organisation in Wärmevorgänge übergeführt werden kann, und dazu noch diejenige Menge, die notwendig ist, um die Muskel- und Knochen-Mechanik in Ordnung zu halten. In diesem Falle wird die dem Körper notwendige Wärme erzeugt werden. Tragen die animalischen Kräfte der Ich-Organisation zu wenig Fett zu, so tritt für die Ich-Organisation Wärmehunger ein. Diese muß die ihr notwendige Wärme den Tätigkeiten der Organe entziehen. Dadurch werden diese gewissermaßen in sich brüchig,

inner activities of the body, at the earliest by pancreatic secretions.

The occurrence of fat in human milk points to a very remarkable activity of the organism. The body does not consume this fat; it allows its transition into a product of secretion. But, along with this the ego organization goes over into *this* fat as well. This is what the plastic sculptural[7] force of mother's milk is based on. The mother thereby transfers her own plastic sculptural ego organization forces to the child, and thus adds something more to the form-giving forces that were already passed on by heredity.

A healthy course is taken when, in the development of warmth, the human plastic sculptural forces consume the fat stores present in the body. In an unhealthy course, fat is not used up by the ego organization in processes of warmth, but is carried unused into the organism. Such fat forms an excessive potential for generating warmth here and there in the organism. That kind of warmth is not enveloped by the ego organization and interferes misleadingly with other life processes here and there in the organism. Parasitic foci of warmth are, as it were, engendered. These bear within themselves the tendency towards inflammatory conditions. The origin of such foci must be sought in the fact that the body develops a tendency to make more fat than the ego organization requires for its life in inner warmth.

In the healthy organism, the animalic (astral) forces will generate or take up whatever fat can be transferred into warmth processes by the ego organization and, in addition, what is required to keep the mechanics of muscle and bone in order. In that case, the required warmth will be generated for the body. If the animalic forces supply the ego organization with too little fat, then the ego organization develops a hunger for warmth. It must withdraw the warmth it requires from the activities of organs. The organs then become, as it were,

versteift. Ihre notwendigen Vorgänge spielen sich träge ab. Man wird dann da oder dort Krankheitsprozesse auftreten sehen, bei denen es sich darum handeln wird, zu erkennen, ob sie in einem allgemeinen Fettmangel ihre Ursachen haben.

Tritt der schon erwähnte andere Fall ein, das Zuviel an Fettgehalt, so daß parasitäre Wärmeherde sich bilden, dann werden Organe so erfaßt, daß sie sich über ihr Maß hinaus betätigen. Es werden dadurch Neigungen erzeugt zu überreichlicher, den Organismus überlastender Nahrungsaufnahme. Es ist gar nicht nötig, daß dies so sich entwickelt, daß die in Frage kommende Person ein Zuviel-Esser wird. Es kann sein, daß z. B. bei der Stoffwechseltätigkeit im Organismus einem Kopforgan zuviel Substanz zugeführt unt dadurch solche den Unterleibsorganen und Absonderungsvorgängen entzogen wird. Dann tritt herabgestimmte Tätigkeit bei den schlecht versorgten Organen ein. Die Drüsenabsonderungen können mangelhaft werden. Die flüssigen Bestandteile des Organismus geraten in ein ungesundes Mischungsverhältnis. Es kann z. B. die Gallenabsonderung im Verhältnis zur Absonderung der Bauchspeicheldrüse zu groß werden. Wieder wird es darauf ankommen, daß man erkenne, wie ein lokal auftretender Symptomenkomplex in seinem Hervorgehen aus ungesunder Fett-Betätigung zu beurteilen ist.

inwardly brittle, stiff. The processes they require take place sluggishly. It will be essential to recognize whether the appearance of pathological processes that one sees here and there, may be caused by a general fat deficiency.

In the already mentioned other case, when there is an excess of fat and when parasitic foci of warmth are formed, organs will be taken hold of in such a way that they become active beyond their measure. Through that, tendencies toward excessive food intake are generated that overload the organism. It is not at all necessary that this develops in such a way that the person in question becomes an overeater. It may be that the organism's metabolic activity supplies an organ of the head with too much substance, which is therefore withdrawn from organs of the lower body and from the processes of secretion. As a result, the activity in the deprived organs is reduced. Glandular secretions may become inadequate. The fluid constituents of the organism become mixed in an unhealthy, disproportionate way. Bile secretion, for example, may become too copious in relation to the secretion of the pancreatic gland. Again it will be important to recognize how a local symptoms complex is to be judged as coming from an unhealthy mode of fat activity.

XI
DIE GESTALTUNG DES MENSCHLICHEN KÖRPERS UND DIE GICHT

Die Aufnahme des Eiweißes ist ein Vorgang, der mit der *einen* Seite der inneren Betätigung des menschlichen Organismus zusammenhängt. Es ist dies *die* Seite, die auf Grund der Stoffaufnahme zustande kommt. Jede derartige Betätigung hat zu ihrem Ergebnis Formbildung, Wachstum, Neubildung von substantiellem Inhalt. Alles, was mit den unbewußten Verrichtungen des Organismus zusammenhängt, gehört hierher.

Diesen Vorgängen stehen diejenigen gegenüber, die in Ausscheidungen bestehen. Es können Ausscheidungen sein, die nach außen gehen; es können auch solche sein, wo das Ausscheidungsprodukt im Innern weiter verarbeitet wird in der Formung oder Substanzierung des Körpers. Diese Vorgänge bilden die materielle Grundlage der bewußten Erlebnisse. Durch die Vorgänge der ersteren Art wird die Kraft des Bewußtseins herabgestimmt, wenn sie über das Maß dessen hinausgehen, was durch die Vorgänge der zweiten Art im Gleichgewicht gehalten werden kann.

Ein besonders bemerkenswerter Ausscheidungsvorgang ist derjenige der Harnsäure. Bei dieser Ausscheidung ist der astralische Leib tätig. Dieselbe muß durch den ganzen Organismus hindurch geschehen. In besonderem Maße geschieht sie durch den Harn. In einer ganz fein verteilten Weise z.B. im Gehirn. Bei der Harnsäureabsonderung durch den Harn ist in der Hauptsache der astralische Leib betätigt; die Ich-Organisation ist in untergeordneter Weise daran beteiligt. Bei der Harnsäureabsonderung im Gehirn ist in erster Linie die Ich-Organisation maßgebend, der astralische Leib tritt zurück.

Nun ist im Organismus der astralische Leib der Vermittler der Tätigkeit der Ich-Organisation für ätherischen und physischen Leib. Diese muß in die Organe die leblosen Substanzen und Kräfte tragen. Nur durch diese Imprägnierung der Organe mit Unorganischem kann der Mensch das bewußte Wesen sein, das er ist. Organische

CHAPTER XI

The Form of the Human Body and Gout

Protein intake is a process connected with *one* side of the inner activities of the human organism. This is the side which comes about on the basis of the intake of matter. Every activity of this kind results in building up form, in growth, in the creation of new substantial content. Everything connected to the unconscious actions of the organism belongs here.

These processes are the opposite of those consisting of excretions. The excretions may be outwards; they may also be such that the excretion product is further elaborated internally in the forming of, or bringing substance to, the body. These processes provide the material foundation for conscious experiences. Processes of the first kind reduce the force of consciousness if they exceed what can be held in balance by processes of the second kind.

A most remarkable excretory process is that of uric acid. The astral body is active in this excretion, which has to occur throughout the whole organism. It occurs through the urine in an especially ample measure. In a very finely distributed way it happens, for example, in the brain. Mainly the astral body is active in the secretion of uric acid in the urine; the ego organization has only a secondary part in it. In the secretion of uric acid in the brain, the ego organization is primarily the determining factor; the astral body recedes to the background.

Now, in the organism, the astral body is the mediator of the activity of the ego organization for the etheric and the physical body. The ego organization must carry the lifeless substances and forces into the organs. Only through this impregnation of the organs with inorganic material can the human being become the conscious being that he is. Organic

Substanz und organische Kraft würde das menschliche Bewußtsein zum tierischen herabdämpfen.

Der astralische Leib macht durch seine Tätigkeit die Organe geneigt, die unorganischen Einlagerungen der Ich-Organisation aufzunehmen. Er ist gewissermaßen für sie der Wegmacher.

Man sieht: in den unteren Teilen des menschlichen Organismus hat die Tätigkeit des astralischen Leibes die Oberhand. Es dürfen da die Harnsäuresubstanzen von dem Organismus nicht aufgenommen werden. Sie müssen reichlich ausgeschieden werden. Da muß unter dem Einfluß dieser Ausscheidung die Imprägnierung mit Unorganischem verhindert werden. Je mehr Harnsäure ausgeschieden wird, desto reger ist die Tätigkeit des astralischen Leibes, desto geringer die der Ich-Organisation und damit die Imprägnierung mit Unorganischem.

Im Gehirn ist die Tätigkeit des astralischen Leibes gering. Es wird wenig Harnsäure ausgeschieden, dafür um so mehr Unorganisches im Sinne der Ich-Organisation eingelagert.

Große Harnsäuremengen bewältigt die Ich-Organisation nicht; sie müssen der Tätigkeit des astralischen Leibes verfallen; kleine Harnsäuremengen gehen in die Ich-Organisation über und bilden dann die Grundlage für die Formung des Unorganischen im Sinne dieser Organisation. Es muß im gesunden Organismus die rechte Ökonomie herrschen in der Harnsäureverteilung für die einzelnen Gebiete. Für alles, was Nerven-Sinnesorganisation ist, muß eine nur so große Harnsäuremenge geliefert werden, als durch die Ich-Tätigkeit gebraucht werden kann; für die Stoffwechsel-Gliedmaßenorganisation muß diese Tätigkeit unterdrückt werden; die astralische Tätigkeit muß in der reichlichen Harnsäureabsonderung sich entfalten können.

Da nun der astralische Leib der Wegmacher für die Ich-Tätigkeit in den Organen ist, so muß man die richtig verteilte Harnsäureablagerung als ein ganz wesentliches Glied der menschlichen Gesundheit ansehen. Denn in ihr kommt zum Ausdrucke, ob zwis-

substance and organic force would lower human consciousness to the dim level of the animal.

Through its activity, the astral body brings the organs to the point that they are inclined to take up the inorganic deposits of the ego organization. Its function is in fact to prepare the way for them.

One may note: the activity of the astral body has the upper hand in the lower parts of the human organism. Here the uric acid substances must not be taken up by the organism. They must be amply excreted. Under the influence of this excretion the impregnation with inorganic material must be prevented there. The more uric acid is excreted, the more lively the activity of the astral body, and the less that of the ego organization and consequently the impregnating with inorganic materials.

In the brain, astral body activity is modest. Little uric acid is excreted, and all the more inorganic material is deposited in accordance with the ego organization in its stead.

The ego organization cannot master large quantities of uric acid; those must be left to the activity of the astral body. Small quantities of uric acid pass over into the ego organization and then provide the foundation for the forming of the inorganic in accordance with this organization.

In the healthy organism an appropriate economy in the distribution of uric acid to the individual regions must prevail. For the whole nerve-sense organization, only the amount of uric acid must be provided that the ego activity can make use of. For the metabolic-limb organization this ego activity must be suppressed; astral activity must be able to unfold in ample secretion of uric acid.

Since the astral body paves the way for ego activity in the organs, a proper distribution of uric acid deposits must be seen as an essential factor in human health. For what comes to

chen der Ich-Organisation und dem astralischen Leib in irgendeinem Organ oder Organsysteme das rechte Verhältnis besteht.

Man nehme nun an, in irgendeinem Organe, in dem die Ich-Organisation vorherrschen sollte gegenüber der astralischen Tätigkeit, beginne die letztere die Oberhand zu haben. Es kann dies nur ein Organ sein, in dem die Ausscheidung der Harnsäure durch die Einrichtung des Organes über einen gewissen Grad hinaus unmöglich ist. Es wird dann dieses Organ mit Harnsäure überladen, die von der Ich-Organisation nicht bewältigt wird. Der astralische Leib beginnt dann damit, die Ausscheidung dennoch zu bewirken. Und da die Ausführungsorgane an den betreffenden Stellen fehlen, so wird die Harnsäure statt nach außen, im Organismus selbst abgelagert. Gelangt sie an Stellen des Organismus, wo die Ich-Organisation nicht genügend eingreifen kann, so ist da Unorganisches, d. h. solches, das nur der Ich-Organisation zugehört, aber von dieser der astralischen Tätigkeit überlassen wird. Es entstehen Herde, wo in den menschlichen Organismus untermenschliche (animalische) Vorgänge eingeschoben werden.

Man hat es mit der *Gicht* zu tun. Wenn gesagt wird, diese entwickle sich vielfach auf Grund vererbter Anlage, so geschieht das eben deswegen, weil beim Vorherrschen der Vererbungskräfte das Astralisch-Animalische besonders tätig wird, und dadurch die Ich-Organisation zurückgedrängt wird.

Man wird aber die Sache besser durchschauen, wenn man die wahre Ursache darin sucht, daß in den menschlichen Körper durch die Nahrungsaufnahme Substanzen gelangen, die durch dessen Tätigkeit ihre Fremdheit innerhalb des Organismus nicht verlieren können. Sie werden durch eine schwache Ich-Organisation nicht in den Ätherleib übergeführt, verbleiben daher in der Region der astralischen Tätigkeit. Ein Gelenkknorpel oder eine Bindegewebspartie können mit Harnsäure nur überladen und dadurch die Überbürdung mit Unorganischem in ihnen bewirkt werden, daß in diesen Körperteilen die Ich-Tätigkeit hinter der Astralwirksamkeit zurückbleibt. Da die ganze Form des menschlichen Organismus

expression in it is whether the right relationship exists between ego organization and astral body in any particular organ or organ system.

Assume that in some organ, in which the ego organization should predominate over astral activity, the latter begins to gain the upper hand. This can only be an organ in which excretion of uric acid is impossible beyond a certain measure because of the organization of the organ. This organ then becomes overloaded with uric acid which cannot be mastered by the ego organization. The astral body then nevertheless begins to bring about an excretion of uric acid. And since, in the relevant places, the organs that carry it out are lacking, uric acid is deposited in the organism itself instead of outside. If it reaches places in the body where the ego organization cannot sufficiently engage, then inorganic material is present there, i.e., something that appertains only to the ego organization, but that is left by this to astral activity. Foci originate where sub-human (animalic) processes integrate themselves into the human organism.

One is dealing with *gout*. When it is said that gout frequently develops on the basis of an inherited tendency, then this is simply because the astral-animalic becomes especially active when inheritance forces predominate and repress the ego organization.

One shall, however, see through the matter better if one looks for the true cause in the fact that by ingesting food, man introduces substances into the body that cannot lose their foreign nature in the organism through the body's activity. Because of a weak ego organization they are not transferred to the ether body, and thus they remain in the region of astral activity. An articular cartilage or connective tissue area will only become overloaded with uric acid, and thus be overburdened with inorganic material, when ego activity lags behind astral functioning in these parts of the body. Since the whole

ein Ergebnis der Ich-Organisation ist, so muß durch die gekennzeichnete Unregelmäigkeit eine Deformierung der Organe eintreten. Der menschliche Organismus strebt da aus seiner Form heraus.

form of the human organism is a consequence of the ego organization, the characterized abnormality must cause organ deformation. Then the human organism strives away from its proper form.

XII
AUFBAU UND ABSONDERUNG DES MENSCHLICHEN ORGANISMUS

Der menschliche Körper bildet sich wie andere Organismen aus dem halbflüssigen Zustand heraus. Doch ist zu seiner Bildung stets die Zufuhr von luftförmigen Stoffen nötig. Der wichtigste ist der durch die Atmung vermittelte Sauerstoff.

Man betrachte zunächst einen festen Bestandteil, z. B. ein Knochengebilde. Es wird aus dem Halbflüssigen abgeschieden. In dieser Abscheidung ist die Ich-Organisation tätig. Jeder kann sich davon überzeugen, der die Ausbildung des Knochensystems verfolgt. Es entwickelt sich in dem Maße, als der Mensch durch die Embryonal- und Kindheitszeit seine menschliche Form, den Ausdruck der Ich-Organisation, bekommt. Die Eiweißverwandlung, die dabei zugrunde liegt, scheidet zunächst die (astralischen und ätherischen) Fremdkräfte von der Eiweißsubstanz ab; das Eiweiß geht durch den Zustand des Unorganischen hindurch; es muß dabei flüssig werden. In diesem Zustand wird es von der Ich-Organisation, die sich in der Wärme betätigt, erfaßt und dem eigenen menschlichen Ätherleib zugeführt. Es wird Menschen-Eiweiß. Bis zu der Verwandlung in die Knochensubstanz hat es noch einen weiten Weg.

Es ist nach seiner Verwandlung in Menschen-Eiweiß notwendig, daß es zur Aufnahme und Umformung von kohlensaurem und phosphorsaurem Kalk usw. reif gemacht wird. Dazu muß es eine Zwischenstufe durchmachen. Es muß unter den Einfluß der Aufnahme von Luftförmigem kommen. Dieses trägt die Umwandlungsprodukte der Kohlehydrate in das Eiweiß hinein. Es entstehen dadurch Substanzen, die die Grundlage für die einzelnen Organbildungen abgeben können. Man hat es da nicht mit fertigen Organsubstanzen, nicht mit Leber- oder Knochensubstanz z. B. zu tun, sondern mit einer allgemeineren Substanz, aus der heraus alle die einzelnen Organe des Körpers gebildet werden können. In der Bildung der fertigen Organgestalten ist die Ich-Organisation tätig.

CHAPTER XII

Upbuilding and Secretion in the Human Organism

The human body, like other organisms, is formed out of the semifluid state, but an influx of gaseous elements is constantly required for its formation. The most important one is oxygen, which is mediated by breathing.

Consider first a solid component, e.g., a bone structure. It is densified out of semifluid material. The ego organization is active in this process. Anyone following the development of the skeletal system can verify this. During the embryonal time and in childhood it develops to the extent that the human being receives his human form, the expression of the ego organization. The conversion of protein which underlies this development first eliminates the foreign (astral and etheric) forces from the protein; then protein passes through the inorganic state and it must become fluid in the process. In this condition it is taken hold of by the ego organization, which is active in the element of warmth, and is introduced into the human being's own ether body. It becomes human protein. It has yet to go a long way before it is converted into bone substance.

After its conversion into human protein it must mature to be able to take up and transform calcium carbonate, calcium phosphate, etc. To this end it must undergo an intermediate stage. It must be influenced by the assimilation of a gaseous element. The latter carries the transformation products of carbohydrates into protein. This brings substances into being which can provide the basis for the formation of individual organs. One is not dealing here with finished organ substance, not with, for example, liver or bone substance, but with a more general substance out of which all the individual organs of the body can be built up. The ego organization is active in forming the final organ shape. In the characterized, still undifferentiated

In der gekennzeichneten, noch undifferenzierten Organsubstanz ist der astralische Leib tätig. Beim Tiere nimmt dieser astralische Leib auch die fertige Organgestaltung auf sich; beim Menschen bleibt die Tätigkeit des astralischen Leibes und damit die animalische Natur nur als der allgemeine Untergrund der Ich-Organisation bestehen. Die Tierwerdung kommt beim Menschen nicht zu Ende; sie wird auf ihrem Wege unterbrochen und ihr das Menschliche durch die Ich-Organisation gewissermaßen aufgesetzt.

Diese Ich-Organisation lebt ganz in Wärmezuständen. Sie holt aus der allgemeinen Astralwesenheit die einzelnen Organe heraus. Sie betätigt sich dabei an der allgemeinen, durch das Astralische herbeigeführten Substanz so, daß sie den Wärmezustand eines sich vorbereitenden Organs entweder erhöht oder vermindert.

Vermindert sie ihn, so treten unorganische Substanzen in einem sich verhärtenden Vorgang in die Substanz ein, und es ist die Grundlage zur Knochenbildung gegeben. Es werden Salzsubstanzen aufgenommen.

Erhöht sie ihn, so werden Organe gebildet, deren Tätigkeit in einer Auflösung des Organischen besteht, in einer Überführung in Flüssiges oder Luftförmiges.

Man nehme nun an, die Ich-Organisation finde im Organismus nicht so viel Wärme entwickelt, daß die Erhöhung des Wärmezustandes für die Organe, denen er nötig ist, im hinreichenden Maße erfolgen kann. Es geraten dadurch Organe, deren Tätigkeit nach der Richtung der Auflösung hin erfolgen soll, in die Tätigkeit des Verhärtens. Sie erhalten die Neigung als krankhafte, die in den Knochen die gesunde ist.

Nun ist der Knochen, wenn er von der Ich-Organisation geformt ist, ein Organ, das von dieser aus ihrem Bereich entlassen wird. Er kommt in einen Zustand, in dem er nicht mehr innerlich ergriffen wird von der Ich-Organisation, sondern nur noch äußerlich. Er ist aus dem Wachstums- und Organisationsbereich herausgeführt und dient noch mechanisch der Ich-Organisation bei Ausführung der Körperbewegungen. Nur ein Rest von innerer

organ substance, the astral body is active. Within the animal, this astral body also takes the task upon itself of giving the final organ shape; within the human being astral body activity (and with it animalic nature) only continues to exist as a general underlying principle of the ego organization. Animal development is not carried to its conclusion in the human being; it is interrupted in its course and human nature is, as it were, superimposed upon it by the ego organization.

This ego organization lives entirely in states of warmth. It derives the individual organs from the general astral essence. It works upon the general substance provided by the astral, by either raising or lowering the state of warmth of an organ in preparation.

If it lowers the warmth state, then inorganic materials enter into the substance in a process of hardening, and the basis for bone formation is provided. Saline substances are taken up.

If it raises the warmth state, then organs are formed whose activity consists in dissolving organic substance, in bringing it into the liquid or gaseous state.

Assume now that the ego organization does not find enough warmth developed in the organism, to increase the warmth state adequately in those organs requiring it. This will bring organs that should have their proper activity in the direction of dissolving, to hardening activity. For them, the tendency which is healthy in the bones becomes pathological.

Now, bone is an organ which, once it has been formed by the ego organization, is released by it from its sphere. It comes into a state where it is no longer taken hold of by the ego organization from within, but only from without. It is removed from the sphere of growth and organization, and merely serves the ego organization in a mechanical capacity by performing body movements. Only a remainder of inner ego organization activity continues to permeate bone throughout life because,

Tätigkeit der Ich-Organisation durchsetzt ihn die ganze Lebenszeit hindurch, weil er ja doch auch Organisationsglied innerhalb des Organismus bleiben muß und aus dem Leben nicht herausfallen darf.

Die Organe, die aus dem angegebenen Grunde in eine knochenähnliche Bildungstätigkeit übergehen können, sind die Adern. Bei ihnen tritt dann die sogenannte Verkalkung (Sclerosis) auf. Es wird aus diesen Organsystemen die Ich-Organisation gewissermaßen ausgetrieben.

Der entgegengesetzte Fall tritt ein, wenn die Ich-Organisation nicht auf die notwendige Verminderung des Wärmezustandes für das Knochengebiet trifft. Dann werden die Knochen den Organen ähnlich, die eine auflösende Tätigkeit entwickeln. Sie vermögen dann wegen der mangelnden Verhärtung keine Grundlage abzugeben für die Salzeingliederung. Es findet also die letzte Entfaltung der Knochengebilde, die in den Bereich der Ich-Organisation gehört, nicht statt. Die astralische Tätigkeit wird nicht an dem rechten Punkte ihres Weges aufgehalten. Es müssen Neigungen zur Gestalt-Mißbildung auftreten; denn die gesunde Gestaltbildung kann nur im Bereiche der Ich-Organisation erfolgen.

Man hat es mit den rachitischen Erkrankungen zu tun. Aus alledem ersieht man, wie die menschlichen Organe mit ihren Tätigkeiten zusammenhängen. Der Knochen entsteht im Bereiche der Ich-Organisation. Ist seine Bildung zum Abschlusse gekommen, so dient er dieser Ich-Organisation, die ihn fortan nicht mehr bildet, sondern zu den willkürlichen Bewegungen benützt. Ebenso ist es nun mit dem, was im Bereiche der astralischen Organisation entsteht. Es werden da undifferenzierte Substanzen und Kräfte gebildet. Diese treten als die Grundlage der differenzierten Organbildungen überall im Körper auf. Die astralische Tätigkeit führt sie bis zu einer gewissen Stufe; dann benützt sie sie. Es ist der ganze menschliche Organismus vom Halbflüssigen durchdrungen, in dem astralisch orientierte Tätigkeit waltet.

after all, it must also stay an integral part within the organism and must not be allowed to fall out of the sphere of life.

Organs that for the above-mentioned reason may go into a formative activity similar to bones are the arteries. Then the so-called calcification (sclerosis) appears in them. In a certain sense the ego organization is driven out of these organ systems.

The opposite is the case when the ego organization does not meet the bones with the required lowering of the state of warmth for the region. Bones then become similar to organs which develop dissolving activity. Due to the lack of hardening they are not capable of providing the basis for the integration of salt. Thus the final step in the development of bone structure, which belongs in the sphere of the ego organization, fails to take place. Astral activity is not stopped at the right point along the way. Tendencies towards malformation of shape must appear, for healthy formation of shape can only occur within the sphere of the ego organization.

One is dealing here with diseases like rickets. From all this it becomes evident in which way human organs are related to their activities. Bone comes into being in the sphere of the ego organization. When its formation has been concluded, then bone serves this ego organization, which from now on no longer forms it but uses it for voluntary movements. Then it is the same for what comes into being in the sphere of the astral organization. Here undifferentiated substances and forces are formed. These occur throughout the body as the basis for differentiated organ formation. Astral activity carries them up to a certain level; then it makes use of them. The entire human organism is permeated by semifluid material, in which astrally oriented activity is at work.

Diese Tätigkeit lebt sich aus in Absonderungen, die in der Bildung des Organismus nach der Richtung seiner höheren Glieder hin ihre Verwendung finden. Man hat eine so gerichtete Absonderung in den Drüsenerzeugnissen zu sehen, die in der Ökonomie der Organismuswirksamkeit ihre Rolle spielen. Man hat dann neben diesen Absonderungen nach dem Innern des Organismus diejenigen, die eigentliche Abscheidungen nach außen sind. Man irrt, wenn man in diesen nichts weiter sieht als dasjenige, was der Organismus von den aufgenommenen Nahrungsstoffen nicht brauchen kann und deshalb nach außen wirft. Es kommt nämlich nicht darauf an, daß der Organismus Stoffe nach außen absondert, sondern daß er diejenigen Tätigkeiten vollzieht, die zu den Ausscheidungen führen. In der Verrichtung dieser Tätigkeiten liegt etwas, das der Organismus für seinen Bestand *braucht*. Diese Tätigkeit ist ebenso notwendig wie diejenige, die Stoffe in den Organismus aufnimmt oder in ihm ablagert. Denn in dem gesunden Verhältnis der *beiden* Tätigkeiten liegt das Wesen der organischen Wirksamkeit.

So erscheint in den Ausscheidungen nach außen das Ergebnis der astral orientierten Tätigkeit. Und sind Stoffe in die Ausscheidungen eingelagert, die bis zum Unorganischen getrieben sind, dann lebt in diesen auch die Ich-Organisation. Und *dieses* Leben der Ich-Organisation ist sogar von ganz besonderer Wichtigkeit. Denn die Kraft, die auf solche Ausscheidungen verwendet wird, erzeugt gewissermaßen einen Gegendruck nach innen. Und dieser ist für das gesunde Sein des Organismus notwendig. Die Harnsäure, die durch den Harn abgesondert wird, erzeugt als solchen Gegendruck nach innen die richtige Neigung des Organismus für den Schlaf. Zu wenig Harnsäure im Harn und zuviel im Blut erzeugt einen so kurzen Schlaf, daß dieser für die Gesundheit des Organismus nicht hinreicht.

This activity expresses itself in secretions which find their use where the formation of the organism is on the way to its higher members. A secretion tending in this direction can be seen in the glandular products, which play a role in the economy of the organism's functioning. Then in addition to these secretions into the inner organism, there are those that are actual eliminations to the outside. One is mistaken if one regards these as nothing else but the part of the ingested nutritive substances which the organism cannot make use of and therefore discards. It is actually not important that the organism secretes substances to the outside, but rather, that it accomplishes the activities which result in excretions. Something lies in carrying out these activities that the organism *needs* for its continued existence. *This* activity is just as necessary as the one which takes up substances into the organism or stores them in it. For the essence of organic functioning lies in the healthy relationship of *both* activities.

The result of astrally oriented activity thus appears in excretions to the outside. And if substances, which have been driven to the inorganic state, are embedded in the excretions, then the ego organization also lives in these excretions. And *this* life of the ego organization is of exceptional importance. For the force that is used for such excretions creates, as it were, a counterpressure going inward. And this is necessary for the healthy existence of the organism. The uric acid which is secreted through the urine creates, in such a counterpressure going inward, the proper inclination for sleep of the organism. Too little uric acid in the urine and too much in the blood generates such a short sleep that it does not suffice for the health of the organism.

XIII
VOM WESEN DES KRANKSEINS UND DER HEILUNG

Schmerz, der irgendwo im Organismus auftritt, ist Erlebnis im astralischen Leib und im Ich. Beide, sowohl der astralische Leib wie das Ich sind in den physischen Leib und den ätherischen Leib in einer entsprechenden Art eingeschaltet, so lange der Mensch im wachenden Zustande ist. Tritt der Schlaf ein, so verrichten der physische und der ätherische Leib allein die organische Tätigkeit. Der astralische Leib und das Ich sind von ihnen abgetrennt.

Im Schlafen kehrt der Organismus zu den Betätigungen zurück, die am Ausgangspunkte seiner Entwicklung liegen, in der Embryonal- und ersten Kindheitszeit. Im Wachen herrschen diejenigen Vorgänge vor, die am Ende dieser Entwicklung liegen, im Altern und Sterben.

Im Anfange der Menschenentwicklung liegt das Vorherrschen der Tätigkeit des ätherischen Leibes über diejenige des astralischen; allmählich wird die Tätigkeit des letzteren immer intensiver, die des ätherischen Leibes tritt zurück. Im Schlafen erhält dann der ätherische Leib nicht etwa die Intensität, die er im Lebensanfange gehabt hat. Er behält diejenige, die er im Verhältnis zum Astralischen im Laufe des Lebens entwickelt hat.

Für jedes Organ des menschlichen Körpers entspricht in jedem Lebensalter eine bestimmte Stärke der auf das Organ entfallenden ätherischen Tätigkeit einer ebensolchen der astralischen. Daß das rechte Verhältnis vorhanden ist, davon hängt es ab, ob der astralische Leib sich in den ätherischen entsprechend einschalten kann oder nicht. Kann er das wegen Herabstimmung der ätherischen Tätigkeit nicht, so entsteht Schmerz; entwickelt der ätherische Leib eine über sein Normalmaß hinausgehende Tätigkeit, so wird die Durchdringung der astralischen und der ätherischen Betätigung besonders intensiv. Es entsteht Lust, Wohlbehagen. Man muß sich nur klar sein darüber, daß Lust beim Wachsen über ein gewisses Maß hinaus in Schmerz und umgekehrt Schmerz in Lust übergeht. Beachtet man dies nicht, so könnte dies

CHAPTER XIII

On the Essential Nature of Being Ill and of Healing

Pain occuring somewhere in the organism is an experience in the astral body and in the I. Both, astral body as well as I, each in their respective ways, are engaged in the physical body and the etheric body for as long as the human being is in the waking state. When sleep sets in, the physical and the etheric body perform the organic activities alone. The astral body and the I are separated from them.

In sleeping, the organism returns to those modes of activity which are present at the starting point of its development, during the embryonal time and in early infancy. In waking, those processes predominate which are present at the end of this development, during aging and dying.

At the beginning of human development, there is a predominance of the activity of the etheric body over that of the astral; gradually the activity of the latter becomes more and more intense, and that of the etheric body recedes. Then in sleep the etheric body does not obtain the degree of intensity it had at the beginning of life. It retains the intensity it has developed in relation to the astral in the course of life.

For every organ of the human body at every age of life a certain intensity of etheric activity allotted to the organ is in conformity with a certain intensity of astral activity. The presence of a proper relationship determines whether the astral body can appropriately fit in with the etheric or not. If it is unable to do so because of a reduction of etheric activity, then pain originates; if the etheric body develops an activity beyond its normal measure, then the interpenetration of the astral and the etheric mode of activity becomes especially intense. Then pleasure, a feeling of comfort arises. One must simply be clear about the fact that pleasure which grows beyond a certain

hier Gesagte im Widerspruch mit früher Ausgeführtem erscheinen.

Ein Organ erkrankt, wenn sich die ihm zukommende ätherische Tätigkeit nicht entfalten kann. Man nehme z. B. die aus dem Verdauungsvorgange sich in den ganzen Organismus fortsetzende Stoffwechseltätigkeit. Werden die Erzeugnisse des Stoffwechsels überall restlos übergeführt in die Tätigkeit und Substanzgestaltung des Organismus, so ist dies ein Zeichen dafür, daß der ätherische Leib in entsprechender Weise arbeitet. Lagern sich aber auf den Stoffwechselwegen Substanzen ab, die nicht in das Tun des Organismus übergehen, dann ist der Ätherleib herabgestimmt in seiner Tätigkeit. Diejenigen physischen Vorgänge, die sonst vom astralischen Leib angeregt werden, aber nur in ihrem Gebiete dem Organismus seine Dienste leisten, greifen über ihr Gebiet hinaus in dasjenige der ätherischen Tätigkeit hinüber. Es entstehen auf diese Art Vorgänge, die dem Vorherrschen des astralischen Leibes ihr Dasein verdanken. Es sind das Vorgänge, die ihre rechte Stelle da haben, wo das Altern, der Abbau des Organismus eintritt.

Es handelt sich nun darum, die Harmonie zwischen der ätherischen und der astralischen Tätigkeit herbeizuführen. Der ätherische Leib muß verstärkt, der astralische geschwächt werden. Es kann dies dadurch geschehen, daß die physischen Substanzen, welche der Ätherleib verarbeitet, in einen Zustand gebracht werden, in dem sie sich leichter der Tätigkeit fügen, als dies im kranken Zustande geschieht. Ebenso muß der Ich-Organisation Kraft zugeführt werden, denn der astralische Leib, der in seiner Tätigkeit animalisch orientiert ist, wird durch die Verstärkung der Ich-Organisation nach der Richtung der menschlichen Organisation mehr gehemmt als ohne diese.

Der Weg, diese Dinge erkennend zu durchschauen, wird sich finden, wenn man beobachtet, was für Wirkungen auf den Stoffwechselwegen irgend eine Substanz entfaltet. Man nehme den Schwefel. Er ist im Eiweiß enthalten. Er liegt also dem ganzen Vorgang zugrunde, der sich bei der Aufnahme der Eiweißnahrung

measure turns into pain and, vice versa, pain into pleasure. If one does not bear this in mind then what is said here might seem in contradiction with what was elaborated earlier.

An organ becomes diseased when the etheric activity which belongs to it cannot unfold. Take for example metabolic activity, which continues from the digestive process into the whole organism. When the products of metabolism are entirely transferred into the organism's activity and its shaping of substance everywhere, then this is a sign that the etheric body is working appropriately. If, however, substances are deposited along metabolic pathways that do not become part of the doings of the organism, then the etheric body is reduced in its activity. Such physical processes, as serve the organism only in their own domain and which the astral body usually stimulates, reach beyond their limits into the domain of etheric activity. In this way processes originate which owe their existence to the predominance of the astral body. These processes have their proper place where aging, where breakdown of the body occurs.

Now it is essential to bring harmony between etheric and astral activity. The etheric body must be strengthened, the astral toned down. This can be made to happen by bringing the physical substances, which the etheric body is processing, into a condition in which they accommodate activity more easily than when a state of disease is present. Likewise strength must be brought to the ego organization, for the astral body, which is oriented toward the animalic in its activity, will be more inhibited and on the way to human organization through the strengthening of the ego organization, than without this.[8]

One will find the means to see through these matters with insight by observing the functions which a particular substance displays along metabolic pathways. Take sulfur. It is present in protein. It is therefore fundamental to the whole process which

abspielt. Er geht von der fremden ätherischen Art durch den Zustand des Unorganischen über in die ätherische Tätigkeit des menschlichen Organismus. Er findet sich im Faserstoff der Organe, im Gehirn, in Nägeln und Haaren. Er geht also durch die Stoffwechselwege bis an die Peripherie des Organismus. Er erweist sich damit als eine Substanz, die bei der Aufnahme der Eiweißstoffe in das Gebiet des menschlichen Ätherleibes eine Rolle spielt.

Es entsteht nun die Frage, ob denn der Schwefel auch bei dem Übergang von dem Gebiet der ätherischen Wirksamkeit in das der astralischen eine Bedeutung hat, und ob er etwas mit der Ich-Organisation zu tun hat. Er verbindet sich nicht merklich mit den in den Organismus eingeführten unorganischen Substanzen zu Säuren und Salzen. In einer solchen Verbindung würde die Grundlage für eine Aufnahme der Schwefelprozesse in den astralischen Leib und die Ich-Organisation liegen. Der Schwefel dringt also nicht dahin. Er entfaltet seine Wirksamkeit im Bereiche des physischen und des Ätherleibes. Das zeigt sich auch darin daß erhöhte Schwefelzufuhr in dem Organismus Schwindelgefühle, Bewußtseins-Dämpfungen hervorruft. Auch der Schlaf, also der Körperzustand, in dem der astralische Leib und die Ich-Organisation als seelische Wesenheiten nicht wirken, wird durch vermehrte Schwefelzufuhr intensiver.

Man kann daraus ersehen, daß der Schwefel, als Heilmittel zugeführt, die physischen Tätigkeiten des Organismus dem Eingreifen der ätherischen geneigter macht, als sie im kranken Zustande sind.

Anders liegt die Sache beim Phosphor. Er findet sich im menschlichen Organismus als Phosphorsäure und phosphorsaure Salze im Eiweiß, im Faserstoff, im Gehirn, in den Knochen. Er drängt zu den unorganischen Substanzen hin, die in dem Bereich der Ich-Organisation ihre Bedeutung haben. Er regt die bewußte Tätigkeit des Menschen an. Dadurch bedingt er auf entgegengesetzte Art wie der Schwefel, nämlich nach der Anregung der bewußten Tätigkeit, den Schlaf; der Schwefel dagegen bedingt diesen durch

happens in the assimilation of proteinaceous food. It passes from the foreign etheric mode through the inorganic state on into the etheric activity of the human organism. It is found in the fibrinogen of the organs, in the brain, in nails and hair. Thus it goes along metabolic pathways right to the periphery of the organism. In this way it proves to be a substance which plays a part in the assimilation of proteinaceous substances in the domain of the human ether body.

Now comes the question whether sulfur also has significance in the transition from the region of etheric function into that of astral function, and if it has anything to do with the ego organi-zation. It does not noticeably combine with the inorganic substances introduced into the organism to form acids and salts. Such combination would be the basis for an assimilation of sulfur processes into the astral body and ego organization. But sulfur does not reach that far. It functions in the sphere of the physical and ether body. This is also apparent from the fact that an increased supply of sulfur evokes feelings of dizziness, suppression of consciousness in the organism. Sleep, the state of the body in which the astral body and ego organization are not at work as soul beings, also becomes more intensive when the sulfur supply is increased.

One can learn from this that sulfur, introduced as a medication, will increase the disposition of the physical activities for intervention of the organism's etheric activities more so than when a state of disease is present.

The matter is different for phosphorus. It is found in the human organism as phosphoric acid and phosphoric salts in protein, in fibrinogen, in the brain, in bones. It strives towards the inorganic substances, which are significant in the sphere of the ego organization. It stimulates the conscious activity of the human being. It thereby causes sleep in a way that is opposite to sulfur, namely after stimulation of conscious activity;

Erhöhung der unbewußten physischen und ätherischen Tätigkeit. Der Phosphor ist im phosphorsauren Kalk der Knochen, also derjenigen Organe, die der Ich-Organisation unterliegen, wenn diese sich der äußeren Mechanik zur Körperbewegung bedient, nicht wenn sie von innen, in Wachstum, Stoffwechselregulierung usw. wirkt.

Als Heilmittel wird daher der Phosphor wirken, wenn der krankhafte Zustand in dem Überwuchern des astralischen Gebietes über die Ich-Organisation besteht und die letztere gestärkt werden muß, damit die astralische zurückgedrängt wird.

Man betrachte die Rachitis. Es wurde im früheren ausgeführt, wie sie in einem Überwuchern der ätherisch-astralischen Tätigkeit beruht und wie sie zu einer mangelhaften Betätigung der Ich-Organisation führt. Behandelt man sie zuerst mit Schwefel in entsprechender Weise, so wird die ätherische gegenüber der astralischen Tätigkeit verstärkt; läßt man, nachdem dies geschehen ist, eine Phosphorbehandlung eintreten, so wird, was man in der Äther-Organisation vorbereitet hat, zu derjenigen des Ich hinübergeleitet; und man kommt der Rachitis von zwei Seiten entgegen. (Es ist uns bekannt, daß die Phosphorheilung bei Rachitis angezweifelt wird; allein, man hatte es bei den bisherigen Heilversuchen *nicht* mit der hier beschriebenen Methode zu tun.)

sulfur, in contra-distinction, causes sleep by increasing unconscious physical and etheric activity. Phosphorus is present in calcium phosphate in the bones, that is in those organs that are subject to the ego organization as it employs outer mechanics to move the body, not when it works from within, in growth, regulation of metabolism, etc.

Phosphorus will therefore act as a medication when the pathological condition consists in a hypertrophy of the astral region over the ego organization and the latter needs to be strengthened so that the astral is pushed back.

Consider rickets. It was discussed earlier how it has its root in a proliferation of etheric-astral activity and how it leads to an inadequate mode of activity of the ego organization. If it is first treated appropriately with sulfur, then etheric in relation to astral activity is strengthened; if one allows a phosphorus treatment to take place after this has happened, then what was prepared in the ether organization is led further to the organization of the "I." One confronts the rickets from two sides. (We are aware that phosphorus treatment for rickets is called into question, but until now attempts at treatment have *not* had anything to do with the method described here.)

XIV
VON DER THERAPEUTISCHEN DENKWEISE

Die Kieselsäure trägt ihre Wirkungen durch die Stoffwechselwege bis in diejenigen Partien des menschlichen Organismus, in denen das Lebendige zum Leblosen wird. Sie findet sich im Blute, durch das hindurch die Gestaltungskräfte ihren Weg nehmen müssen; und sie kommt in den Haaren vor, also dort, wo sich die Gestaltung nach außen abschließt; man trifft sie in den Knochen, in denen die Gestaltung nach innen ihr Ende findet. Sie erscheint im Harn als Absonderungsprodukt.

Sie bildet die physische Grundlage der Ich-Organisation. Denn diese wirkt gestaltend. Diese Ich-Organisation braucht den Kieselsäureprozeß bis in diejenigen Teile des Organismus hinein, in denen die Gestaltung, die Formgebung an die äußere und innere (unbewußte) Welt grenzt. In dem Umkreis des Organismus, wo die Haare die Kieselsäure tragen, wird die menschliche Organisation an die unbewußte Außenwelt angeschlossen. In den Knochen wird diese Organisation an die unbewußte Innenwelt angeschlossen, in der der Wille wirkt.

Zwischen den beiden Wirkungsfeldern der Kieselsäure muß sich im gesunden menschlichen Organismus die physische Grundlage des Bewußtseins entfalten. Die Kieselsäure hat eine zweifache Aufgabe. Sie setzt im Innern den bloßen Wachstums-, Ernährungs- etc. Vorgängen eine Grenze. Und sie schließt nach außen die bloßen Naturwirkungen von dem Innern des Organismus ab, so daß dieser innerhalb seines Bereiches nicht die Naturwirkungen zur Fortsetzung bringen muß, sondern seine eigenen entfalten kann.

Der menschliche Organismus ist in seiner Jugend an den Stellen, wo die mit den Gestaltungskräften versehenen Gewebe liegen, am meisten mit Kieselsäure ausgestattet. Von da aus entfaltet die Kieselsäure ihre Tätigkeit nach den beiden Grenzgebieten hin und schafft zwischen ihnen den Raum, in dem sich die Organe des bewußten Lebens bilden können. Im gesunden Organismus sind das vornehmlich die Sinnesorgane. Aber man muß eingedenk dessen

CHAPTER XIV

About the Therapeutic Way of Thinking

Silicic acid carries its activities along metabolic pathways right into those parts of the human organism where what is alive becomes lifeless. It is present in the blood, through which the form-giving forces have to make their way, and it occurs in hair, where giving form outwardly comes to a close. One also finds it in the bones, where form giving ends inwardly. It appears in the urine as an excretory product.

It constitutes the physical basis of the ego organization. For this works by creating form. This ego organization needs the silicic acid process right into those regions of the organism in which shaping, giving form, borders on the outer and inner (unconscious) world. In the circumference of the organism where the hairs carry silicic acid, the human organization is connected to the unconscious outer world. In the bones, this organization is connected to the unconscious inner world, in which the will is working.

Between the two fields of action of silicic acid the physical foundation of consciousness must unfold in the healthy human organism. Silicic acid has a twofold task. Inwardly, it sets a border to processes such as growth, nutrition, etc. To the outside it closes the mere effects of nature off from the inner organism, so that it does not have to continue the workings of nature within its own sphere, but is able to unfold its own.

The human organism is most richly supplied with silicic acid in its youth wherever tissues are provided with form-giving forces. From there the silicic acid unfolds its activity towards the two border areas, creating between them the space in which the organs of conscious life can form themselves. In the healthy organism these are chiefly the sense organs. But one must bear in mind that sensory life permeates the whole

sein, daß das Sinnesleben den ganzen menschlichen Organismus durchzieht. Die Wechselwirkung der Organe beruht darauf, daß immer ein Organ die Wirkung des andern wahrnimmt. Bei denjenigen Organen, die nicht in der eigentlichen Bedeutung Sinnesorgane sind, z. B. Leber, Milz, Niere etc., ist die Wahrnehmung eine so leise, daß sie im gewöhnlichen wachen Leben unter der Schwelle des Bewußtseins bleibt. Jedes Organ ist außerdem, daß es dieser oder jener Funktion im Organismus dient, noch Sinnesorgan.

Aber es ist doch der ganze menschliche Organismus von sich gegenseitig beeinflussenden Wahrnehmungen durchzogen und muß es sein, damit alles in ihm gesund zusammenwirkt.

Alles das aber beruht auf der richtigen Verteilung der Kieselsäurewirkungen. Man kann geradezu von einem dem Gesamt-Organismus eingegliederten speziellen Kieselsäure-Organismus sprechen, auf dem die der gesunden Lebenstätigkeit zugrunde liegende gegenseitige Empfindlichkeit der Organe und deren richtiges Verhältnis nach innen zu der Seelen- und Geist-Entfaltung und nach außen für den richtigen Abschluß der Naturwirkungen beruht.

Dieser Spezial-Organismus wird nur richtig wirken, wenn die Kieselsäure in einer solchen Menge im Organismus vorhanden ist, daß der Ich-Organismus in voller Art sie ausnützen kann. Für alle übrige Kieselsäuremenge muß die astralische Organisation, die unter der Ich-Organisation liegt, die Kraft haben, sie durch den Harn oder auf andere Art auszuscheiden.

Die nicht ausgeschiedenen überschüssigen, von der Ich-Organisation nicht erfaßten Kieselsäuremengen müssen im Organismus als Fremdstoffe sich ablagern und wegen ihrer Neigung zur Gestaltung, durch die sie – in richtiger Menge – gerade der Ich-Organisation dienen, diese stören. Zu viel Kieselsäure dem Organismus beigebracht, gibt daher Anlaß zu Magen- und Darmverstimmungen. Die Aufgabe des Verdauungsgebietes besteht dann darin, abzuscheiden, was zur überschüssigen Gestaltung drängt. Wo das Flüssige vorherrschen soll, wird Vertrocknung bewirkt. Am deutlichsten zeigt sich dies, wenn die Störungen des seelischen Gleich-

human organism. The interaction of the organs is based on the fact that at all times an organ is perceiving the action of another organ. Within those organs which are not sense organs in the real meaning of the word, e.g., liver, spleen, kidneys, etc., the perception is so subtle that in ordinary waking life it stays below the threshold of consciousness. Every organ, besides serving this or that function in the organism, is also a sense organ.

But indeed, the whole human organism is, and has to be, permeated with perceptions which influence each other reciprocally so that everything in it works together in a healthy way.

All this is, however, based on the right distribution of silicic acid actions. One can actually speak of a special silicic acid organism, integrated into the organism as a whole, on which rests the basis of healthy life activity, the reciprocal sensitivity of the organs and their right relationship inwardly to the unfolding of soul and spirit, and outwardly towards the right closing off of the effects of nature.

This special organism will work properly only if silicic acid is present in the organism in such quantity that the ego organization is able to make full use of it. For the whole remaining quantity of silicic acid, the astral organization, which lies below the ego organization, must have the force to excrete it through the urine or in another way.

Excessive quantities of silicic acid which are neither excreted, nor taken hold of by the ego organization, cannot but be deposited as foreign substances in the body, interfering with the ego organization through their form-giving tendency, by means of which—in the right quantity—they precisely serve it. Too much silicic acid introduced into the organism will therefore cause gastrointestinal upsets. It is then the task of the digestive tract to eliminate the excessive formative tendency. Where the fluid element should predominate, a desiccation is

gewichtes, hinter denen die organischen unverkennbar sind, bei zu reichlicher Kieselsäurezufuhr stattfinden. Man fühlt Schwindel-Gefühle, kann sich vor dem Verfallen in den Schlafzustand nicht behüten, empfindet Unlenkbarkeit der Gehör- und Gesichtswahrnehmungsvorgänge; ja man kann geradezu etwas verspüren, wie wenn sich die Wirkungen der Sinne vor der Fortsetzung in das Innere des Nervensystems stauten. Das alles zeigt, daß sich die Kieselsäure nach dem Umkreis des Körpers drängt, aber, wenn sie zu reichlich dorthin kommt, die Normal-Gestaltung durch eine Fremdneigung zur Gestaltung stört. Ebenso tritt nach der Seite des inneren Abschlusses der Gestaltung die Störung ein. Man empfindet Unlenkbarkeit des Bewegungssystems, Gelenkschmerzen. Das alles kann dann übergehen in entzündliche Vorgänge, die dort entstehen, wo die Fremdgestaltung der Kieselsäure zu stark eingreift.

Man wird dadurch auf das verwiesen, was die Kieselsäure im menschlichen Organismus an Heilkraft entwickeln kann. Man nehme an, ein Organ, das nicht eigentliches Sinnesorgan ist, werde in seiner unbewußten Wahrnehmefähigkeit für die außer ihm gelegenen Organismuspartien überempfindlich. Man wird dann bemerken, daß in den Funktionen dieses Organs eine Störung auftritt. Ist man in der Lage, durch Zuführung von Kieselsäure die Überempfindlichkeit zu beheben, dann wird man dem krankhaften Zustand beikommen können. Es wird sich nur darum handeln, die organische Körperwirkung so zu beeinflussen, daß die Kieselsäurezufuhr gerade um das krankhaft gewordene Organ herum wirkt, und nicht durch eine Allgemeinwirkung im Sinne des oben Geschilderten den ganzen Organismus beeinflußt.

Durch die Kombination der Kieselsäure mit anderen Mitteln kann man es dahin bringen, daß die Kieselsäure beim Einführen in den Organismus gerade an dasjenige Organ herangelangt, in dem sie benötigt wird, und von dort auch wieder als Ausscheidung nach außen zu befördern ist, ohne daß sie anderen Organen zum Schaden wird.

caused. This is most evident, when, with excessive uptake of silicic acid, disturbances of the balance of the soul take place behind which the organic disturbances are unmistakable. One feels dizziness, is unable to keep from falling asleep, feels unable to direct the perceptive processes of hearing and sight; one may even have a feeling as though the functioning of the senses became congested where it continues into the inner nervous system. All this shows that silicic acid presses out towards the periphery of the body, but that when it gets there in excessive quantities, it disturbs normal form-giving by introducing an alien form-giving tendency. Similarly, the disturbance occurs towards the inner closing off of form giving. One feels unable to direct one's movement system, and experiences pain in the joints. All this may progress to inflammatory processes, originating where the alien form giving of silicic acid takes hold too strongly.

One is thereby referred to the healing forces that silicic acid can develop in the human organism. Assume that an organ which is not strictly speaking a sense organ becomes oversensitive, in its unconscious faculty of perception, to the parts of the organism external to it. Then one will observe that a disturbance occurs in the functions of this organ. If one is able to remedy the over-sensitivity by administering silicic acid then one can get somewhere with the pathological condition. But it will be a matter of influencing the organic bodily functioning in such a way that the administration of silicic acid acts directly around the diseased organ, and does not influence the whole body through a systemic effect, in the sense of what was portrayed above.

By combining silicic acid with other preparations one can have the silicic acid, when introduced into the organism, reach directly to that organ in which it is needed, and also from there have it be stimulated to excretion outward again without becoming harmful to other organs.

Ein anderer Fall ist derjenige, in dem ein Organ für die Wirkungen der anderen Organe in seiner Empfindlichkeit herabgestimmt wird. Dann hat man es mit einer Anhäufung von Kieselsäurewirkung im Umkreis des Organs zu tun. Man hat dann nötig, auf die Kieselsäurewirkung des ganzen Organismus zu einem solchen Einfluß zu gelangen, daß die lokale Wirkung ihre Kraft verliert, oder man kann auch durch Ausscheidemittel die Fortschaffung der Kieselsäure fördern. Das erstere ist vorzuziehen, weil die Anhäufung der Kieselsäure an einem Orte in der Regel einen Mangel an einem anderen hervorruft. Die Verteilung der lokalisierten Kieselsäurewirkung auf den ganzen Organismus wird man z. B. durch eine Schwefelkur bewirken können. Man wird einsehen, warum das der Fall ist, wenn man die Schwefelwirkungen im Organismus an einer andern Stelle dieses Buches nachliest.

Another case occurs when the sensitivity of an organ for the functions of the other organs is reduced. Then one is dealing with an accumulation of silicic acid in the surroundings of the organ. Then the function of silicic acid in the whole organism needs to be influenced in such a way that the local action loses its force, or one can also stimulate the removal of silicic acid with medications that encourage excretion. The first method is to be preferred, since the accumulation of silicic acid in one place, as a rule, evokes a deficit somewhere else. Distribution of the localized silicic acid function over the whole organism may be brought about, for example, by a course of sulfur. One realizes why this is the case when one reads again, elsewhere in this book, about how sulfur functions in the organism.

XV
DAS HEILVERFAHREN

Die Erkenntnis der Heilmittelwirkungen beruht auf dem Durchschauen der in der außermenschlichen Welt vorhandenen Kraftentwickelungen. Denn, um einen Heilvorgang zu veranlassen, muß man Substanzen in den Organismus einführen, die in diesem sich so ausbreiten, daß der Krankheitsvorgang allmählich in einen normalen übergeht. Nun liegt eben das Wesen des krankhaften Vorganges darin, daß innerhalb des Organismus sich etwas abspielt, das sich nicht eingliedert in die Gesamttätigkeit desselben. Das hat ein solcher Vorgang gemeinsam mit einem solchen der äußeren Natur.

Man kann sagen: entsteht im Innern des Organismus ein Vorgang, der einem solchen der äußeren Natur ähnlich ist, so tritt Erkrankung ein. Ein solcher Vorgang kann den physischen oder den ätherischen Organismus ergreifen. Es muß dann entweder der astralische Leib oder das Ich eine Aufgabe erfüllen, die sie sonst nicht vollbringen. Sie müssen sich in einem Lebensalter, in dem sie in freier seelischer Tätigkeit sich entfalten sollten, zurückschrauben in ein früheres Lebensalter – in vielen Fällen sogar in das Embryonalalter – und an der Bildung von physischen und ätherischen Gestaltungen mitwirken, die bereits übergegangen sein sollten in den Bereich des physischen und des ätherischen Organismus; das heißt, die im ersten menschlichen Lebensalter vom astralischen Leib und der Ich-Organisation besorgt, später aber vom physischen und ätherischen Organismus allein übernommen werden. Denn *alle* Entwicklung des menschlichen Organismus beruht darauf, daß ursprünglich die Gesamtgestaltung des physischen und ätherischen Leibes aus der Tätigkeit des Astralischen und der Ich-Organisation sich ergibt; daß aber mit zunehmendem Alter die astralische und Ich-Tätigkeit in der physischen und ätherischen Organisation weiterlaufen. Tun sie das nicht, so müssen der astralische Leib und die Ich-Organisation in einem Stadium

CHAPTER XV
The Method of Healing

Insight into how medicines work is based on an understanding of how forces become active in the world outside the human being. For, in order to allow a process of healing to begin, one has to introduce substances into the organism which distribute themselves in it in such a way that the pathological process gradually turns into a normal one. Now the nature of a pathological process is precisely that something is going on within the organism which does not integrate itself into the organism's activity as a whole. That is something which such a process has in common with a similar process in outer nature.

One could say: if a process similar to one in outer nature originates in the inner organism, then illness sets in. Such a process can take hold of the physical or the etheric organism. Then either the astral body or the I has to fulfil a task which they do not otherwise accomplish. In a period of life in which they should be unfolding in free activity of soul, they have to turn back to an earlier age—in many cases even the embryonal age—and have to participate in building physical and etheric forms which should already have passed over into the domain of the physical and the etheric organism, that is to say, those forms that in the first period of human life are provided by the astral body and ego organization but later are taken over by the physical and etheric organism alone. For *all* development of the human organism is based on the fact that originally the whole physical and etheric body form results from astral and ego organization activity; but with increasing age astral and ego activity proceed of their own accord in the physical and etheric organization. If they do not do so, then astral body and ego organization have to intervene at a stage of their

ihrer Entwickelung in einer Art eingreifen, zu der sie in diesem Stadium nicht mehr geeignet sind.

Man nehme an, es treten Unterleibsstockungen auf. Die physische und ätherische Organisation vollziehen nicht die ihnen im vorangehenden Lebensalter übertragenen Tätigkeiten in dem entsprechenden Teile des menschlichen Körpers. Die astralische und Ich-Tätigkeit müssen eingreifen. Dadurch schwächen sich diese ab für andere Aufgaben im Organismus. Sie sind nicht da, wo sie sein sollten, z. B. in der Gestaltung der in die Muskeln gehenden Nerven. Die Folge sind Lähmungserscheinungen in gewissen Teilen des Organismus.

Es handelt sich darum, solche Substanzen in den menschlichen Organismus einzuführen, welche der astralischen und der Ich-Organisation die ihnen nicht zukommende Tätigkeit abnehmen können. Man kann nun finden, daß die Prozesse, die in der Bildung starker ätherischer Öle im Pflanzenorganismus, insbesondere in der Blütenbildung wirken, dieses Abnehmen bewirken können. Auch Substanzen, die Phosphor enthalten, können das. Man muß nur dafür sorgen, daß man den Phosphor durch Zusammenmengen mit andern Substanzen dazu bringe, daß er seine Wirkung im Darm entfalte, nicht in dem über den Darm hinausliegenden Stoffwechsel.

Hat man es zu tun mit Entzündungserscheinungen der Haut, so entfalten da astralischer Leib und Ich-Organisation eine abnorme Tätigkeit. Sie entziehen sich dann den Wirkungen, die sie auf mehr nach innen gelegene Organe ausüben sollten. Sie vermindern die Empfindlichkeit innerer Organe. Diese hinwiederum hören wegen ihrer herabgestimmten Empfindlichkeit auf, die ihnen obliegenden Vorgänge auszuführen. Es können dadurch z. B. abnorme Zustände in der Lebertätigkeit auftreten. Und die Verdauung kann dann in unrechtmäßiger Weise beeinflußt werden. Bringt man nun Kieselsäure in den Organismus, so werden die auf die Haut entfallenden Tätigkeiten des astralischen und des Ich-Organismus entlastet. Die nach innen erfolgende Tätigkeit dieser

development in a way for which they are no longer suited at this stage.

Assume that congestions occur in the lower abdomen. Physical and etheric organization do not then perform the activities that were transferred to them in a preceding period of life in the part of the human body in question. Astral and ego activity must intervene. This weakens them for other tasks in the organism. They are not present where they should be, e.g., in giving form to the nerves that go to the muscles. Paralytic symptoms in certain parts of the organism are the consequence.

It is a matter then of introducing substances into the body which can relieve astral and ego organization of the activity that does not befit them. Now one may discover that processes which are at work in forming strong etheric oils in the plant organism, particularly in the forming of the flower, are able to effect this relief. Substances containing phosphorus can also do that. All one must do is to assure that phosphorus is mixed with other substances so that it unfolds its action within the intestine, not in the metabolism that lies beyond the intestine.

If one is dealing with symptoms of inflammation of the skin, then astral body and ego organization unfold an abnormal activity there. Then they withdraw from functions which they should perform in organs that are more internal. They lessen the sensitivity of internal organs. As a consequence of their reduced sensitivity, these again cease to perform their normal functions. For example, abnormal conditions in liver activity may arise. Consequently the digestion may be adversely influenced. If now silicic acid is introduced into the organism, then the activities of the astral and the ego organism that have been diverted to the skin are relieved. The activity of these organisms directed inwardly becomes free again, and a healing process arises.

Organismen wird wieder freigegeben; und ein Gesundungsprozeß tritt ein.

Steht man vor krankhaften Zuständen, die sich in abnormem Herzklopfen offenbaren, so wirkt eine nicht regelmäßige Tätigkeit des astralischen Organismus auf den Gang der Blutzirkulation. Diese Tätigkeit schwächt sich dann für die Hirnvorgänge ab. Es treten epileptische Zustände ein, weil durch die abgeschwächte astralische Tätigkeit im Kopforganismus die dort hingehörige ätherische zu stark angespannt wird. Bringt man den aus Levisticum (Liebstöckel) zu gewinnenden gummiartigen Stoff – etwa in Teeform, noch besser in etwas verarbeiteter Form in einem Präparat – in den Organismus, dann wird die für die Blutzirkulation unrecht verbrauchte Tätigkeit des astralischen Leibes freigegeben, und die Stärkung für die Gehirnorganisation tritt ein.

Man muß in allen diesen Fällen durch eine entsprechende Dagnose die Richtung der Krankheitswirkungen feststellen. Man nehme den letzten Fall. Er kann so liegen, daß die Ursache von einem gestörten Wechselwirken zwischen ätherischem und atralischem Leib in der Blutzirkulation ausgeht. Die Hirnerscheinungen sind dann die Folge. Man wird mit der Heilung so vorgehen können, wie es beschrieben worden ist.

Die Sache kann aber auch umgekehrt liegen. Die Unregelmäßigkeit kann ursächlich zwischen der astralischen und ätherischen Tätigkeit im Gehirnsystem auftreten. Dann ist die unregelmäßige Blutzirkulation mit der abnormen Herztätigkeit die Folge. Dann muß man z. B. schwefelsaure Salze in den Stoffwechselvorgang bringen. Diese wirken auf die ätherische Organisation des Gehirns so, daß sie in dieser eine Anziehungskraft zu dem astralischen Leibe hervorrufen. Man kann das daran beobachten, daß die Denk-Initiative, die Willenssphäre und die ganze Geschlossenheit des Wesens eine Umwandlung nach dem Besseren erfahren. Es wird dann wahrscheinlich nötig sein, die astralischen Kräfte in ihrer neu zu erwerbenden Wirkung auf das Zirkulationssystem etwa durch ein Kupfersalz zu unterstützen.

When confronted with pathological conditions that manifest in palpitations, then one has irregular activity of the astral organism acting on the movement of the blood circulation. This astral activity then weakens in relation to brain processes. Epileptiform conditions arise, because the weakened astral activity in the head organism puts too much strain on the etheric activity belonging to this area. If the gumlike substance that can be extracted from levisticum (lovage) is introduced into the organism—perhaps in the form of a tea, or even better in a somewhat processed preparation—then the activity of the astral body that was improperly used for the blood circulation is set free and becomes strengthened for the brain organization.

In all these cases an appropriate diagnosis must determine the direction of the pathological functions. Take the last case. It could be that the cause lies in a disturbed interaction between the etheric and astral body in the blood circulation. Then the brain symptoms are the consequence. One may proceed with the treatment as was described.

But the situation may also be the other way around. The irregularity may originate between astral and etheric activity in the cerebral system. Then the irregular blood circulation with abnormal cardiac activity is the consequence. In that case one must introduce, for example, sulfates into the metabolic process. These work on the etheric organization of the brain by way of evoking in it a force of attraction for the astral body. One may observe this from the fact that the thought initiative, the will sphere, and the whole integrity of the individual, experience a change for the better. In addition it will probably be necessary to support the influence of the astral forces on the circulatory system, which they have to acquire anew, with a copper salt perhaps.

Man wird bemerken, daß der Gesamt-Organismus in seine regelmäßige Tätigkeit dann wieder eintritt, wenn man die durch den physischen und ätherischen Organismus bewirkte Übertätigkeit des astralischen und Ich-Organismus in irgend einem Gliede des Leibes ersetzt durch eine von außen bewirkte. Der Organismus hat die Tendenz, seine Mängel auszugleichen. Deshalb stellt er sich wieder her, wenn man eine Unregelmäßigkeit eine Zeitlang künstlich so reguliert, daß man den innerlich hervorgerufenen Vorgang, der aufhören muß, bekämpft durch einen ähnlichen Vorgang, den man von außen her bewirkt.

One may observe that the organism as a whole returns to its regular activity when the excessive activity of the astral and ego organism caused by the physical and etheric organism in some part of the body, is replaced by an activity caused from outside. The organism has the tendency to balance out its deficiencies. Therefore it restores itself when an irregularity can be artificially regulated for a time in such a way that the process evoked internally, which must cease, is combatted with a similar process which one brings about from outside.

XVI
HEILMITTEL – ERKENNTNIS

Man muß die Substanzen, deren Verwendung als Heilmittel in Betracht kommen soll, zunächst in der Art kennen, daß man die in ihnen enthaltenen möglichen Kräftewirkungen außerhalb und innerhalb des menschlichen Organismus beurteilen kann. Dabei kann es sich nur in einem geringen Grade darum handeln, die Wirkungsmöglichkeiten ins Auge zu fassen, die von der gewöhnlichen Chemie erforscht werden, sondern es kommt darauf an, *die Wirkungen zu beobachten, die sich aus dem Zusammenhange der inneren Kräftekonstitution einer Substanz im Verhältnis zu den Kräften ergeben, die von der Erde ausstrahlen oder in sie einstrahlen.*

Man betrachte von diesem Gesichtspunkte aus z. B. den Antimonglanz. Das Antimon hat eine starke Verwandtschaft zu den Schwefelverbindungen anderer Metalle. Der Schwefel hat eine Summe von Eigenschaften, die sich in verhältnismäßig nur engen Grenzen konstant erhält. Er ist empfindlich gegen die Prozesse der Natur wie Erwärmung, Verbrennung usw. Das macht ihn fähig, auch eine bedeutende Rolle innerhalb der sich völlig aus den Erdenkräften herauslösenden und in die ätherischen Wirkungen sich einspannenden Eiweißsubstanzen zu spielen. Indem das Antimon sich verwandtschaftlich an den Schwefel bindet, macht es diese Einspannung in die Ätherwirkungen leicht mit. Es ist daher leicht in die Tätigkeit des Eiweißes im menschlichen Körper hineinzubringen, und diesem zu einer Ätherwirkung zu verhelfen, wenn dieser Körper durch irgendeinen krankhaften Zustand eine von außen eingeführte Eiweißsubstanz nicht selbst so verwandeln kann, daß sie seiner eigenen Tätigkeit sich eingliedert.

Aber das Antimon zeigt noch andere Eigentümlichkeiten. Wo es nur kann, strebt es die büschelförmige Gestaltung an. Es gliedert sich damit in Linien, die von der Erde weg- und den Kräften entgegenstreben, die im Äther wirken. Man bringt mit dem Antimon somit etwas in den menschlichen Organismus, das

CHAPTER XVI

Insight into Medications

One must first of all have insight into the substances which have to be considered for use as medication, so that one can assess the potential sphere of working of the forces they embody, outside and within the human organism. In this connection it could only to a small extent be a matter of looking into the possible reactions which ordinary chemistry investigates. The point is, on the contrary, to observe *those* functions which result in the context of the substance's inner constitution of forces in relation to the forces that radiate from the earth or stream in towards it.

Consider, for example, antimonite from this point of view. Antimony has a strong affinity for the sulfur compounds of other metals. Sulfur has a number of properties which remain constant within relatively narrow limits. It is sensitive to processes of nature such as heating, combustion, etc. This also makes it capable of playing a significant role in proteinaceous substances which completely free themselves from earth forces and subject themselves to etheric functions. Since antimony has an affinity for the sulfur to which it bonds, it readily partakes in this subjection to the ether functions. Therefore it is easily introduced into the activity of protein in the human body. It helps the latter to an ether function when, due to some pathological condition, the body itself is unable to convert a proteinaceous substance introduced from outside and to integrate it into its own activity.

But antimony shows still other unique characteristics. Wherever possible it strives for sheaflike forms. It arranges itself in lines which strive away from the earth and toward the forces that work in the ether. With antimony one thus introduces something into the human organism that goes

der Wirkung des Ätherleibes auf halbem Wege entgegenkommt. Auch dasjenige, was im Seigerprozeß mit dem Antimon vor sich geht, weist auf die Äther-Verwandtschaft dieses Stoffes hin. Es wird durch diesen Prozeß feinfaserig. Nun ist der Seigerprozeß ein solcher, der gewissermaßen unten physisch beginnt und oben in das Ätherische übergeht. Das Antimon gliedert sich in diesen Übergang hinein.

Des weiteren zeigt das Antimon, das beim Glühen oxydiert, beim Verbrennen einen aus ihm entstehenden weißen Rauch, der an kalten Körpern sich anlegt und die Antimonblumen erzeugt.

Ferner hat das Antimon eine gewisse Abwehrkraft gegen die elektrischen Wirkungen. Wird es elektrolytisch in einer gewissen Art behandelt und an die Kathode als Niederschlag gebracht, so explodiert dieser bei Berührung mit einer Metallspitze.

Alles dieses zeigt, daß im Antimon die Tendenz enthalten ist, in das Ätherelement in dem Augenblick *leicht* überzugehen, in dem dazu die Bedingungen auch nur in geringem Grade vorhanden sind. Dem geistigen Schauen gelten alle diese Einzelheiten nur als Andeutungen; denn dieses nimmt die Beziehung zwischen Ich-Tätigkeit und Antimon-Wirksamkeit unmittelbar so wahr, daß die Antimonprozesse, in den menschlichen Organismus gebracht, *so* wirken, wie die Ich-Organisation.

Im menschlichen Organismus zeigt das Blut in seiner Strömung eine Tendenz, zu gerinnen. Diese Tendenz ist diejenige, die unter dem Einfluß der Ich-Organisation steht und unter ihr die Regulierung erfahren muß. Blut ist ein organisches Mittelprodukt. Was im Blute entsteht, hat Vorgänge durchgemacht, die auf dem Wege sind, solche des menschlichen Vollorganismus, d. h. der Ich-Organisation zu werden. Es muß noch Vorgänge durchmachen, die in die Gestaltung dieses Organismus sich einfügen. Welcher Art diese sind, kann aus Folgendem erkannt werden. Indem das Blut beim Entfernen aus dem Körper gerinnt, zeigt es, daß es durch sich selbst die Tendenz zum Gerinnen hat, aber im menschlichen Organismus an diesem Gerinnen fortdauernd ver-

halfway to meet the function of the ether body. Also what goes on with antimony in the Seiger process[9] points to this substance's kinship to ether. In this process it becomes filamentous. Now the Seiger process begins, as it were, physically from below, and above it makes a transition to the etheric. Antimony integrates itself into this transition.

Moreover antimony, which oxidizes when red-hot, gives off, in the process of combustion, a white vapor which precipitates on cold surfaces, generating the so-called "flowers of antimony."

Furthermore antimony has a certain resistance to electrical effects. When it undergoes electrolysis in a specific way and precipitates on the cathode, it will explode on contact with a metallic needle.

All this shows that antimony has a tendency to go over *easily* into the ether element the moment the conditions are favorable in the slightest degree. To spiritual vision all these particulars only count as indications, for this vision directly perceives the relationship between ego activity and antimony function to be such that antimony processes introduced into the human organism function in the *same* way as the ego organization.

As it flows through the human organism, blood shows a tendency to coagulate. This tendency is subject to the influence of the ego organization and must be regulated by it. Blood is an intermediary organic product. What arises in blood has undergone processes which are on the way to become part of the fully human organism, i.e., of the ego organization. It still must undergo processes which adapt to the form of this organism. The nature of these processes can be gleaned from the following. Since blood coagulates when it is removed from the body, it shows that it has the inherent tendency to coagulate, but it must continually be prevented from coagulating within the human organism. The force by which it integrates

hindert werden muß. Was Blut am Gerinnen verhindert, ist die Kraft, durch die es der Organismus sich eingliedert. Es gliedert sich in die Körpergestaltung durch die Formkräfte ein, die gerade noch vor dem Gerinnen liegen. Würde das Gerinnen eintreten, wäre das Leben gefährdet.

Hat man es daher im Organismus mit einem krankhaften Zustande zu tun, der in einem Mangel dieser nach der Blutgerinnung hinzielenden Kräfte besteht, so wirkt das Antimon in dieser oder jener Form als Heilmittel.

Die *Gestaltung* des Organismus ist im wesentlichen eine solche Verwandlung der Eiweißsubstanz, durch die diese zum Zusammenwirken mit mineralisierenden Kräften kommt. Solche sind z. B. in dem Kalk enthalten. Was hier in Betracht kommt, zeigt anschaulich die Schalenbildung der Auster. Die Auster muß sich desjenigen, was in der Schalenbildung vorliegt, entledigen, um die Eiweißsubstanz in ihrer Eigenart zu behalten. Ähnliches ist auch bei der Schalenbildung des Eies vorhanden.

Bei der Auster wird das Kalkartige *abgesondert,* um es der Eiweißbildung *nicht* einzugliedern. Im menschlichen Organismus muß diese Eingliederung stattfinden. Die bloße Eiweißwirkung muß in eine solche umgewandelt werden, in der mitwirkt, was im Kalkartigen durch die Ich-Organisation an gestaltenden Kräften hervorgerufen werden kann. Das muß sich innerhalb der Blutbildung abspielen. Das Antimon wirkt der kalkausscheidenden Kraft entgegen und führt das Eiweiß, das seine Form bewahren will, durch seine Verwandtschaft mit dem Äther-Elemente in die Formlosigkeit hinüber, die für die Einflüsse des Kalkartigen oder Ähnlichem empfänglich ist.

Beim Typhus ist es klar, daß der krankhafte Zustand in einer mangelnden Überführung der Eiweißsubstanz in gestaltungsfähige Blutsubstanz besteht. Die Form der Diarrhöen, die auftritt, zeigt, daß schon im Darm die Unfähigkeit zu dieser Umwandlung beginnt. Die schweren Bewußtseins-Beeinträchtigungen, die sich einstellen, zeigen, daß die Ich-Organisation aus dem Körper

itself into the human organism is what prevents the blood from coagulating. It integrates itself into the body's form by means of the formative forces which lie just before coagulation. If coagulation were to occur, life would be endangered.

If one therefore has a pathological condition in the organism in which there is a deficiency of these forces working toward coagulation of the blood, then antimony in one form or another works as medication.

Form giving in the organism is essentially a kind of conversion of proteinaceous substance through which it comes to work together with mineralizing forces. The latter are, for example, contained in limestone. What comes into consideration here is graphically shown in the shell formation of the oyster. The oyster must rid itself of the shell-forming element, in order to preserve the inherent nature of proteinaceous substance. Something similar is also present in the forming of the eggshell.

In the oyster calcareous constituents are *secreted* so as *not* to integrate them into protein. In the human organism this integration must take place. The pure protein working must be transformed into one in which also works what the ego organization can evoke from the calcareous as form-creating forces. This must take place within blood formation. Antimony counteracts the force that excretes calcium carbonate and guides the protein, which wants to preserve its form, through its kinship with the ether element into a formlessness which is receptive to the influences of calcareous or similar substances.

It is clear that the pathology of typhoid fever consists of an inadequate transition of proteinaceous substance into blood substance that has form-giving quality. The form of the diarrheas occurring here shows that the incapacity for this transformation already begins in the intestinal tract. The severe impairments of consciousness that take place show that the ego organization is driven out of the body and cannot be active.

herausgetrieben wird und nicht wirken kann. Das ist aus dem Grunde, weil die Eiweißsubstanz nicht an die mineralisierenden Kräfte, in denen die Ich-Organisation wirken kann, herankommt. Ein Beweis für diese Anschauung ist auch die Tatsache, daß die Entleerungen die Ansteckungsgefahr bringen. In diesen erweist sich die Tendenz zur Zerstörung der gestaltenden Kräfte gesteigert.

Wendet man bei typhösen Erscheinungen Antimonpräparate in entsprechender Zusammensetzung an, so erweisen sich diese als Heilmittel. Sie entkleiden die Eiweißsubstanz ihrer Eigenkräfte und machen sie geneigt, den Gestaltungskräften der Ich-Organisation sich einzufügen.

Man wird von Gesichtspunkten aus, die in der Gegenwart vielfach üblich sind, sagen: solche Ansichten wie die hier über das Antimon angedeutete, seien nicht exakt; und man wird dagegen auf die Exaktheit der gewöhnlichen chemischen Methoden hinweisen. Aber für die Wirkung im menschlichen Organismus kommen in Wahrheit die chemischen Wirkungen der Stoffe so wenig in Betracht wie die chemische Zusammensetzung eines Farbstoffes für die Handhabung dieses Stoffes durch den Maler. Gewiß, der Maler tut gut, von dem chemischen Ausgangspunkt etwas zu wissen. Aber *wie* er die Farbstoffe im Malen behandelt, das kommt von einer andern Methodik. Und so ist es für den Therapeuten. Dieser kann die Chemie als eine Grundlage betrachten, die für ihn etwas bedeutet; die Wirkungsweise der Stoffe im menschlichen Organismus hat aber nichts mehr mit diesem Chemischen zu tun. Wer Exaktheit nur in dem sieht, was die Chemie – auch die pharmazeutische – feststellt, der vernichtet die Möglichkeit, Anschauungen darüber zu gewinnen, was im Organismus bei Heilungsvorgängen geschieht.

This is due to the situation that the proteinaceous substance cannot approach the mineralizing forces in which the ego organization is able to work. This view is also evidenced by the fact that the evacuations are contagious. In them the tendency to destruction of the form-creating forces proves to be enhanced.

When properly compounded antimony preparations are administered for typhoid symptoms, they prove to be medications. They divest the proteinaceous substance of its inherent forces and make it inclined to adapt to the form-giving forces of the ego organization.

From points of view that are frequently encountered today one could say: views like the ones outlined here about antimony are not exact, and one will instead refer to the exactitude of customary chemical methods. But when it comes to their function within the human organism, chemical reactions of substances actually have as little significance as the chemical composition of a paint has for the handling of this substance by the painter. Surely the painter would do well to know something about the chemical starting point. But *how* he deals with the paints as he is painting stems from another methodology. And so it is for the therapist. He may regard chemistry to be a basis which means something to him; the mode of action of substances within the human organism, however, no longer has anything to do with this chemical aspect. Whoever sees exactitude only in the data ascertained by chemistry—its pharmaceutical branch as well—eradicates the possibility of gaining ways of looking at what takes place in processes of healing in the organism.

XVII
SUBSTANZ-ERKENNTNIS ALS GRUNDLAGE DER HEILMITTEL-ERKENNTNIS

Wer die Wirkung von Heilmitteln beurteilen will, muß ein Auge haben für die Kräftewirkungen, die sich im menschlichen Organismus ergeben, wenn eine Substanz, die außer demselben gewisse Wirkungen zeigt, in irgend einer Art in ihn eingeführt wird.

Ein klassisches Beispiel kann man in der Ameisensäure finden. Sie tritt als eine ätzende, Entzündung bewirkende Substanz im Körper der Ameisen auf. Da erscheint sie als ein Absonderungsprodukt. Ein solches muß der entsprechende tierische Organismus erzeugen, damit er seine Tätigkeit in angemessener Weise ausführen kann. Das Leben liegt in der absondernden Tätigkeit. Ist das Absonderungsprodukt erzeugt, so hat es keine Aufgabe mehr im Organismus. Es muß ausgeschieden werden. Im Tun liegt das Wesen des Organismus, nicht in seinen Substanzen. Die Organisation ist nicht ein Stoffzusammenhang, sondern eine Tätigkeit. Der Stoff trägt den Anreiz zur Tätigkeit in sich. Hat er diesen Anreiz verloren, so hat er für die Organisation keine weitere Bedeutung.

Im menschlichen Organismus entsteht auch die Ameisensäure. Da aber hat sie ihre Bedeutung. Sie dient der Ich-Organisation. Durch den astralischen Leib werden aus der organischen Substanz Teile ausgesondert, die dahin zielen, leblos zu werden. Die Ich-Organisation braucht diesen Übergang der organischen Substanz in den leblosen Zustand. Aber sie braucht eben den Vorgang des Überganges; nicht, was dann durch den Übergang entsteht. Ist nun das nach dem Leblosen hin sich Entwickelnde gebildet, so wird es im Innern des Organismus zur Last. Es muß entweder unmittelbar abgesondert werden, oder aufgelöst, um mittelbar hinwegzukommen.

Geschieht nun für etwas, das aufgelöst werden sollte, diese Auflösung nicht, so häuft es sich im Organismus an und kann die Grundlage für gichtische oder rheumatische Zustände bilden. Da

CHAPTER XVII

Insight into Substance as Basis for Insight into Medications

Whoever wants to assess the effect of medications, must have an eye for the resultant force activity in the human organism when a substance, which shows certain functions outside of the human organism, is introduced somehow into it.

One can find a classic example in formic acid. It occurs as a corrosive, inflammation-inducing substance in the body of ants. It appears there as a product of secretion. The animal organism in question must generate this if it is to carry out its activity properly. Life lies in the activity of secretion. Once the secretory product has been produced it has no further task within the organism. It must be excreted. The essence of the organism lies in the doing, not in its substances. The organization is not a conglomeration of matter, it is an activity. Matter holds the stimulus for activity within it. Once it has lost this stimulus, it has no further significance for the organization.

Formic acid is also generated in the human organism. But here it has significance. It serves the ego organization. The astral body separates out from the organic substance parts that tend to become lifeless. The ego organization needs this transition of organic substance to the lifeless state. But it needs the very process of transition; not what then comes into being through the transition. Once what is becoming lifeless has been formed, it is a burden to the inner organism. It either must be excreted directly, or be dissolved to get away indirectly.

If the dissolution of something that should be dissolved does not happen, then it accumulates within the organism forming the basis for gouty or rheumatic conditions. Here the

tritt nun im menschlichen Organismus auflösend die sich bildende Ameisensäure ein. Wird sie in der notwendigen Menge erzeugt, so enfernt der Organismus die zum Leblosen zielenden Produkte in richtiger Art. Ist die Erzeugungskraft zu schwach, so entstehen die gichtischen oder rheumatischen Zustände. Führt man sie dem Organismus von außen zu, so unterstützt man ihn, indem man ihm gibt, was er nicht selbst erzeugen kann.

Man kann solche Wirkungsarten kennen lernen, wenn man die eine Substanz mit der andern in ihrem Fortwirken im menschlichen Organismus vergleicht. Man nehme die Kleesäure. Sie kann unter gewissen Verhältnissen in die Ameisensäure übergehen. Die letztere stellt in ihren Wirkungen eine Metamorphose der Kleesäure dar. Die Kleesäure ist Absonderung des Pflanzlichen wie die Ameisensäure des Tierischen. Die Kleesäure-Erzeugung stellt im pflanzlichen Organismus eine Tätigkeit her, die der von der Ameisensäure-Erzeugung im Tierischen analog ist. Das heißt, die Kleesäure-Erzeugung entspricht dem Gebiet des Ätherischen, die Ameisensäure-Erzeugung dem des Astralischen. Die in gichtischen und rheumatischen Zuständen sich offenbarenden Erkrankungen schreiben sich von einer mangelhaften Tätigkeit des astralischen Leibes her. Es gibt andere Zustände, die sich so darstellen, daß die Ursachen, die bei Gicht und Rheumatismus aus dem astralischen Organismus stammen, in den ätherischen Organismus zurückverlegt sind. Dann entstehen nicht bloß Kräftestockungen nach dem Astralischen hin, welche der Ich-Organisation hemmend in den Weg treten, sondern Hinderniswirkungen im Ätherischen, die von der astralischen Organisation nicht bewältigt werden können. Sie zeigen sich in einer trägen Tätigkeit des Unterleibes, in Hemmungen der Leber- und Milztätigkeit, in steinartigen Ablagerungen der Galle und Ähnlichem. Führt man in diesen Fällen Kleesäure zu, so unterstützt man in entsprechender Art den ätherischen Organismus in seiner Tätigkeit. Man erhält durch Kleesäure eine Verstärkung des ätherischen Leibes, weil die Kraft der Ich-Organisation durch

formic acid which is forming in the human organism comes into play, dissolving. If it is generated in sufficient quantity, then the organism will correctly remove the products tending to be lifeless. If the generating force is too weak, then the gouty or rheumatic conditions come about. One supports the organism by bringing formic acid to it from outside, since one then provides what it is unable to generate for itself.

One can get to know such modes of action when one compares the ongoing functioning in the human organism of one substance with another. Take oxalic acid. Under certain conditions it can turn into formic acid. The functions of the latter represent a metamorphosis of oxalic acid. As oxalic acid is a secretion of the plant world, so formic acid is of the animal world. Oxalic acid production establishes an activity in the plant organism which is analogous to that of formic acid production in the animal. That is to say, oxalic acid production corresponds to the domain of the etheric, formic acid production to that of the astral. Illness which comes to expression in gouty and rheumatic conditions can be ascribed to an inadequate activity of the astral body. Other conditions present in such a way that the causes, which stem from the astral organism in gout and rheumatism, lie further back in the etheric organism. Then not only force congestions towards the astral emerge, which inhibit the ego organization, but also inhibitory effects in the etheric which cannot be mastered by the astral organization. They manifest in sluggish lower abdominal activity, in inhibited activity of liver and spleen, in stonelike deposits in the gall bladder and the like. If one gives oxalic acid in such cases, then the etheric organism is supported appropriately in its activity. Through oxalic acid the etheric body is strengthened since the force of the ego organization is converted by this acid to a force of the astral body which then works more strongly on the ether body.

diese Säure in eine Kraft des astralischen Leibes verwandelt wird, der dann verstärkt auf den Ätherleib wirkt.

Von solchen Beobachtungen ausgehend, kann man die Wirkung der dem Organismus heilsamen Stoffe kennen lernen. Die Beobachtung kann vom Pflanzenleben ausgehen. In der Pflanze wird die physische Tätigkeit von der ätherischen durchsetzt. Man lernt an ihr kennen, was durch die ätherische Tätigkeit erreicht werden kann. Im tierisch-astralischen Organismus wird diese Tätigkeit in die astralische übergeführt. Ist sie als ätherische zu schwach, so kann sie durch Hinzufügung der von einem eingeführten Pflanzenprodukt herrührenden verstärkt werden. Dem menschlichen Organismus liegt das Tierische zugrunde. Für dasjenige, was sich zwischen dem menschlichen ätherischen und astralischen Leibe abspielt, gilt *innerhalb gewisser Grenzen* dasselbe wie im Tierischen.

Man wird mit Heilmitteln aus dem Pflanzenreiche das zwischen der ätherischen und der astralischen Tätigkeit gestörte Verhältnis herstellen können. Man wird aber mit solchen Mitteln nicht zustande kommen, wenn irgend etwas in der physischen, ätherischen und astralischen menschlichen Organisation in Bezug auf ihr Wechselverhältnis zu der Ich-Organisation gestört ist. Die Ich-Organisation muß ihre Tätigkeit auf Vorgänge lenken, die nach dem Mineralischwerden hinzielen.

Deshalb ist bei den entsprechenden krankhaften Zuständen auch nur Mineralisches als Heilmittel brauchbar. Um die Heilwirkung eines Mineralischen kennen zu lernen, ist notwendig, eine Substanz daraufhin zu untersuchen, inwiefern sie abgebaut werden kann. Denn im Organismus muß das von außen zugeführte Mineralische abgebaut und aus den organischen Eigenkräften in neuer Form wieder aufgebaut werden. In einem solchen Ab- und Aufbauen muß die Heilwirkung bestehen. Und was sich da ergibt, muß in der Linie liegen, daß eine mangelhafte Eigentätigkeit des Organismus von der Tätigkeit der zugeführten Heilmittel übernommen wird.

Starting from such observations one can get to know the action of substances that have a healing effect on the organism. Observation may start from plant life. In the plant physical activity is permeated by etheric activity. One gets to know from the plant what etheric activity can do. In the animal-astral organism this activity is carried over to astral activity. If it is too weak as etheric activity, one may strengthen it by adding etheric activity from a plant product that is administered. Animal nature lies at the basis of the human organism. The same applies to what proceeds between the human etheric and astral body as in the animal, *within certain limits*.

One may restore the disturbed relation between etheric and astral activity with medications from the plant world. But one will come to nothing with such preparations when something or other in the physical, etheric and astral human organization is disturbed in its interrelation with the ego organization. The ego organization must direct its activity to processes that tend to become mineral.

Therefore only mineral substances are useful as medication in the pathological conditions in question. To get to know the medicinal function of a mineral substance it is necessary to investigate to what extent the substance can be broken down. For the mineral introduced from outside has to be broken down and then be built up again in a new form in the organism by the inherent organic forces. The medicinal function must consist in such breaking down and building up. And the result must go in the direction that an inadequate inherent activity of the organism is taken over by the activity of the introduced medicine.

Man nehme das Beispiel einer übermäßigen Periode. Bei ihr ist die Kraft der Ich-Organisation abgeschwächt. Sie wird einseitig in der Blutbereitung verbraucht. Es bleibt von ihr für die Absorptionskraft des Blutes im Organismus zu wenig übrig. Der Weg, den Kräfte im Organismus gehen sollen, die nach dem Leblosen hin liegen, ist zu kurz, weil diese Kräfte zu heftig wirken. Sie erschöpfen sich auf dem halben Wege.

Man kommt ihnen zu Hilfe, wenn man dem Organismus Calcium in irgend einer Verbindung zuführt. Dieses bildet an der Blutentstehung mit. Der Ich-Tätigkeit wird dieses Gebiet abgenommen. und sie kann sich der Blutabsorption zuwenden.

Take the example of excessive menstruation. Here the force of the ego organization is weakened. It is expended one-sidedly in making blood. Too little of it is left for the blood's absorptive force in the organism. The path which the forces going towards the lifeless are to take in the organism is too short, because these forces work too vehemently. They exhaust themselves halfway.

One can come to their assistance by administering calcium in some compound to the organism. This joins in with blood formation. The ego activity is relieved from this domain and can turn to blood absorption.

XVIII
HEIL – EURYTHMIE

Innerhalb des Gebietes unserer Therapie spielt noch eine besondere Rolle die sogenannte «*Heil-Eurythmie*». Sie ist herausgebildet aus der Anthroposophie durch Dr. Rudolf Steiner, zunächst als eine *neue Kunst*.

Sie ist in ihrer Wesenheit als eurythmische Kunst von Dr. Steiner oft geschildert worden und hat auch als Kunst schon eine weite Verbreitung gefunden.

Sie stellt sich auf die Bühne hin in dem bewegten Menschen; ist aber keine Tanzkunst. Das zeigt sich schon darinnen, daß am Menschen vorzüglich die Arme und Hände in Bewegung sind. Menschengruppen in Bewegungen erheben das Ganze zu einem in sich künstlerisch wirkenden Bühnenbild.

Alle Bewegungen beruhen auf der inneren Wesenheit der Menschen-Organisation. Aus dieser fließt in den ersten Jahren des menschlichen Lebens die Sprache. So wie sich nun der Laut in der Sprache der Konstitution des Menschen entringt, so können bei einer wirklichen Erkenntnis dieser Konstitution Bewegungen aus dem Menschen und aus den Menschengruppen herausgeholt werden, die eine *wirkliche* sichtbare Sprache oder ein sichtbarer Gesang sind. Dabei ist in den Bewegungen so wenig etwas willkürliches wie in der Sprache selbst. Wie in einem Worte nicht ein *O* intoniert werden kann, wo ein *I* hingehört, so kann auch in dem Eurythmischen für ein *I* oder ein *Cis* nur eine eindeutige bewegte Gebärde erscheinen. Es ist damit die Eurythmie eine wirkliche Offenbarung der Menschennatur, die nicht unbewußt wie die Sprache oder der Gesang aus ihr sich entwickelt, die aber durch wirkliche Menschen-Erkenntnis bewußt entwickelt werden kann.

Bei der Darstellung hat man auf der Bühne den bewegten Menschen oder Menschengruppen. Die Dichtung, die nun in die sichtbare Sprache umgesetzt wird, wird gleichzeitig rezitiert. Man hört den Inhalt der Dichtung und schaut ihn zugleich mit dem

CHAPTER XVIII
Curative Eurythmy

Within our therapeutic approach, the movement therapy called *"curative eurythmy"*[10] plays a special role. It was initially developed out of anthroposophy by Dr. Rudolf Steiner as a *new art form*.

In its essence as an art, eurythmy has often been described by Dr. Steiner,[11] and indeed as an art form it has already found wide recognition.

It is presented on stage by the human being in movement, but is not an art of dance. This becomes apparent already from the fact that particularly the arms and hands of the human being are in movement. Groups of people in movement elevate the whole to a stage setting that has an artistic effect in itself.

All movements are based on the inner nature of the human organization. In the first years of life, speech flows from the human organization. Just as in speech the sound wrests itself from the constitution of the human being, so with the help of a true insight into this constitution one can elicit movements from the human being and from groups of human beings which represent a *truly* visible speech or visible song. In this the movements are no more arbitrary than speech itself. As in the spoken word an *O* cannot be pronounced where an *I* belongs, so, in eurythmy only one distinct gesture can appear for an *I* or for a *C-sharp*. Eurythmy is thus a true manifestation of human nature that does not derive from it unconsciously like speech or music, but which may be developed consciously by means of a true insight into the human being.

In the performance, a person or groups of people are moving on the stage. The poem, now transposed into visible speech, is simultaneously recited. One hears the content of the poem, and

Auge. Oder es wird ein Musikalisches dargeboten, das in den bewegten Gebärden wieder erscheint als sichtbarer Gesang.

Es ist in der Eurythmie eine bewegte Plastik gegeben, die das Gebiet des Künstlerischen wesentlich erweitert.

Es kann nun, was da in künstlerischer Art gefunden worden ist, nach zwei anderen Seiten hin ausgebildet werden. Eine dieser Seiten ist die pädagogische. In der Waldorfschule in Stuttgart, die von Emil Molt begründet worden ist, und die unter der Leitung von Rudolf Steiner steht, wird pädagogische Eurythmie neben der Gymnastik durch alle Klassen hindurch getrieben. Es kommt dabei in Betracht, daß bei der gewöhnlichen Gymnastik nur die Dynamik und Statik des physischen Körpers entwickelt wird. Bei der Eurythmie strömt sich der ganze Mensch, nach Körper, Seele und Geist in Bewegung aus. Das fühlt der heranwachsende Mensch, und er erlebt diese eurythmischen Übungen mit ganz derselben Natürlichkeit als eine Äußerung der menschlichen Natur, wie er in jüngeren Jahren das Sprechenlernen erlebt.

Die andere Seite ist die therapeutische. Werden die Bewegungs-Gebärden der Kunst- und pädagogischen Eurythmie modifiziert, so daß sie aus der kranken Wesenheit des Menschen *so* fließen, wie die anderen aus der gesunden, so entsteht die Heil-Eurythmie.

Bewegungen, die so ausgeführt werden, wirken auf die erkrankten Organe zurück. Man sieht, wie hier äußerlich Ausgeführtes sich gesundend in die Organe hinein fortsetzt, wenn einer Organerkrankung die bewegte Gebärde genau angepaßt ist. Weil diese Art, durch Bewegung in dem Menschen zu wirken, auf Körper, Seele und Geist geht, wirkt sie in intensiverer Art in das Innere des kranken Menschen hinein, als alle andere Bewegungs-Therapie.

Dafür kann Heil-Eurythmie aber auch nie eine Laiensache werden, und darf nicht als eine solche betrachtet oder behandelt werden.

sees it at the same time. Or a piece of music is offered which reappears in the moving gestures as visible music.

A sculptured movement is given in eurythmy which is an essential extension for the artistic sphere.

What has been discovered here as an artistic form can now be developed in two other directions. One of these directions is pedagogical. In the Waldorf School, which was founded by Emil Molt in Stuttgart and which stands under the direction of Rudolf Steiner, pedagogical eurythmy is practiced in all classes in addition to gymnastics. One has to take into consideration here that ordinary gymnastics only develops the dynamics and statics of the physical body. In eurythmy, the full human being, in body, soul and spirit, flows into the movement. The growing human being feels this and experiences these eurythmy exercises quite naturally as an expression of human nature, just as he has experienced learning to speak in earlier years.

The other direction is therapeutic. When the gestures of artistic and pedagogical eurythmy are modified, so that they flow from the diseased nature of the human being *just* as the others flow from a healthy nature, then curative eurythmy comes into being.

Movements that are done in this way work back on the diseased organs. One sees how what is done here outwardly continues inwardly into the organs, restoring health when the moving gesture is exactly adapted to an organ pathology. Since this way of working into the human being through movement addresses body, soul and spirit, it affects the inner nature of the diseased human being more intensively than all other movement therapy.

For this very reason, though, curative eurythmy can never become the business of lay people, and may not be regarded or treated as such.

Der Heil-Eurythmist, der gut geschult in der Erkenntnis der menschlichen Organisation sein muß, kann nur im Zusammenhange mit dem Arzte handeln. Alles Herumdilettieren kann nur zu Übeln führen.

Nur auf Grundlage einer sachgemäßen Diagnose kann die heileurythmische Handlung ausgeführt werden. Es sind auch die praktischen Erfolge der Heileurythmie solche, daß man sie durchaus als ein segensreiches Glied unserer hier dargestellten therapeutischen Denkweise ansprechen kann.

The curative eurythmist, who must be well trained in the understanding of the human organization, can only work in association with the physician. Dilettantism in any form can only lead to problems.

A pertinent diagnosis is the only basis for the practice of curative eurythmy. The practical results of curative eurythmy are indeed such that one can altogether call it a beneficial part of the therapeutic way of thinking presented in this book.

XIX
CHARAKTERISTISCHE KRANKHEITSFÄLLE

In diesem Kapitel möchten wir aus der Praxis des klinisch-therapeutischen Institutes in Arlesheim eine Reihe von Krankheitsfällen beschreiben. Dieselben werden zeigen, wie versucht werden kann, mit Zuhilfenahme der Erkenntnis vom geistigen Menschen ein durchgreifendes Bild des krankhaften Zustandes so zu gewinnen, daß die Diagnose unmittelbar lehrt, welches Arzneimittel angewendet werden muß. Dabei liegt eine Anschauung zugrunde, die Erkrankungs- und Gesundungsprozeß als einen einzigen Kreisprozeß ins Auge faßt. Die Erkrankung beginnt mit einer Irregularität in der Zusammensetzung des menschlichen Organismus mit Bezug auf seine in diesem Buch beschriebenen Teile. Sie ist an einem bestimmten Punkte angekommen, wenn man den Kranken in Behandlung bekommt. Man hat nun dafür zu sorgen, daß alle Vorgänge, die sich seit dem Beginn der Krankheit im menschlichen Organismus abgespielt haben, wieder zurückverlaufen, so daß man zuletzt bei dem Zustande der Gesundheit anlangt, in dem der Organismus vorher war. Ein solcher Prozeß, der in sich selbst zurückläuft, ist nicht zum Vollzug zu bringen, ohne daß im Gesamtorganismus ein Verlust an Wachstumskräften vor sich geht, die gleichwertig sind den Kräften, welche der menschliche Organismus während der Kindheitszeit braucht, um sein Volumen zu vergrößern. Die Heilmittel müssen daher so beschaffen sein, daß sie nicht nur den Krankheitsprozeß zurücklaufen lassen, sondern auch die sich herabstimmende Vitalität wieder unterstützen. Einen Teil der letzteren Wirkung wird man der Krankheitsdiät überlassen müssen.

Doch ist in der Regel bei ernsteren Krankheitsfällen der Organismus nicht gestimmt, in der Verarbeitung der Nahrungsmittel genügend Vitalität zu entwickeln. Es wird daher notwendig sein, auch die eigentliche Therapie so einzurichten, daß der Organismus in dieser Beziehung seine Unterstützung findet. Bei den typischen Mitteln, die von den klinisch-therapeutischen Instituten ausgehen, ist durchaus diese Einrichtung getroffen. Man wird deshalb nur bei

CHAPTER XIX
Characteristic Case Histories

In this chapter we would like to describe a number of cases from the practice of the Clinical-Therapeutic Institute in Arlesheim.[12] They will show how one can, with the help of insight into the spiritual aspect of the human being, try to gain a thorough picture of the pathological condition so that the diagnosis directly teaches us which medication should be used. Fundamental to this is a view which looks at the process of illness and healing as one complete cycle. The illness begins with an irregularity in the composition of the human organism with regard to the parts that were described in this book. It has reached a certain stage when the patient comes in for treatment. Now one must see to it that all processes which have taken place in the human organism since the beginning of the disease are reversed, so that one eventually arrives at the state of health which the organism had previously. A process of this kind, reversing on itself, cannot be accomplished without the experience of a loss of growth forces in the organism as a whole, forces which are equivalent to the forces that the human organism needs during childhood to increase in size. Medications must therefore be so constituted that they not only reverse the pathological process but also support the reducing vitality again. Part of the latter function must be left to dietary measures. But in the more serious cases the organism is, as a rule, not in the position to develop sufficient vitality in the assimilation of food. Therefore it will be necessary to regulate the actual treatment as well in such a way that the organism is supported in this respect. In the typical medications that have been brought out by the Clinical-Therapeutic Institute,[13] this provision has been made altogether. Only on closer inspection will one therefore realize

genauerem Zusehen bei einem Präparat erkennen, warum es bestimmte Bestandteile enthält. Im Krankheitsverlaufe ist nicht nur der lokalisierte Krankheitsprozeß, sondern die Gesamtveränderung des Organismus zu berücksichtigen und diese in den rückläufigen Prozeß einzubeziehen. Wie das im Einzelnen zu denken ist, werden bestimmte Fälle, die wir nun charakterisieren wollen, zeigen. Nach deren Beschreibung wollen wir mit den allgemeinen Betrachtungen fortfahren.

Erster Fall

Man hat es mit einer 26-jährigen Patientin zu tun. Der ganze Mensch zeigt einen außerordentlich labilen Zustand. Die Patientin läßt deutlich erkennen, daß derjenige Teil ihres Organismus, den wir in unserem Buche Astralleib genannt haben, in einem Zustand der übermäßigen Tätigkeit ist. Man sieht, daß dieser Astralleib von der Ich-Organisation nur mangelhaft beherrscht werden kann. Schickt sich die Patientin an, eine Arbeit zu verrichten, so gerät der Astralleib sofort in Wallungen. Die Ich-Organisation sucht sich geltend zu machen, wird aber fortwährend zurückgestoßen. Das bewirkt, daß in einem solchen Falle erhöhte Temperatur eintritt. Die geregelte Verdauungstätigkeit ist beim Menschen im eminentesten Sinne von der normalen Ich-Organisation abhängig. Die Ohnmacht dieser Ich-Organisation drückt sich bei der Patientin in hartnäckiger Obstipation aus. Eine Folge dieser gestörten Verdauungstätigkeit sind dann die migräneartigen Zustände und das Erbrechen, an dem sie leidet. Im Schlafe zeigt sich, daß die ohnmächtige Ich-Organisation eine mangelhafte organische Tätigkeit von unten nach oben bewirkt und die Ausatmung schädigt. Die Folge davon ist übermäßige Anhäufung von Kohlensäure im Organismus während des Schlafes, was organisch durch das Herzklopfen beim Aufwachen, psychisch durch Angstgefühl und Aufschreien zutage tritt. Die körperliche Untersuchung kann nichts anderes ergeben als einen Mangel an solchen Kräften, die den regelmäßigen Zusammenhang von Astralleib, Ätherleib und physischem Leib bewirken. Die übermäßige Eigentätig-

why a given preparation contains certain ingredients. In the course of a disease one should take into consideration not only the localized pathological process, but as well the change in the organism as a whole, and the latter is to be included in the reversal process. How this is to be thought of in detail will be made clear in specific cases, which we will now characterize. After describing them we shall continue the more general considerations.

First Case[14]

The patient is a twenty-six-year-old woman. The whole state of her being is extraordinarily labile. It is clear from looking at the patient that the part of the organism that we have called the astral body in our book is in a state of excessive activity. One may perceive that the astral body is but inadequately controlled by the ego organization. As soon as the patient gets ready to do some work, the astral body becomes agitated. The ego organization tries to make itself felt, but is constantly pushed back. This causes the temperature to rise in such a case. A well-regulated digestion depends above all on a normal ego organization in the human being. The impotence of the ego organization expresses itself in a persistent constipation in this patient. This disturbance in the digestive activity has a further consequence in the migrainous conditions and vomiting from which she suffers. In sleep the impotent ego organization is seen to cause an inadequate organic activity from below upward, impairing the outbreathing. This results in an excessive accumulation of carbonic acid in the organism during sleep and manifests organically in palpitations on awakening, and psychologically in anxiety and crying out. Physical examination could show nothing other than a lack of those forces which bring about the normal coherence of astral body, ether body and physical body. The

keit des Astralleibes bewirkt, daß zu wenig Kräfte von diesem in den physischen und Ätherleib überströmen. Die letzteren bleiben daher während der Wachstumsperiode in ihrer Entwicklung zart. Das hat sich auch bei der Untersuchung dadurch gezeigt, daß die Patientin einen grazilen schwächlichen Körper hatte und über häufige Rückenschmerzen klagte. Die letzteren entstehen, weil in der Rückenmarkstätigkeit gerade die Ich-Organisation sich am stärksten geltend machen muß. Patientin spricht auch von vielen Träumen. Das ist eine Folge davon, daß der astralische Leib, wenn er beim Schlafe vom physischen und Ätherleib getrennt ist, seine übermäßige Eigentätigkeit entfaltet. Man hat nun davon auszugehen, daß die Ich-Organisation verstärkt und die Tätigkeit des Astralischen herabgemindert werden muß. Das erste erreicht man, wenn man ein Arzneimittel wählt, das geeignet ist, die in dem Verdauungstrakt schwachwerdende Ich-Organisation zu unterstützen. Man kann im Kupfer ein solches Arzneimittel erkennen. Wendet man es in Form eines Kupfersalbenverbandes, der in die Lendengegend gelegt wird, an, so wirkt das Kupfer verstärkend auf die von der Ich-Organisation mangelhaft ausgehende Wärmeentwicklung. Man wird dies bemerken an der zurückgehenden abnormen Herztätigkeit und an dem Weichen der Angstgefühle. Die übermäßige Eigentätigkeit des Astralleibes läßt sich bekämpfen durch kleinste Dosen von Blei, innerlich genommen. Blei zieht den Astralleib zusammen und weckt in ihm die Kräfte, durch die er sich stärker mit dem physischen Leib und dem Ätherleib verbindet. (Bleivergiftung besteht in einer zu starken Verbindung des astralischen mit dem Äther- und physischen Leib, so daß die letzteren einem zu starken Abbauprozesse unterliegen.) Patientin erholte sich sichtlich bei dieser Kur. Der labile Zustand wich einer gewissen inneren Festigkeit und Sicherheit. Die Gemütsverfassung wurde von einer zerrissenen zu einer innerlich befriedigten. Die Erscheinungen der Verstopfung und der Rückenschmerzen verschwanden, die migräneartigen Zustände und Kopfschmerzen gleichfalls. Patientin wurde ihre Arbeitsfähigkeit wieder zurückgegeben.

excessive inherent activity of the astral body causes too little of its forces to flow over into the physical and etheric body. During the period of growth therefore, the latter two remained delicate in their development. This showed itself also on examination in that the patient had a graceful, weakly body and complained of frequent back pains. The latter come about because in the activity of the spinal cord it is precisely the ego organization which asserts itself most strongly. In addition the patient speaks of many dreams. This is caused by the astral body, which unfolds its excessive inherent activity when separated from the physical and ether body in sleep. One has to start from the fact that the ego organization needs to be strengthened and the activity of the astral body reduced. One achieves the first by selecting a medication that is suited to support the ego organization as it is weakened in the digestive tract. Copper can be identified as such a medication. Applied in the form of a copper ointment bandage to the lumbar region, copper has a strengthening effect on the inadequate development of warmth by the ego organization. This will be noticed in a diminution of abnormal heart activity and dissipation of the anxiety. The excessive inherent activity of the astral body is combated by exceedingly minute doses of lead[15] taken orally. Lead draws the astral body together and wakens its forces to join more strongly with the physical body and the ether body. (Lead poisoning consists of the astral connecting too strongly with the ether and physical body, so that the latter two are subject to an excessive breakdown process.) The patient recovered visibly with this treatment. The labile condition was replaced by a certain inner firmness and assurance. From being chaotically fragmented the mood became inwardly contented. The constipation and back pain symptoms disappeared, likewise the migrainous conditions and headaches. The patient regained her capacity to work.

Zweiter Fall

48-jähriger männlicher Patient; war ein kräftiges Kind von seelischer Tüchtigkeit. Gibt an, daß er während des Krieges fünf Monate lang auf Nephritis behandelt und geheilt entlassen wurde. Heiratete mit 35 Jahren, hat fünf gesunde Kinder, ein sechstes starb bei der Geburt. Mit 33 Jahren zeigen sich nach geistiger Überanstrengung Depression, Müdigkeit, Apathie. Diese Zustände verstärken sich fortdauernd. Es tritt parallel damit eine geistige Ratlosigkeit auf. Patient steht vor Fragen. die ihm das Negative seines Berufes zeigen – er ist Lehrer - dem er aber nichts Positives entgegensetzen kann. – Der Krankheitszustand zeigt einen astralischen Leib, der zum Äther- und physischen Leib eine zu geringe Affinität hat und in sich selbst unbeweglich ist. Dadurch machen der physische und Ätherleib ihre eigenen Eigenschaften geltend. Die Empfindung des nicht richtig mit dem Astralleib verbundenen Ätherleibes erzeugt Depressionen; das nicht richtig Verbundensein mit dem physischen Leib Müdigkeit und Apathie. Daß Patient in geistige Ratlosigkeit fällt, rührt davon her, daß der Astralleib ohnmächtig ist, den physischen und Ätherleib zu gebrauchen. Mit alledem hängt zusammen, daß der Schlaf gut ist, weil der Astralleib geringen Zusammenhang mit Äther- und physischem Leib hat. Aus demselben Grunde ist aber das Aufwachen schwer. Der Astralleib will in den physischen nicht hinein. Erst wenn der physische und Ätherleib müde sind am Abend, tritt eine normale Verbindung mit demselben ein. Daher wird Patient erst am Abend recht wach. Der ganze Zustand weist darauf hin. daß man zunächst die Tätigkeit des astralischen Leibes verstärke. Das erreicht man immer. wenn man Arsen innerlich in Form eines Naturwassers gibt. Man wird nach einiger Zeit bemerken, wie der betreffende Mensch mehr Herrschaft über seinen Körper bekommt. Der Zusammenhang zwischen Astralleib und Ätherleib wird stärker, Depression, Apathie und Müdigkeit hören auf. Man muß nun auch dem physischen Körper, der durch die längere zu geringe Verbindung mit dem Astralleibe träge in bezug auf

Second Case[16]

A forty-eight-year-old male patient; he had been a robust child, a capable soul. He states that for five months during the war he was treated for nephritis and was discharged as cured. He married at the age of thirty-five, has five healthy children, a sixth child died at birth. At the age of thirty-three he becomes depressed, tired and apathetic after mental overexertion. These conditions get progressively stronger. At the same time spiritual despair arises. The patient is confronted with questions which show him the negative side of his profession—he is a teacher—and he cannot meet them with anything positive.—The pathological condition demonstrates an astral body with insufficient affinity to ether and physical body and with an inherent rigidity. Therefore the physical and ether body assert their own qualities. The experience of the ether body as not being soundly connected to the astral body results in depressions; the unsound connection with the physical body results in fatigue and apathy. That the patient falls into spiritual despair has its origin in the astral body's impotence in making use of the physical and ether body. Connected with all this is that sleep is good, since the astral body has little connection with ether and physical body. However, for the same reason, waking up is difficult. The astral body is loath to enter the physical. Not until the evening, when the physical and ether body are tired, does a normal connection begin with them. Therefore the patient does not really wake up until the evening. The whole condition points to the need first of all to strengthen the activity of the astral body. This one always achieves by giving arsenic in the form of a mineral water.[17] One will notice after some time that the particular person gains more control over his body. The cohesion of astral body and ether body is strengthened; depression, apathy and fatigue cease to exist. One must now also help the physical body, which has become sluggish in its movements through its long,

Beweglichkeit geworden ist, durch eine Phosphorkur in schwacher Dosis zu Hilfe kommen. Der Phosphor unterstützt die Ich-Organisation, so daß diese den Widerstand des physischen Körpers überwinden kann. Rosmarinbäder werden den abgelagerten Stoffwechselprodukten einen Abfluß eröffnen. Heileurythmie kann die Harmonie der einzelnen Glieder (Nerven-Sinnessystem, rhythmisches System, motorisches und Stoffwechselsystem) des menschlichen Organismus, die durch die Untätigkeit des Astralleibes gestört worden ist, wieder herstellen. Gibt man dem Patienten noch Fliedertee, so wird der träge Stoffwechsel, der sich nach und nach durch die Untätigkeit des Astralleibes eingestellt hat, wieder normal gemacht. Wir konnten bei diesem Patienten eine vollständige Heilung konstatieren.

Dritter Fall

31-jähriger Patient, Künstler, suchte während einer Konzertreise unsere Klinik auf, ist in einem Zustande starker entzündlicher Funktionsstörung der Harnorgane; katarrhalische Erscheinungen, Fieber, übermüdeter Körper, allgemeine Schwäche, Arbeitsunfähigkeit.

Die Anamnese ergibt, daß der gleiche Zustand wiederholentlich bei dem Patienten vorhanden war. Die Untersuchung der geistigen Beschaffenheit des Patienten ergibt einen überempfindlichen, zermürbten Astralleib. Als eine Folge davon erweist sich die leichte Anfälligkeit des physischen und des Ätherleibes für katarrhalische und entzündliche Zustände. Patient hatte schon als Kind einen schwächlichen, vom Astralleib unversorgten physischen Leib. Daher Masern, Scharlach, Wasserpocken, Keuchhusten, oft Angina; mit 14 Jahren Harnröhrenentzündung, die mit 29 Jahren kombiniert mit einer Blasenentzündung sich wiederholte. Mit 18 Jahren trat eine Lungen- und Brustfellentzündung auf; mit 29 Jahren bei einem Grippeanfall Rippenfellentzündung; mit 30 Jahren Stirnhöhlenkatarrh. Es ist eine fortwährende Neigung zu Bindehautkatarrh der Augen vorhanden. – Die Fie-

inadequate connection to the astral body, by treating it with a course of phosphorus in a weak dosis.[18] Phosphorus supports the ego organization to overcome the resistance of the physical body. Rosemary baths will open the way for drainage of the accumulated products of metabolism. Curative eurythmy can reestablish the harmony of the individual members of the human organism (nerve-sense system, rhythmic system, metabolic-limb system), which was impaired by the inactivity of the astral body. If one gives the patient elder flower tea as well, then the metabolism, which, due to the inactivity of the astral body has gradually become sluggish, is restored back to normal again. We could witness a complete cure in this patient.

Third Case[19]

A thirty-one-year-old male patient, musician, visiting our clinic during a concert tour, has a condition of severe inflammatory functional disturbances of the urinary tract; he has catarrhal[20] symptoms, fever, is physically overtired, has generalized weakness, and is unable to work.

The past history reveals that the patient has repeatedly had the same condition. Examination of the patient's nonphysical state reveals a hypersensitive, worn-down astral body. Consequently, the physical and ether body are strongly susceptible to catarrhal and inflammatory conditions. Already as a child the patient had a delicate physical body, not maintained by the astral body. Therefore he had measles, scarlet fever, chicken pox, whooping cough and frequent sore throats; at age fourteen he had urethritis, which recurred combined with cystitis at age twenty-nine. At the age of eighteen he had pneumonia and pleurisy; at age twenty-nine pleurisy with a bout of the flu; and at the age of thirty catarrh of the frontal sinuses. There is a constant inclination to catarrh of the conjunctivae.—During

berkurve war während des zweimonatigen Aufenthaltes des Patienten in der Klinik anfangs bis zu 38.9, ging dann herunter, um am 14. Tage wieder zu steigen; wurde später wellig zwischen 37 und 36, stieg zuweilen auch über 37 und ging bis 35 herunter. Diese Fieberkurve ist ein deutliches Bild der wechselnden Stimmungen in der Ich-Organisation. Es entsteht eine solche Kurve, wenn die Wirkungen der halb bewußten Inhalte der Ich-Organisation in den Wärmeprozessen des physischen und Ätherleibes sich ausleben, ohne durch den astralischen Leib auf einen normalen Rhythmus reduziert zu werden. Die Gesamtaktionsfähigkeit des astralischen Leibes ist in diesem Falle auf das rhythmische System konzentriert und lebt sich in demselben durch die künstlerische Begabung aus. Die anderen Systeme kommen dabei zu kurz. Eine wichtige Folge davon ist eine starke Müdigkeit und Schlaflosigkeit während der Sommerzeit. Im Sommer wird der astralische Leib durch die äußere Welt sehr in Anspruch genommen. Seine innere Aktionsfähigkeit tritt zurück. Die Kräfte des physischen und Ätherleibes werden vorherrschend. In der allgemeinen Lebensempfindung tritt das als starke Ermüdung auf. Die beeinträchtigte Aktionsfähigkeit des Astralleibes hindert denselben, sich vom physischen Leibe zu trennen. Daher tritt Schlaflosigkeit ein. Die nur mangelhafte Trennung des Astralleibes vom Ätherleibe lebt sich in aufregenden und unangenehmen Träumen aus, die von einer Empfindsamkeit dieses Leibes gegenüber den Schädigungen des physischen Organismus herrühren. Charakteristisch ist, daß die Träume diese Schädigungen des physischen Leibes in den Bildern menschlicher Verstümmelungen symbolisieren. Das Schreckhafte derselben ist ihre naturgemäße Gefühlsbetonung. Eine Folge des im Stoffwechselsystem mangelhaft funktionierenden Astralleibes ist die Neigung zur Obstipation. Durch die Selbständigkeit des Ätherleibes, der vom astralischen Leib zu wenig beeinflußt wird, kann das mit der Nahrung aufgenommene Eiweiß nicht vom pflanzlichen und tierischen Eiweiß vollständig in menschliches Eiweiß umgewan-

the two months he spent at our clinic, the patient's temperature curve rose at first to 38.9°C, then it came down, only to rise again on the fourteenth day. It then fluctuated between 37° and 36°, occasionally rising above 37° or dropping to 35°C. This temperature curve gives a clear picture of the changing conditions in the ego organization. Such a curve develops when the effects of the semiconscious contents of the ego organization are expressed in warmth processes of the physical and ether body without having been reduced to a normal rhythm by the astral body. In this case the whole capacity for action of the astral body concentrates on the rhythmic system and expresses itself there in artistic talent. Then the other systems do not get enough. An important consequence of this is the severe fatigue and insomnia during summertime. In summer considerable demands are made by the outer world on the astral body. Its inner capacity for action diminishes. The forces of the physical and ether body become predominant. In the general sense of well-being this is perceived as severe fatigue. The impaired capacity for action of the astral body hinders its separation from the physical body. Therefore insomnia sets in. The but inadequate separation of the astral body from the ether body is expressed in exciting and unpleasant dreams that stem from the sensitivity of the astral body to the damages in the physical organism. Characteristically the dreams symbolize these damages of the physical body in images of human mutilations. The terrifying nature of these images is due to the accompanying quality of feelings that is so natural. A consequence of the astral body's inadequate functioning in the metabolic system is the tendency to constipation. Because of the independence of the ether body, which is insufficiently influenced by the astral body, the protein consumed as food cannot be completely transformed from vegetable and animal protein into human protein. Thus protein is excreted in the urine, so that the urinalysis is

delt werden. Es wird daher im Urin Eiweiß ausgeschieden, so daß die Eiweißreaktion positiv ist. Funktioniert der astralische Leib mangelhaft, so treten im physischen Leibe Prozesse auf, die Fremdprozesse im menschlichen Organismus sind. Das Ergebnis solcher Prozesse ist die Eiterbildung. Die stellt gewissermaßen einen außermenschlichen Vorgang im Menschen dar. Es ergab sich daher im Urinsediment reiner Eiter. Diese Eiterbildung hat einen seelischen Parallelprozeß. Es verarbeitet der Astralleib ebensowenig seelisch die Lebenserfahrungen, wie physisch die Stoffe. Bilden sich außermenschliche Stoffbildungen als Eiter, so auch seelische Inhalte mit außermenschlichem Charakter als Interesse für abnorme Lebenszusammenhänge, Ahnungen, Wahrzeichen usw. – Es handelte sich für uns nun darum, auf den astralischen Leib ausgleichend, reinigend, kräftigend einzuwirken. Da die Ich-Organisation eine sehr regsame ist, so kann ihre Tätigkeit gewissermaßen als Träger der Heilmittelwirkung benutzt werden. Man kommt der Ich-Organisation, die auf die Außenwelt eingestellt ist, am besten bei, wenn man von außen nach innen gerichtete Wirkungen anstrebt. Das erreicht man durch Umschläge. Wir gaben in den Umschlag zuerst Melilotus. Dieser wirkt auf den Astralleib so, daß derselbe in der Verteilung seiner Kräfte eine Ausgleichung erfährt und der einseitigen Hinlenkung auf das rhythmische System entgegengewirkt wird. Natürlich darf man die Umschläge nicht auf jenen Teil des Organismus legen, in dem das rhythmische System besonders konzentriert ist. Wir legten sie um die Organe, in denen der Stoffwechsel und das motorische System konzentriert sind. Kopfumschläge vermieden wir aus dem Grunde, weil der Stimmungswechsel der Ich-Organisation, der vom Kopfe ausgeht, die Wirkung paralysieren mußte. Es handelte sich deshalb nun darum, den astralischen Leib und die Ich-Organisation, die für die Wirkung der Melilotus zusammengespannt werden mußten, zu fördern. Das suchten wir zu erreichen durch einen oxalsauren Zusatz, der der Klettenwurzel entnommen war. Oxalsäure wirkt so, daß die Tätigkeit der Ich-

positive for protein. If the astral body functions inadequately then processes will appear in the physical body which are foreign processes in the human organism. The result of those processes is the formation of pus. This represents, as it were, an extra-human process within the human being. Therefore pure pus could be found in the urinary sediment. This pus formation has a parallel process in the soul. The astral body digests life experiences in the soul as little as it digests substances physically. In the same way that extra-human substances develop in the form of pus so also soul contents of an extra-human character develop in the form of an interest in abnormal life contexts, premonitions, omens etc.—For us it was now a question of exerting a balancing, purifying and strengthening effect on the astral body. Since the ego organization is very agile, its activity can be used as a carrier, as it were, for medicinal action. It is focussed on the external world and thus one can best access the ego organization by striving for effects oriented from without inward. One achieves this with poultices. We first put melilotus[21] in the poultice. This works on the astral body so that it experiences balancing of the distribution of its forces and counteracting of its one-sided disposition toward the rhythmic system. Naturally the poultices must not be applied to that part of the organism in which the rhythmic system is especially concentrated. We applied them to the organs where the metabolic and movement systems are concentrated. We avoided poultices around the head, because the changing conditions of the ego organization which proceed from the head would have paralyzed the effect. Therefore it was now important to stimulate astral body and ego organization, which have to be pulled together for the melilotus to take effect. This we sought to do by adding oxalic acid, derived from burdock root.[22] Oxalic acid works in such a way that it transforms the activity of the ego organization into one of the astral body. In addition, we gave oral medications in

Organisation in eine solche des Astralleibes umgewandelt wird. Zu allem dem gaben wir innere Mittel in sehr schwacher Dosierung, welche die Aufgabe hatten, die Absonderungen in eine regelmäßige Eingliederung in die Astralleib-Wirkungen zu bringen. Die Absonderungen, die von der Kopforganisation aus dirigiert werden, suchten wir zu normalisieren durch schwefelsaures Kalium. Diejenigen Vorgänge, die vom Stoffwechselsystem im engeren Sinne abhängen, suchten wir durch kohlensaures Kalium zu beeinflussen. Die Harnabsonderung regelten wir durch Teucrium. Wir gaben deshalb ein Präparat, das zu gleichen Teilen bestand aus schwefelsaurem Kalium, kohlensaurem Kalium und Teucrium. Die ganze Behandlung mußte mit einem sehr labilen Gleichgewicht des physischen, seelischen und geistigen Gesamtorganismus rechnen. Es mußte daher durch dauerndes Bettliegen für physisches, durch seelische Ruhe für geistiges Gleichgewicht gesorgt werden, das ein Ineinanderwirken der verschiedenen Heilmittel erst möglich machte. Bewegung und Aufregung machen einen so komplizierten Heilungsprozeß fast unmöglich. – Patient war nach Beendigung der Kur körperlich kräftig und gestärkt und seelisch in guter Verfassung. Daß bei einem so labilen Gesundheitszustand bei irgend einer äußeren Attacke die eine oder andere Störung wieder eintreten kann, ist selbstverständlich. Es gehört zur Gesamtheilung, daß in einem solchen Falle solche Attacken vermieden werden.

Vierter Fall

Ein Kind, das uns zweimal in die Klinik gebracht wurde, erst mit 4 Jahren, dann mit 5½ Jahren. Dazu dessen Mutter und die Schwester der Mutter. Die Diagnose führte von der Erkrankung des Kindes sowohl zu derjenigen der Mutter wie zu der der Schwester hinüber. Für das Kind konnten wir das Folgende feststellen: Es ist ein Zwillingskind, sechs Wochen zu früh geboren. Das andere Kind war im letzten Embryonalstadium abgestorben. Mit sechs Wochen erkrankte das Kind, schrie außerordentlich viel

very weak dosage to integrate the secretions normally into the functions of the astral body. With the sulfate of potassium we tried to normalize the secretions that are under the control of the head organization. With the carbonate of potassium we sought to influence those processes that depend on the metabolic system in the narrower sense of the word. With teucrium we regulated the secretion of urine. Thus we gave a preparation, consisting of equal parts of potassium sulfate, potassium carbonate and teucrium.[23] The entire treatment had to reckon with a very labile balance in the whole physical, soul and spiritual organism. Thus one had to provide for physical balance through complete bed rest and for spiritual balance through mental quiet. This alone made the interaction of the various medicines possible. Movement and excitement render such a complicated therapeutic process almost impossible.— On completion of the treatment the patient was restored to bodily strength and vigor, and was mentally in a good disposition. It goes without saying that when there is such a labile state of health any external disruption may bring on a recurrence of one or another disturbance. It is part of the total healing that in such a case such events should be avoided.

Fourth Case[24]

A child which was brought to our clinic twice, first at the age of four, and then at age five and a half. The mother of the child and the mother's sister came along. The diagnosis led us from the child's illness to that of both the mother and the sister. In regard to the child, we were able to ascertain the following: she is one of twins, born six weeks prematurely. The other child had died in the last stage of fetal life. At the age of six weeks, the child became ill, cried an unusual amount and was admitted to a hospital. There pyloric stenosis was

und wurde in ein Hospital verbracht. Dort stellte man die Diagnose Pylorospasmus. Das Kind wurde teilweise von einer Amme, teilweise künstlich ernährt. Mit acht Monaten wird es vom Hospital entlassen. Zu Hause angekommen, hatte es am ersten Tage einen Krampfanfall, der sich in den ersten zwei Monaten täglich wiederholte. Das Kind wurde dabei steif und verdrehte die Augen. Vor dem Anfall trat Ängstlichkeit und Weinen ein. Auch schielte das Kind mit dem rechten Auge und hatte Erbrechen, bevor der Anfall kam. Mit 2½ Jahren trat wieder ein Anfall ein, der fünf Stunden dauerte. Das Kind wurde wieder steif und lag wie tot da. Mit vier Jahren trat ein Anfall ein, der ½ Stunde dauerte. Für diesen wurde uns zum erstenmal die Begleitung mit Fiebererscheinungen gemeldet. Nach den Konvulsionen, die nach dem Zurückbringen aus dem Hospital eintraten, merkten die Eltern eine Lähmung des rechten Armes und des rechten Beines. Mit 2½ Jahren kommt das Kind zum ersten Gehversuch, der so ausfällt, daß nur das linke Bein schreiten kann und das rechte nachgezogen wird. Auch der rechte Arm bleibt willenlos. Der gleiche Zustand war noch vorhanden, als uns das Kind gebracht wurde. Es handelte sich darum, festzustellen, wie es mit den Organisationsgliedern des Kindes stand. Dies wurde unabhängig von dem Symptomenkomplex versucht. Es stellte sich eine starke Atrophie des Ätherleibes heraus, der in gewissen Teilen nur einen sehr geringen Einfluß des astralischen Leibes aufnahm. Die Gegend der rechten Brusthälfte war im Ätherleibe wie gelähmt. Dagegen zeigte sich etwas wie eine Hypertrophie des Astralleibes in der Magengegend. Nun handelte es sich darum, den Symptomenkomplex mit diesen Befunden in Einklang zu bringen. Es ist zweifellos durch den astralischen Leib eine starke Inanspruchnahme des Magens bei der Verdauung vorhanden, die sich aber wegen der Lähmung des Ätherleibes beim Übergange vom Darm in die Lymphgefäße staut. Dadurch ist das Blut unterernährt. Wir müssen die Brechreizerscheinungen daher als besonders wichtige Symptome nehmen. Krämpfe treten immer ein, wenn der ätheris-

diagnosed. The child was partly breastfed by a wet nurse and partly had artificial feedings. At the age of eight months she was discharged from the hospital. On the first day after her arrival home she had a convulsion, which for the next two months recurred on a daily basis. During the seizure the child would become stiff and roll her eyes. The attacks were preceded by fearfulness and crying. Before the attack began the child also would squint with the right eye and vomit. At the age of two and a half there was another attack lasting five hours. The child again became stiff and lay there as though dead. At the age of four there was an attack which lasted one-half hour. We were advised that this was the first attack which was accompanied by fever. After the convulsions, which had set in on returning from the hospital, the parents noticed a paralysis of the right arm and the right leg. At two and a half the child made her first attempt to walk, during which it turned out that only the left leg was able to step out and the right leg dragged behind. The right arm, too, remained without will. The same condition was still present when the child was brought to us. It was essential to assess the state of the members of the child's organization. This was attempted independently of the complex of symptoms. A severe atrophy of the ether body became apparent and in certain parts the ether body took up only a very slight influence from the astral body. The area of the right half of the chest was as though lamed in the ether body. By comparison, the area of the stomach had sort of a hypertrophy of the astral body. Now it was a matter of reconciling the complex of symptoms with these findings. There is no doubt that the astral body makes a strong demand on the stomach in the digestion. The latter, however, is congested at the transition from the intestines to the lymph vessels due to the paralysis of the ether body. Therefore the blood is undernourished. We therefore must consider the appearances of nausea very significant symptoms.

che Leib atrophisch wird und der astralische Leib einen unmittelbaren Einfluß auf den physischen Leib erlangt ohne Vermittlung des Ätherleibes. Das war bei dem Kinde im höchsten Maße vorhanden. Wenn dieser Zustand während der Wachstumsperiode, wie es hier der Fall war, dauernd wird, so fallen diejenigen Vorgänge aus, welche das motorische System zur normalen Aufnahme des Willens geeignet machen. Das zeigte sich bei dem Kinde in der Unbrauchbarkeit der rechten Seite. – Wir mußten nun den Zustand des Kindes mit dem der Mutter in Verbindung bringen. Diese ist 37 Jahre alt, als sie zu uns kommt. Sie gibt an, mit 13 Jahren schon so groß gewesen zu sein wie gegenwärtig. Sie hatte früh schlechte Zähne, litt als Kind an Gelenkrheumatismus, behauptet rachitisch gewesen zu sein. Die Menses traten verhältnismäßig früh ein. Die Patientin erklärt, mit 16 Jahren eine Nierenkrankheit gehabt zu haben, und spricht auch von krampfartigen Zuständen, die sie gehabt hat. Mit 25 Jahren Obstipation wegen Krampf des Sphinkter ani, der gedehnt werden mußte. Hat auch jetzt bei der Entleerung Krampf. – Der ohne Schlußfolgerung aus dem Symptomenkomplex in unmittelbarer Anschauung festgestellte Befund ergibt eine außerordentliche Ähnlichkeit mit dem des Kindes. Nur erweist sich alles in viel milderer Form. Man muß berücksichtigen, daß der Ätherleib des Menschen zwischen dem Zahnwechsel und der Geschlechtsreife seine besondere Entwickelung erfährt. Dies kommt bei der Patientin dadurch zum Ausdruck, daß die verfügbaren Kräfte des Ätherleibes, die wenig stark sind, ein Wachstum nur bis zur Geschlechtsreife möglich machen. Mit dieser beginnt die besondere Entwickelung des Astralleibes, der mit seiner Hypertrophie nun den Ätherleib überwuchert und zu stark in die physische Organisation eingreift. Das tritt in dem stehenbleibenden Wachstum mit dem 13. Jahre zutage. Dabei ist die Patientin keineswegs zwerghaft, sondern sehr groß, was davon herrührt, daß die zwar geringen, aber vom Astralleibe ungehemmten Wachstumskräfte des Ätherleibes eine starke Volumenausdehnung des physischen Körpers bewirkten.

Cramps always occur when the etheric body becomes atrophied and the astral body gains direct influence over the physical body without the ether body mediating. This was present to the highest degree in the child. When this situation becomes permanent during the period of growth as was the case here, then those processes are lacking which make the movement system suited to a normal receptivity for the will. This became apparent in the child in that the right side was not usable.—We now had to relate the condition of the child to that of the mother. The latter is thirty-seven years old when she comes to us. She states that at the age of thirteen she had already reached her present size. She had bad teeth at an early age, had suffered in childhood from articular rheumatism, and maintains that she had rickets. Menstruation began comparatively early. The patient explains that at the age of sixteen she had kidney disease and she also speaks of having had cramping conditions. At the age of twenty-five she had constipation which was due to a cramp in the anal sphincter that had to be dilated. Even now she has cramping on evacuation.—The directly perceived findings, before drawing any conclusions from the complex of symptoms, reveal an extraordinary similarity with those of the child. But everything appears in a much milder form. One must keep in mind that the human ether body experiences its particular development between the change of teeth and puberty. This expresses itself in the patient in the fact that the available forces of the ether body, since they are not very strong, only enable her to grow until puberty. At this moment the particular development of the astral body begins, and through the latter's hypertrophy, the ether body is now overwhelmed and the astral body intervenes too strongly in the physical organization. This manifests in the arrested growth in the thirteenth year. At the same time the patient is by no means dwarflike but on the contrary very tall, which stems from the effect of the growth forces of the ether body which, although

Diese Kräfte konnten dann noch nicht regulär in die Funktionen des physischen Leibes eingreifen. Das zeigte sich in dem Auftreten des Gelenkrheumatismus und später in den Krampfzuständen. Durch die Schwäche des Ätherleibes tritt eine besonders starke Wirkung des Astralleibes auf den physischen Leib ein. Diese Wirkung ist eine abbauende. Sie wird in der normalen Lebensentwicklung durch die Aufbaukräfte im Schlafe, wenn der Astralleib von dem physischen und Ätherleib getrennt ist, ausgeglichen. Ist der Ätherleib zu schwach, wie im Falle unserer Patientin, so tritt ein Überschuß des Abbaues ein, was sich bei ihr darin zeigte, daß die Zähne schon im 12. Jahre die erste Plombe notwendig machten. Wird der Ätherleib noch besonders in Anspruch genommen, wie in der Schwangerschaft, so tritt jedesmal eine Verschlechterung der Zähne ein. Die Schwäche des Ätherleibes in Bezug auf seine Verbindung mit dem Astralleibe zeigt sich noch besonders in der Häufigkeit der Träume und im gesunden Schlaf, der bei der Patientin vorhanden ist. trotz aller Unregelmäßigkeit. Die Schwäche des Ätherleibes zeigt sich auch darinnen, daß im physischen Körper durch den Ätherleib nicht bewältigte Fremdprozesse sich abspielen, die im Urin als Eiweiß, vereinzelte hyaline Zylinder und Salze sich zeigen. – Merkwürdig ist die Verwandtschaft dieser Krankheitsprozesse mit denen der Schwester der Mutter. Der Befund in Bezug auf die Zusammensetzung der Teile der menschlichen Wesenheit ist fast ganz derselbe. Schwach wirkender Ätherleib, daher Überwiegen des Astralleibes. Nur ist der Astralleib selbst schwächer als bei der Schwester. Es kommt daher ebenso wie bei dieser zum frühen Eintritt der Menses, aber es treten bei ihr statt der Entzündungen bloße Schmerzen auf, die von einer Irritierung der Organe, z. B. der Gelenke herrühren. In den Gelenken muß der Ätherleib besonders tätig sein, wenn die Vitalität normal vor sich gehen soll. Ist die Tätigkeit des Ätherleibes schwach, so wird die Tätigkeit des physischen Leibes überwiegend, was sich hier in Schwellungen und in chronischer Arthritis zeigt. Auf die Schwäche des

limited, had worked uninhibited by the astral body, bringing on a large increase in the size of the physical body. But these forces were not able to engage normally in the functions of the physical body. This became apparent when arthritic rheumatism occurred and later cramping. The weakness of the ether body causes a particularly strong effect of the astral body on the physical body to set in. This effect is catabolic. In the normal course of development in life it is offset by regenerative forces in sleep, when the astral body is separated from the physical and ether body. If the ether body is too weak, as is the case in our patient, then an excess of breaking down begins, which became apparent in her teeth already needing their first filling in the twelfth year. When besides this special demands are made on the ether body as in pregnancy, then at every such instance the teeth get worse. In addition, the weakness of the ether body with respect to its connection with the astral body becomes particularly apparent in the frequency of dreams and in the sound sleep which the patient enjoys in spite of all irregularity. The weakness of the ether body also becomes apparent in that foreign processes are enacted in the physical body which are not mastered by the ether body, and which show themselves in the urine as protein, isolated hyaline casts, and salts.—These disease processes in the mother were remarkably akin to those of her sister. The findings regarding the composition of the human being's members are almost exactly the same: a delicately functioning ether body, therefore preponderance of the astral body. The astral body itself is, however, weaker than that of her sister. Accordingly, as in the latter, menstruation begins early, but, instead of inflammations, she only has pains that stem from an irritation of the organs, e.g., the joints. In the joints the ether body must be particularly active if the vitality is to get on normally. When the ether body activity is weak, then the physical body activity becomes predominant; this becomes apparent here in joint

Astralleibes, der zu wenig auf das subjektive Empfinden wirkt, weist die Vorliebe zu süßen Speisen hin, welche das Empfinden des Astralleibes erhöhen. Ist der schwache Astralleib durch das Tagesleben noch dazu abgenutzt, so treten, wenn das Schwachsein erhalten bleibt, die Schmerzen bedeutender auf. Patientin klagt über die Zunahme der Schmerzen abends. – Der Zusammenhang der Krankheitszustände der drei Patienten weist in der Aszendenz auf die den beiden Schwestern vorangegangene Generation hin, insbesondere auf die Großmutter des Kindes. Bei dieser muß die Ursache gesucht werden. Das gestörte Gleichgewicht zwischen Astral- und Ätherleib bei allen drei Patienten kann nur in einem ebensolchen bei der Großmutter des Kindes begründet sein. Diese Unregelmäßigkeit muß in der mangelhaften Ausbildung der embryonalen Ernährungsorgane, insbesondere der Allantois durch Astral- und Ätherleib der Großmutter bedingt sein. Diese mangelhafte Ausbildung der Allantois muß bei allen drei Patienten gesucht werden. Bei uns wurde sie zunächst auf rein geisteswissenschaftliche Art festgestellt. Die physische Allantois metamorphosiert sich, ins Geistige hinübergehend, in der Tüchtigkeit der Kräfte des Astralleibes. Eine degenerierte Allantois erzeugt eine verminderte Tüchtigkeit des Astralleibes, die sich insbesondere in allen motorischen Organen äußert. Alles dieses ist bei den drei Patienten der Fall. Man kann wirklich aus der Beschaffenheit des Astralleibes diejenige der Allantois erkennen. Man wird daraus ersehen, daß unser Hinweis auf die Aszendenz nicht einer gewagten Phantasie-Schlußfolgerung, sondern einer wirklichen geisteswissenschaftlichen Beobachtung entstammt.

Wen diese Wahrheit irritiert, dem möchten wir sagen, daß unsere Ausführungen durchaus nicht dem Triebe zum Paradoxen, sondern dem Verlangen, die nun einmal vorhandene Erkenntnis niemandem vorzuenthalten, entsprungen sind. Die mystischen Begriffe der Vererbung werden ja stets dunkel bleiben, wenn man sich scheut, die Metamorphose vom Physischen zum Geistigen und umgekehrt in der Folge der Generationen anzuerkennen.

swelling and in chronic arthritis. The weakness of the astral body, which functions too little in subjective experience, is indicated by the preference for sweets, which enhance the experience of the astral body. When besides this the weak astral body is worn out at the end of the day, the pains will increase in intensity if the weakness continues. The patient complains of increasing pain in the evening.—The correlation of the pathological conditions of the three patients points to antecedents in the generation preceding that of the two sisters, and particularly to the grandmother of the child. The real cause must be looked for in her. The disturbed equilibrium between astral and ether body in all three patients can only be based on a similar situation in the grandmother of the child. This irregularity must be based on inadequate development of the embryonal organs of nutrition, particularly the allantois, by the astral and ether body of the grandmother. This inadequate development of the allantois must be looked for in all three patients. It was assessed initially in a purely spiritual-scientific way by us. The physical allantois goes through a metamorphosis, passing into the spiritual, constituting the strength and vigor of the forces of the astral body. A degenerated allantois gives rise to reduced abilities of the astral body which expresses itself particularly in all the organs for movement. All this is the case in the three patients. One actually can apprehend the constitution of the allantois by looking at that of the astral body. One can gather from this that our reference to the preceding generation was not born of a far-fetched fantastic conclusion, but of a real spiritual-scientific observation.

To whomever is irritated by this truth we would say that our elaborations do not spring at all from a bent for the paradoxical but rather from the wish not to withhold from anyone the insight that is after all available. The mystical conceptions of heredity will ever remain dark when one shrinks from recognizing the metamorphosis from the physical

Therapeutisch kann eine solche Einsicht ja nur dazu führen, eine Ansicht zu bekommen, an welchem Punkte man mit dem Heilungsprozeß anzusetzen hat. Würde man nicht in einer solchen Art an das Hereditäre verwiesen worden sein, sondern einfach die Unregelmäßigkeit im Zusammenhange zwischen Ätherleib und Astralleib bemerkt haben, so hätte man Heilmittel angewendet, welche auf diese beiden Teile des Menschen wirken. Diese würden aber in unserem Falle unwirksam geblieben sein, weil die Schädigung, die durch Generationen hindurch geht, zu tief liegt, um in diesen Gliedern der menschlichen Organisation selbst ausgeglichen zu werden. Man muß in einem solchen Falle auf die Ich-Organisation wirken und in dieser alles zur Auswirkung bringen, was auf die Harmonisierung und Stärkung von Äther- und Astralleib Bezug hat. Man kann das erreichen, wenn man in gewissermaßen verstärkten Sinnesreizen (Sinnesreize wirken auf die Ich-Organisation) der Ich-Organisation beikommt. – Bei dem Kinde wurde dies auf folgende Art versucht: es wurde eine Bandage der rechten Hand mit einer 5-prozentigen Pyritsalbe und gleichzeitig Einreiben der linken Kopfhälfte mit Kaiserschwammsalbe angewendet. Der Pyrit, eine Verbindung von Eisen und Schwefel, wirkt äußerlich angewendet so, daß er die Ich-Organisation anregt, den Astralleib lebhafter zu machen und seine Affinität zum Ätherleib zu vergrößern. Die Kaiserschwammsubstanz mit ihrem besondern Inhalte an organisiertem Stickstoff wirkt so, daß eine Wirkung vom Kopfe ausgeht, die durch die Ich-Organisation den Ätherleib lebhafter macht und dessen Affinität zum Astralleibe erhöht. Der Heilungsprozeß wurde unterstützt durch Heileurythmie, die die Ich-Organisation als solche in rege Tätigkeit versetzt. Dadurch wird, was äußerlich angewendet wird, in die Tiefen der Organisation geleitet. Der damit eingeleitete Heilungsprozeß wurde dann noch verstärkt durch Mittel, welche Astral- und Ätherleib besonders empfindlich machen sollten für die Wirkung der Ich-Organisation. In rhythmischer Tagesfolge wurden dazu angewendet Bäder mit einer Auskochung von Soli-

to the spiritual, and vice versa, in the sequence of the generations.

Therapeutically, such an insight must of course lead to the idea of where to make a start with the healing process. If one had not thus been referred to the hereditary aspect, but instead had simply observed the irregularity in the association between ether body and astral body, then one would have used medicines which affect both these members of the human being. However, these would have remained ineffective in our case, since the damage, running through the generations, is too deep-seated to be offset within the members of the human organization themselves. In a case like this, one must work on the ego organization and here one must bring everything into effect which relates to the harmonizing and strengthening of the etheric and astral body. One can achieve this if one makes an impression on the ego organization with intensified sensory stimuli (sensory stimuli work on the ego organization). For the child this was attempted in the following way: a bandage was applied to the right hand with a 5% pyrite ointment and simultaneously an embrocation was done of the left half of the head with ointment of Amanita caesarea (golden agaric). Pyrite, a compound of iron and sulfur, externally applied, has the effect of stimulating the ego organization to bring the astral body more to life and to increase its affinity with the ether body. The golden agaric substance, with its particular content of organized nitrogen, acts in such a way that an effect coming from the head makes the ether body more lively through the ego organization and increases its affinity with the astral body. The healing process was supported by curative eurythmy,[25] which brings the ego organization as such into lively activity. Through this what is applied externally is guided into the depths of the organization. The healing process introduced in this way was then further intensified through preparations which should make the astral and ether body particularly

dago, Rückenabreibungen mit Auskochung von Stellaria media und innerlich Tee von Weidenrinde (besonders auf die Empfänglichkeit des Astralleibes wirkend) und Stannum 0.001 (besonders den Ätherleib empfänglich machend). Wir gaben auch noch Mohnsaft in schwacher Dosierung, um die geschädigte Eigenorganisation gegenüber den Heilwirkungen zurücktreten zu lassen.

Bei der Mutter wurde mehr die letzte Therapie angewendet, weil, als in einer Generation höherstehend, die Vererbungskräfte ja weniger gewirkt haben. Das Gleiche gilt für die Schwester der Mutter. – Wir konnten noch, als das Kind in der Klinik war, konstatieren, daß es sich leichter dirigieren ließ und zu einer besseren seelischen Verfassung kam. Es wurde z. B. gehorsamer; und die Bewegungen, die es sonst sehr ungeschickt machte, bewirkte es geschickter. Nachträglich wurde uns von der Tante berichtet, daß mit dem Kinde eine große Veränderung vorgegangen wäre. Es ist ruhiger geworden, das Übermaß unwillkürlicher Bewegungen hat abgenommen; es ist so geschickt geworden, daß es allein spielen kann; und in seelischer Beziehung ist der frühere Eigensinn verschwunden.

Fünfter Fall

Eine 26-jährige Patientin kam in unsere Klinik mit den schweren Folgen einer Grippe, die 1918 mit Lungenkatarrh verbunden durchgemacht worden ist, und die einer 1917 abgelaufenen Brustfellentzündung gefolgt war. Seit der Grippe konnte sich die Patientin nicht mehr so recht erholen. 1920 war sie sehr abgemagert schwach und hatte leichtes Fieber und Nachtschweiße. Bald nach der Grippe setzten Kreuzschmerzen ein, die sich bis ins Spätjahr 1920 fortwährend steigerten; und dann zeigte sich unter heftigen Schmerzen eine Verkrümmung im Kreuz. Auch trat eine Schwellung des rechten Zeigefingers ein. Eine Liegekur brachte angeblich Besserung der Rückenschmerzen. – Als Patientin bei uns ankam, hatte sie einen Senkungsabszeß am

sensitive to the working of the ego organization. For this were used, in rhythmic daily succession, baths with a decoction of Solidago, rubs down the back with a decoction of Stellaria media[26] and orally, willow bark tea (which particularly affects the receptivity of the astral body) and stannum 0.001[27] (which makes the ether body particularly receptive). We also gave poppy juice[28] in weak dosage to allow the patient's own damaged organization to recede in favor of the healing actions.

The latter treatment was employed more for the mother, since the forces of inheritance had of course worked less, being in the preceding generation. The same holds true for the sister of the mother.—While the child was still in the clinic, we were able to establish that she became more easily manageable and that she came into a better state of soul. She became, for example, more obedient, and movements which she had carried out very clumsily, were now accomplished with greater skill. Subsequently the aunt reported to us that a great change had taken place in the child. She had come to rest and the excessive involuntary movements had decreased. She is dexterous enough to be able to play by herself and the earlier stubbornness has disappeared.

Fifth Case[29]

A twenty-six-year-old woman came to our clinic suffering from serious consequences of a flu which she had had in 1918 connected with catarrh of the lungs. This had been preceded in 1917 by pleurisy. Since the influenza the patient has never really recovered. In 1920 she was very emaciated and weak, had a low-grade fever and night sweats. Soon after the flu, lower back pains began which continually worsened until late 1920. Then a curvature of the lumbar spine became apparent which was accompanied by much pain. At the same time there was a swelling of the right index finger. A period of bed rest

rechten Oberschenkel, aufgetriebenen Leib mit etwas Ascites und über den Lungenspitzen katarrhalische Geräusche, sowohl rechts als links. Verdauung und Appetit ist gut. Urin ist konzentriert, zeigt Spuren von Eiweiß. Die geisteswissenschaftliche Untersuchung ergab: Überempfindlichkeit des Astralleibes und der Ich-Organisation; eine solche Abnormität drückt sich zunächst im Ätherleibe dadurch aus, daß derselbe nicht die eigentlichen Ätherfunktionen, sondern einen ätherischen Abdruck der Astralfunktionen entwickelt. Die Astralfunktionen sind abbauende. Es mußten sich daher die Vitalität und der normale Prozeß in den physischen Organen verkümmert zeigen. Das ist immer verbunden mit gewissermaßen außermenschlichen Prozessen, die sich im menschlichen Organismus abspielen. Der Senkungsabszeß, die Rückenschmerzen, die Aufgetriebenheit des Leibes, die katarrhalischen Erscheinungen der Lungen und auch die mangelhafte Eiweißverarbeitung rühren davon her. – Es handelt sich bei der Therapie darum, die Empfindlichkeit des Astralleibes und der Ich-Organisation herabzusetzen. Man erreicht das dadurch, daß man Kieselsäure verabreicht, welche immer die Eigenkraft gegenüber der Empfindlichkeit verstärkt. Wir taten es in diesem Falle, indem wir pulverisierte Kieselsäure in die Speisen taten und als Klistiere gaben. Ebenso leiteten wir die Empfindlichkeit ab, indem wir auf den unteren Rücken Senfpflaster legten. Dessen Wirkung beruht darauf, daß es von sich aus die Empfindlichkeit bewirkt und sie dadurch dem Astralleib und der Ich-Organisation abnimmt. Durch einen Prozeß, der die Überempfindlichkeit des Astralleibes im Verdauungstrakt dämpft, erreichten wir ein Ableiten dieser astralischen Tätigkeit auf den Ätherleib, wo sie normalerweise sein soll. Wir bewirkten das durch geringe Dosen von Kupfer und Carbo animalis. Der Möglichkeit, daß sich der Ätherleib der ihm ungewohnten normalen Verdauungstätigkeit entzieht, begegneten wir, indem wir Pankreassaft gaben.

Der Senkungsabszeß wurde einigemale punktiert. Es entleerten sich durch Aspiration große Eitermengen. Der Abszeß ging

apparently ameliorated the back pains.—When the patient came to us, she had a psoas abscess which had gravitated down to the right thigh, her abdomen was distended with moderate ascites and over the apices of the lungs there were coarse rhonchi. Digestion and appetite is good. The urine is concentrated, with a trace of protein. Spiritual-scientific investigation showed hyper-sensitivity of the astral body and of the ego organization. In the ether body such an abnormality expresses itself, to begin with, by developing an etheric imprint of astral functions instead of true ether functions. Astral functions are catabolic. Therefore, both the vitality as well as the normal process of the physical organs had to appear as withered. This is always connected with processes taking place in the human organism which are in a sense extra-human. From this stem the dependent abscess, the back pains, the distension of the body, the pulmonary catarrhal symptoms, and also the inadequate assimilation of protein.—For therapy it will be a matter of diminishing the sensitivity of the astral body and of the ego organization. One achieves this by administering silicic acid, which always strengthens the inherent forces over and against the sensitivity. In this case we gave powdered silicic acid in the food and in the form of enemas. We also diverted the sensitivity by putting mustard plasters on the lower back. Its effect is based on the fact that it induces sensitivity itself and thereby relieves the astral body and ego organization of it. With a process which dampens down the oversensitivity of the astral body in the digestive tract, we were able to divert this astral activity to the ether body, where it normally belongs. We did this with small doses of copper[30] and *Carbo animalis*. By administering an extract of pancreas, we addressed the possibility that the ether body might withdraw from the normal digestive activity to which it is unaccustomed.[31]

The abscess was tapped several times, yielding large quantities of pus. The abscess became smaller and the

zurück und die Bauchschwellung nahm ab, indem die Eiterbildung stetig nachließ und zuletzt verschwand. Während der Eiter noch floß, wurden wir eines Tages überrascht durch einen erneuten Fieberanstieg. Derselbe erschien uns nicht unerklärlich, da bei der oben geschilderten Konstitution des Astralleibes geringe psychische Aufregungen solches Fieber bewirken können. Man muß aber unterscheiden zwischen der Erklärlichkeit des Fiebers in solchen Fällen und seiner stark schädigenden Wirkung. Denn es ist unter den angegebenen Voraussetzungen solches Fieber geradezu der Vermittler für ein tiefgehendes Eingreifen der Abbauprozesse in den Organismus. Und man muß sogleich für eine Stärkung des Ätherleibes sorgen, damit diese die schädigende Wirkung des Astralleibes paralysiert. Wir wandten hochpotenzierte Silberinjektionen an und erreichten Rückgang des Fiebers. – Patientin hat die Klinik mit 20 Pfund Gewichtszunahme und in gestärktem Zustande verlassen. Wir geben uns keiner Täuschung darüber hin, daß in diesem Falle noch eine Nachkur die Heilung befestigen muß.

Zwischenbemerkung

Durch die bisher behandelten Fälle wollten wir die Prinzipien charakterisieren, nach denen wir aus der Diagnose die Heilmittel suchen. Um die Sache anschaulich zu machen, nahmen wir Fälle, in denen sehr individuell vorgegangen werden mußte. Doch sind von uns auch typische Heilmittel hergestellt worden, die für typische Krankheiten angewendet werden können. Wir wollen nun einige Fälle behandeln, in denen wir solche typischen Mittel anwendeten.

Sechster Fall. Heufieberbehandlung

Wir hatten einen Patienten mit schweren Heufiebererscheinungen. Derselbe litt schon seit Kindheit darunter. Er kam in unsere Behandlung im 40. Lebensjahr. Für diesen Krankheitszustand haben wir unser «*Gencydo*»-Präparat. Dasselbe wurde bei dem Patienten in der Zeit angewendet, in der – es war im Mai – die

abdominal distension decreased during the time that the pus forma-tion steadily subsided and finally disappeared. During the time that the pus was still flowing we were surprised one day by a new rise in temperature. It seemed to us that this could be explained from the constitution of the astral body as sketched above, since in such a situation slight psychological upsets could cause such a fever. However, one must differentiate between the fact that fever can be explained in such cases and the strongly harmful effect it has. Such a fever is the mediator of a far-reaching interference of the catabolic processes in the organism under the indicated preconditions. And one must at once provide for a strengthening of the ether body, so that this lames the harmful effect of the astral body. We gave high potency silver[32] injections and were able to reduce the fever.—The patient left the clinic with a twenty-pound weight gain and in a stronger condition. We are well aware of the need for further treatment in this case to consolidate the healing.

Interim remark

With the cases presented so far we wanted to characterize the principles according to which we search for the medications right out of the diagnosis. For the sake of clarity we selected cases in which it was necessary to proceed very individually. Yet we have prepared typical medications, too, which can be applied in typical diseases. We will now present a few cases where such typical medications were used.

Sixth Case—Hay Fever Treatment

We had a male patient with severe hay fever symptoms. He had suffered with it from childhood. He came for treatment to us in his fortieth year. For this disease we have our "Gencydo" preparation. This was used for the patient at the

Krankheit am heftigsten auftrat. Wir behandelten den Patienten mit Injektionen und lokal durch Pinselung mit der «*Gencydo*»-Flüssigkeit in der Nase. Nachdem eine deutliche Besserung zu einer Zeit eingetreten war, in der der Patient in früheren Jahren von den Heufiebererscheinungen noch schwer geplagt wurde, machte derselbe eine Reise und konnte uns von derselben berichten, daß er sich unvergleichlich wohler als in früheren Jahren befand. Im nächsten Jahre war er zur Heufieberzeit wieder auf einer Reise von Amerika nach Europa und hatte nur einen viel leichteren Anfall als früher. Die Wiederholung der Behandlung ergab für dieses Jahr einen durchaus erträglichen Zustand. Um die Heilung gründlich zu machen, wurde die Behandlung auch im nächsten Jahre vorgenommen, trotzdem ein eigentlicher Anfall nicht vorhanden war. Für ein weiteres Jahr schilderte Patient wörtlich seinen Zustand folgendermaßen: "Im Frühling 1923 begann ich die Behandlung wieder, weil ich neue Attacken erwartete. Ich fand, daß meine Nasenschleimhaut weit weniger empfindlich als früher war. Ich mußte mich arbeitend aufhalten inmitten von Grasblüten und Pollen-erzeugenden Bäumen. Auch ritt ich den ganzen Sommer hindurch über heiße und staubige Straßen. Aber mit Ausnahme eines einzigen Tages traten keinerlei Symptome von Heufieber den ganzen Sommer auf; ja, ich habe allen Grund, zu glauben, daß der einzige Tag mir nur eine Erkältung brachte und keinen Heuschnupfenanfall. Seit 35 Jahren war dies das erste Jahr, daß ich ungehindert mich aufhalten und arbeiten konnte in einer Umgebung, in der ich in früheren Jahren eine wahre Hölle erlebte."

Siebenter Fall. Sklerosebehandlung

Eine 61-jährige Patientin erscheint in unserer Klinik mit Sklerose und Albuminurie. Der augenblickliche Zustand ist ausgelöst durch eine Influenza mit leichtem Fieber und Magen- und Darmstörungen. Seit dem Influenzaanfall fühlt sich Patientin nicht mehr wohl. Sie klagt über Schwere des Atmens beim Aufwachen,

time when the disease was at its worst—it was the month of May. We treated the patient by injection as well as locally by swabbing the inside of the nose with "Gencydo" liquid. After a marked improvement had set in at a time of the year when, in previous years, the patient had still been bothered a lot by the hay fever, he undertook a journey and could report from it that he felt incomparably better than in earlier years. The year after he was travelling again from America to Europe during hay fever season, and still had a much milder attack than in the past. Repetition of the treatment produced an entirely tolerable condition in this year. For a total cure, treatment was also undertaken the following year, even though there was no actual attack. A year later the patient described his condition as follows: "In the spring of 1923, I began the treatment again, since I was expecting new attacks. I found my nasal mucous membranes far less sensitive than in the past. I had to spend time working among flowering grasses and pollen-producing trees. Also, all through the summer, I had to ride along hot and dusty roads. But with the exception of one single day, no symptoms of hay fever appeared at all the whole summer; actually I have every reason to believe that on the single day I only had a cold and not an attack of hay fever. This was the first time in thirty-five years that I could spend time and work unhindered in an environment where in former years I experienced real hell."

Seventh Case—Treatment of Sclerosis

A sixty-one-year-old woman appears in our clinic with sclerosis and albuminuria. The momentary condition was triggered by a flu with a slight fever and stomach and intestinal disturbances. The patient had not felt well again since the flu. She complains of difficulty breathing on

Schwindelanfälle, ein Gefühl von Klopfen in Kopf, Ohren und Händen, das sich besonders beim Aufwachen lästig bemerkbar macht, aber auch beim Gehen und Steigen sich einstellt. Der Schlaf ist gut. Es ist Neigung zur Obstipation vorhanden. Im Urin Eiweiß. Blutdruck 185 mm Quecksilber. Wir gingen zunächst von der Sklerose aus, die an der Übertätigkeit des Astralleibes bemerkbar ist. Der physische Leib und der Ätherleib sind nicht imstande, die volle Tätigkeit des Astralleibes aufzunehmen. Es bleibt in einem solchen Falle eine Übertätigkeit des Astralleibes übrig, die vom physischen und Ätherleibe nicht resorbiert wird. Eine normale feste Haltung der menschlichen Organisation ist nur möglich, wenn diese Resorption eine vollständige ist. Sonst macht sich der nicht resorbierte Teil, wie es hier der Fall ist, durch Schwindel und namentlich durch subjektive Sinnesillusionen, wie Klopfen usw. geltend. Auch ergreift dieser nicht resorbierte Teil die aufgenommenen Substanzen und drängt ihnen Prozesse auf, bevor sie in den normalen Stoffwechsel eingedrungen sind. Das kommt zum Vorschein in der Neigung zur Obstipation und im Eiweißabgang; ebenso in den Magen- und Darmstörungen. Der Blutdruck wird in einem solchen Falle erhöht, weil die Übertätigkeit des Astralleibes auch die Ichtätigkeit erhöht und diese sich im erhöhten Blutdruck offenbart. – Wir behandelten den Fall in der Hauptsache mit unserem «Scleron»; wir fügten nur zur Unterstützung Belladonna in sehr geringer Dosis hinzu, um den Schwindelanfällen auch augenblicklich zu begegnen. Wir gebrauchten Holundertee, um der Verdauung förderlich zu sein, regulierten den Stuhl durch Klistiere und Abführtee und verordneten eine salzlose Diät, weil Salze der Sklerose unterstützend beispringen. Wir erreichten eine verhältnismäßig rasche Besserung. Die Schwindelanfälle gingen zurück, sowie auch das Klopfen. Der Blutdruck ging auf 112 zurück. Das subjektive Befinden besserte sich zusehends. Die Sklerose machte in dem darauffolgenden Jahre keine Fortschritte. Nach einem Jahre kam die Patientin wieder mit einem geringeren Grade der Symptome. Durch

awakening, attacks of dizziness, a pounding sensation in the head, ears and hands, which is particularly troublesome on awakening, but which also happens when she walks and is going uphill. Her sleep is good. There exists a tendency to constipation. There is protein in the urine. Her blood pressure is 185 mm Hg. We began our considerations with the sclerosis, which becomes noticeable from the overactivity of the astral body. The physical body and the ether body are unable to take up the full activity of the astral body. In such a case an excess of activity of the astral body remains that is not resorbed by the physical and ether body. A normal stability of the human organization is only possible when this resorption is complete. Otherwise, the nonresorbed part will make itself felt in dizziness and in particular in subjective sensory illusions, like pounding etc., as in this case. The nonresorbed part also takes hold of the substances that are consumed and forces certain processes upon them before they have entered into the normal metabolism. This becomes apparent in the tendency to constipation and in proteinuria, also in stomach and intestinal disorders. The blood pressure is elevated in such a case since the overactivity of the astral body also heightens the ego activity and this reveals itself in the raised blood pressure.— We treated the patient mainly with our "Scleron;" we supplemented this with very small doses of belladonna, only as a support, to counter also the attacks of dizziness in the moment. We used elder flower tea to help the digestion, regulated the bowels with enemas and laxative tea and ordered a salt free diet, because salts tend to enhance the sclerosis. We achieved a comparatively quick improvement. The attacks of dizziness decreased, likewise the pounding. The blood pressure came down to 112 mm Hg. The subjective feeling improved noticeably. The sclerosis did not progress further in the subsequent year. After a year the patient came again with the same symptoms to a lesser degree. Through a similar treatment, a

eine ähnliche Behandlung trat eine weitere Besserung ein; und an der Patientin ist deutlich bemerkbar, nachdem längere Zeit seit der Behandlung verflossen ist, daß die Sklerose keine weitere Degeneration des Organismus hervorruft. Die für die Sklerose charakteristischen äußern Symptome sind in der Rückbildung begriffen and das schnelle Altern, von dem die Patientin vorher ergriffen war, ist nicht mehr vorhanden.

Achter Fall. Eine Struma-Behandlung

Die Patientin kam im 34. Lebensjahre zu uns. Sie stellt den Typus eines Menschen dar, der in seiner seelischen Gesamtverfassung stark von einer gewissen Schwere und inneren Brüchigkeit des physischen Leibes beeinflußt wird. Es scheint, daß jedes Wort, das sie spricht, eine Anstrengung kostet. Ausserordentlich charakteristisch ist die Konkavität der Gesamtform des Gesichtes; die Nasenwurzel ist wie etwas, was im Organismus zurückgehalten wird. Die Patientin gibt an, daß sie seit Schulzeit schon zart und kränklich war. Von eigentlichen Krankheiten hat sie nur leichte Masern durchgemacht. Sie hat immer blasses Aussehen, viel Müdigkeit and schlechten Appetit gehabt. Sie wurde von Arzt zu Arzt geschickt, wobei nacheinander folgende Diagnosen festgestellt wurden: Lungenspitzenkatarrh, Magenkatarrh, Blutarmut. In ihrem eigenen Bewußtsein hatte die Patientin, dass sie weniger körperlich krank sei, dafür aber mehr seelisch.

Wir wollen nun nach diesem Teil der Anamnese den geisteswissenschaftlichen Teil anführen, um nachher an demselben alles weitere zu prüfen.

Bei der Patientin zeigte sich eine hochgradige Atonie des Astralleibes. Dadurch ist die Ich-Organisation vom physischen and Ätherleib zurückgestaut. Das ganze Bewußtseinsleben ist wie von einer leisen dumpfen Schläfrigkeit durchzogen. Der physische Leib ist den Prozessen ausgesetzt, die von den eingeführten Stoffen herrühren. Dadurch werden diese Stoffe in Teile der menschlichen Organisation umgewandelt. Der Ätherleib wird vom Ich

further improvement set in, and it is clearly noticeable in the patient after a considerable lapse of time since the treatment that the sclerosis causes no further degeneration of the organism. The external symptoms characteristic of sclerosis are being reversed, and the rapid aging of the patient prior to treatment is no longer present.

Eighth Case—A Treatment of Goiter

A female patient came to us in the thirty-fourth year of her life. She represents the type of person who is strongly influenced in her whole frame of mind by a certain heaviness and inner brittleness of the physical body. Every word she speaks seems to take an effort. The concavity in the whole shape of her face is exceptionally characteristic; the root of the nose is as if held back within the organism. The patient indicates that she has been delicate and sickly already since her school time. As far as actual diseases she only had a mild case of the measles. She always had a pale complexion, a lot of fatigue and a poor appetite. She was sent from one doctor to another, and in the process the following were diagnosed successively: catarrh of the lung apices, gastritis, anemia. In her own mind the patient felt that she was not so much physically ill, but rather psychologically ill.

After this part of the history, we now want to indicate the spiritual-scientific finding, in order to check against it all that follows.

A highly atonic state of the astral body is apparent in the patient. Through this the ego organization is held back from the physical and ether body. The whole life of consciousness is as if permeated by a subtle, dull drowsiness. The physical body is exposed to the processes that originate from the substances that are taken in. Therefore these substances

und astralischen Leib in seiner kohärenten Vitalität zu stark herabgedämpft, wodurch die inneren Empfindungen, nämlich das allgemeine Lebensgefühl und das Gefühl der Körperstatik viel zu lebhaft, die Regsamkeit der äußeren Sinne viel zu dumpf werden. Es müssen daher alle körperlichen Funktionen einen Weg nehmen, wodurch sie in Disharmonie zueinander stehen. Es ist nicht anders möglich, als daß bei der Patientin das Gefühl auftritt, sie könne die Funktionen ihres Körpers vom Ich aus nicht zusammenhalten. Das erscheint ihr wie eine seelische Ohnmacht. Deshalb sagt sie, sie sei mehr seelisch als körperlich krank. Steigert sich die Ohnmacht des Ich und astralischen Leibes, so müssen in den verschiedenen Körperteilen Krankheitszustände auftreten, worauf auch die verschiedenen Diagnosen hinweisen. Die Ohnmacht des Ich drückt sich in Unregelmäßigkeiten solcher Drüsen as wie die Schilddrüse, Nebennieren; ferner in Unregelmäßigkeiten des Magen- und Darmsystems. All dies ist bei der Patientin zu erwarten and tatsächlich zu konstatieren. Ihre Struma und die Verfassung des Magen- und Darmsystems entsprechen ganz dem geisteswissenschaftlichen Befund. Sehr charakteristisch ist das Folgende. Durch die Ohnmacht des Ich und des astralischen Leibes wird ein Teil des Schlafbedürfnisses schon während des Wachens absolviert und es ist daher der Schlaf viel weniger tief als beim normalen Menschen. Das erscheint der Patientin als hartnäckige Schlaflosigkeit. Damit hängt es zusammen, daß sie das Gefühl hat, leicht einzuschlafen und leicht aufzuwachen. Ebenso hängt es zusammen, daß sie viele Träume zu haben glaubt, die aber nicht eigentliche Träume sind, sondern Mischungen von Träumen und Wacheindrücken. Sie bleiben deshalb nicht in der Erinnerung und sind nicht stark erregend, weil die Reizstärke herabgestimmt ist. Die Ohnmacht des Ich äußert sich in den innern Organen zuerst in den Lungen. Lungenspitzenkatarrhe sind eigentlich immer der Ausdruck der schwachen Ich-Organisation. Der durch das Ich nicht vollzogene Stoffwechsel offenbart sich in Rheumatismus. Subjektiv kommt das Ganze zum

become transformed into parts of the human organization. The ether body's coherent vitality is excessively dampened down by the I and astral body. Therefore inner sensations, namely the general sense of well-being and proprioception become far too vivid, and the liveliness of the external senses becomes too dull. All body functions thus have to take a course through which they come into disharmony with one another. Inevitably the feeling arises in the patient that she cannot hold the functions of her body together with her I. This appears to her as an impotence of the soul. Therefore she says she is more psychologically than physically ill. As the impotence of the I and astral body increases, disease conditions must appear in various parts of the body, as also the various diagnoses indicate. Impotence of the I expresses itself in irregularities of glands like the thyroid and the adrenals, and also in irregularities of the gastro-intestinal system. All this is to be expected in the patient and can in fact be found. Her goiter and the disposition of the gastrointestinal system correspond entirely with the spiritual-scientific findings. Most characteristic is the following: Due to the impotence of the I and the astral body the need for sleep is partly absolved during waking and therefore the sleep is much less deep than in a normal person. This appears to the patient as refractory insomnia. With this is associated the feeling that she falls asleep easily and wakes up easily. Also associated with this is her belief that she has many dreams, which are, however, not true dreams but mixtures of dreams and impressions while awake. Because the strength of the stimulus is toned down they do not stay in the memory and are not very stimulating. In the inner organs the impotence of the I expresses itself first in the lungs. Catarrhs of the apices of the lungs are in reality always a manifestation of a weak ego organization. The metabolism that does not happen through the I reveals itself in rheumatism. The whole comes to expression subjectively in general fatigue. Menstruation began at the age

Ausdruck in der allgemeinen Müdigkeit. Die Menses traten mit 14 Jahren ein; die schwache Ich-Organisation liefert keine genügende Kraftentfaltung, um den in Fluß gekommenen Menstrualprozeß wieder zurückzuschrauben. Die Arbeit des Ich bei diesem Zurückschrauben kommt als Empfindung durch jene Nerven zum Bewußtsein, die in der Kreuzbeingegend in das Rückenmark münden. Nerven, durch die nicht genügend die Ströme der Ich-Organisation und des Astralleibes gehen, schmerzen. Patientin klagt über Kreuzschmerzen bei der Periode. Das alles führt auf folgende Art zur Therapie. Wir haben gefunden, daß Colchicum autumnale einen starken Reiz auf den Astralleib ausübt und zwar auf denjenigen Teil, welcher der Hals- und Kopforganisation entspricht. Colchicum autumnale wird daher von uns bei allen denjenigen Krankheiten gegeben, die in der Struma ihr wichtigstes Symptom haben. Wir gaben daher Patientin dreimal täglich 5 Tropfen unseres Colchicumpräparates, wodurch die Strumageschwulst zurückgegangen ist und die Patientin sich erleichtert fühlte. Hat man auf diese Weise den Astralleib gestärkt, so vermittelt er auch eine bessere Funktion des Ich-Organismus, wodurch die Mittel, die auf Verdauungs und Fortpflanzungsorgane wirken können, im Organismus ihre Kraft erhalten. Wir haben als solches Mittel angewendet Wermutklistiere, die wir mit Öl versetzten, weil Öl im Verdauungstrakt exzitierend wirkt. Wir haben mit diesem Mittel eine bedeutende Besserung erzielt. Wir glauben, daß diese Therapie ihre besonders günstigen Einwirkungen um das 35. Lebensjahr des Menschen entfalten kann, weil zu dieser Zeit die Ich-Organisation eine starke Affinität zu dem übrigen Organismus hat und auch dann, wenn sie schwach ist, leicht angeregt werden kann. Patientin war, als sie zu uns kam, 34 Jahre alt.

of fourteen; the weak ego organization cannot furnish sufficiently activated forces to scale down the menstrual process again once it has gotten underway. The labor of the I in this scaling down comes to consciousness as a sensation by means of those nerves that reach the spinal cord in the region of the sacrum. Nerves through which the currents of the ego organization and the astral body do not go sufficiently are painful. The patient complains of lower back pain during menstruation. All this leads in the following way to the treatment. We have found that *Colchicum autumnale* exerts a powerful stimulus on the astral body, namely on that part that corresponds to the organization of neck and head. Thus we give *Colchicum autumnale* for all those diseases which have their most important symptom in goiter. We gave the patient three times daily five drops of our colchicum preparation, by which the goiter swelling diminished and the patient felt relieved. When one has thus strengthened the astral body, then it also mediates a better functioning of the ego-organism, so that preparations which can work on the organs of digestion and reproduction keep their strength in the organism. As such a preparation we have used wormwood enemas, which we have mixed with oil, since oil stimulates the digestive tract. With this preparation we obtained a significant improvement. We believe that this treatment can develop its particularly favorable effect at about the thirty-fifth year of life of the human being, since at this age the ego organization has a strong affinity with the rest of the organism and can easily be stimulated, even when it is weak. The patient was thirty-four years old when she came to us.

Neunter Fall
Migräne-artige Zustände im Klimakterium

Die Patientin kam mit 55 Jahren zu uns. Sie gibt an, ein zartes und schwächliches Kind gewesen zu sein; in der Kindheit Masern, Scharlach, Windpocken, Keuchhusten und Mumps gehabt zu haben. Die Menses traten mit 14 – 15 Jahren auf. Die Blutungen waren von Anfang an sehr stark und schmerzhaft. Im 40. Lebensjahre wurde eine Totalexstirpation wegen einer Geschwulst im Unterleibe vollzogen. Die Patientin gibt ferner an, daß sie alle drei bis vier Wochen seit dem 35. Jahre einen dreitägigen migräneartigen Kopfschmerz gehabt, der sich im 46. Jahre zu einer drei Tage dauernden, mit Bewußtlosigkeit verbundenen Kopfkrankheit verstärkte. – Der gegenwärtige geisteswissenschaftliche Befund ist: allgemeine Schwäche der Ich-Organisation, die sich darin äußert, daß die Tätigkeit des Ätherleibes nicht genügend von der Ich-Organisation abgelähmt wird. Dadurch entsteht eine Ausbreitung der vegetativen organischen Tätigkeiten über das Kopf- und Nerven-Sinnes-System, die in einer solchen Stärke bei normaler Ich-Organisation nicht vorhanden ist. Mit diesem Befund stimmen gewisse Symptome zusammen. Ein erstes ist ein häufiger Urindrang. Derselbe rührt davon her, daß dem normal entwickelten Astralleib, welcher die Nierenabsonderung regelt, keine sie normal zurückhaltende, genügend starke Ich-Organisation gegenübersteht. Ein zweites Symptom ist das späte Einschlafen und das müde Aufwachen. Der Astralleib geht schwer aus dem physischen und Ätherleib heraus, weil das Ich ihn nicht genügend stark herauszieht. Ist das Aufwachen erfolgt, so wird die vitale Tätigkeit, die aus dem Schlafe nachwirkt, wegen des schwachen Ichs als Ermüdung empfunden. Ein drittes Symptom sind die wenigen Träume. Die Ich-Organisation prägt dem Astralleibe nur schwache Bilder ein, die sich nicht in lebhaften Träumen äußern können.

Diese Erkenntnisse führen uns zur folgenden Therapie: wir mußten der Ich-Organisation den Weg zum physischen und Äth-

Ninth Case—Migrainous Conditions in Menopause

This patient came to us at the age of fifty-five. She states, that she had been a weak and delicate child; in childhood she had measles, scarlet fever, chicken pox, whooping cough and mumps. Menstruation started at age fourteen to fifteen. Bleeding was very strong and painful from the outset. Due to a tumor in the lower abdomen a total hysterectomy was done in the fortieth year. The patient also states that since the age of thirty-five she has suffered from a migrainous headache every three to four weeks lasting three days, which in her forty-sixth year intensified to a three-day-long cerebral syndrome combined with unconsciousness.—The present spiritual-scientific finding is: generalized weakness of the ego organization, which is expressed in the ether body's activity not being sufficiently suppressed by the ego organization. Therefore the vegetative organic activities start to spread out to the head and nerve-sense system to a degree that is not present when the ego organization is normal. Certain symptoms are congruous with this finding. The first is urinary frequency. This stems from the fact that the normally developed astral body, which regulates the secretion of the kidneys, is not confronted by an ego organization with sufficient strength, which would normally restrain it. A second symptom is falling asleep late and being tired on waking up. The astral body leaves the physical and ether body with difficulty, since the I does not draw it out strongly enough. When waking has occurred, then the vital activity, which is an aftereffect of sleep, is perceived as tiredness on account of the weakness of the I. A third symptom is having few dreams. The ego organization impresses nothing on the astral body but weak images, which cannot express themselves in vivid dreams.

These insights lead us to the following treatment: we had to pave the way for the ego organization to the physical and

erleibe bahnen. Wir taten es durch 2% Kleesalzkompressen auf die Stirn des Abends und Umschläge mit 7% Urtica dioica-Lösung des Morgens am Unterleib, mit 20% Lindenblütenlösung des Mittags an den Füßen. Dadurch soll erreicht werden, daß während der Nacht die vitale Tätigkeit abgeschwächt werde; das Kleesalz, das im Organismus die Funktion der Unterdrückung einer zu großen vitalen Tätigkeit ausübt, bewirkte dieses. Morgens mußten wir dafür sorgen, daß die Ich-Organisation den Weg in den physischen Leib findet. Dies geschieht durch eine Anregung der Blutzirkulation. Die Eisenwirkung der Brennessel ist zu diesem Zwecke angewendet worden. Es blieb also noch übrig, im Laufe des Tages die Durchdringung des physischen Körpers mit der Ich-Organisation zu fördern. Das geschah durch die ableitende Zugwirkung der Lindenblüte am Mittag. Nun traten bei der Patientin die geschilderten Kopfschmerzen mit ihrer Steigerung im 46. Lebensjahr auf. Diese Kopfschmerzen mußten wir in Zusammenhang bringen mit der durch die Exstirpation ausfallenden Periode und die Steigerung mit Bewußtlosigkeit für ein Kompensationssymptom des Klimakteriums. Wir versuchten zunächst Besserung zu erzielen mit Antimon. Dasselbe hätte die Besserung erzeugen müssen, wenn der allgemeine, unter der Regulierung der Ich-Organisation stehende Stoffwechsel in Betracht gekommen wäre. Die Besserung wurde dadurch nicht erzielt. Es war dadurch der Beweis erbracht, daß der relativ selbständige Teil der Ich-Organisation, der vorzüglich die Fortpflanzungsorgane reguliert, in Betracht kommt. Dafür sehen wir in der Wurzel der Potentilla-Tormentilla bei sehr starker Verdünnung ein Spezifikum, und in der Tat, dies wirkte.

ether body. We did this with 2% sorrel salt compresses on the forehead in the evening, wraps in the morning with a 7% solution of *Urtica dioica* on the lower abdomen, and at midday with a 20% solution of linden blossoms on the feet. The goal of this treatment was to weaken the vital activity during the night; this was accomplished by the sorrel salt, which has the function of suppressing excessive vital activity in the organism. In the morning we had to provide for the ego organization to find its way into the physical body. This can be done by stimulating the blood circulation. The iron effect of the stinging nettle was made use of for this purpose. What was left to do was to promote the permeation of the physical body by the ego organization in the course of the day. This was done with the help of the diverting drawing effect of linden blossoms at midday. Now, the portrayed headaches in the patient were intensified in the forty-sixth year of life. We had to associate these headaches with losing the period after the hysterectomy and their intensification with unconsciousness as a compensatory symptom of menopause. We tried at first to realize a change for the better with antimony. This should have brought recovery if the general metabolism, subject to regulation by the ego organization, had been under consideration. The change for the better was not realized. This was proof of the fact that the relatively independent part of the ego organization, that primarily regulates the organs of reproduction is the focus of concern. For that, we consider the root of *Potentilla tormentilla* in a very high dilution as a specific medication, and indeed this was effective.

XX
TYPISCHE HEILMITTEL

Vorbemerkung

Es sollen jetzt einige der von uns zum Teil in den Handel gebrachten, typischen Mittel nach ihrem Heilwerte beschrieben werden. Dieselben sind auch den typischen Krankheitsformen angepaßt, und wenn Typisches im Krankheitszustande in Betracht kommt, so stellt unser Heilmittel dasjenige dar, was im Sinne der Schilderung unseres Buches zur Therapie führen muß. Von diesem Gesichtspunkte aus sollen einige unserer Heilmittel beschrieben werden.

1. Das Mittel «Scleron»

Dasselbe besteht aus metallischem Blei, Honig und Zucker. Das Blei wirkt auf den Organismus so, daß es die Abbauwirkung der Ich-Organisation fördert. Bringt man es also in den Organismus, der eine zu geringe Abbauwirkung der Ich-Organisation hat, so tritt diese Förderung ein, wenn die Dosierung in der genügenden Stärke vorgenommen wird. Wird die Dosierung zu stark vorgenommen, so tritt Hypertrophie der Ich-Organisation ein. Der Körper baut mehr ab, als er aufbaut und muß verfallen. Bei der Sklerose wird die Ich-Organisation zu schwach; sie baut selber nicht genügend ab. Deshalb tritt Abbau allein durch den Astralleib ein. Es fallen die Abbauprodukte aus dem Organismus heraus und liefern Verstärkungen derjenigen Organe, die in Salzsubstanzen bestehen. Blei in gehöriger Dosierung nimmt den Abbau wieder in die Ich-Organisation zurück. Die Abbauprodukte bleiben nicht als Verhärtungen im Körper, sondern werden ausgestoßen. Alle Heilung der Sklerose kann nur darin bestehen, daß man den salzbildenden Prozessen, die sonst im Körper bleiben, den Weg nach außen öffnet. Durch das Blei hat man die *Richtung* der Prozesse der Ich-Organisation bestimmt. Es bedarf des weiteren, daß diese Prozesse in ihrem Verlaufe gewissermaßen flüchtig gehalten werden. Das geschieht durch die Beimengung von Honig. Honig setzt die Ich-Organisation in den

CHAPTER XX

Typical Medications

Introductory remarks

A few of the typical preparations, a number of which were brought on the market by us, shall now be described as to their therapeutic value. These are indeed adapted to typical forms of disease, and when something typical is considered in a state of disease, then our medication represents what needs must bring the cure in the sense explained in this book. From this point of view a few of our medications will be described.

1. The preparation "Scleron"

This consists of metallic lead, honey and sugar. Lead works on the organism by promoting the catabolic function of the ego organization. When lead is introduced into an organism which has insufficient catabolic function of the ego organization, then this is promoted if the dosage that is taken has sufficient strength. If the dosage is too strong, then hypertrophy of the ego organization sets in. The body breaks down more than it can build up and must disintegrate. In sclerosis the ego organization becomes too weak; it does not sufficiently catabolize. Therefore catabolism is only supported by the astral body. The breakdown products fall out of the organism and provide reinforcement to those organs that consist of salt substances. In the right dosage lead draws the catabolic process back into the ego organization again. The products of catabolism do not remain in the body as hardened areas, but are discharged. Any healing of sclerosis can only consist in opening the way out of the organism for salt-forming processes, which otherwise would remain in the body. Through lead the *direction* of the processes of the ego organization is determined. Furthermore, to a certain extent

Stand, die nötige Herrschaft über den Astralleib auszuüben. Er nimmt daher dem Astralleib seine in der Sklerose relative Selbständigkeit. Zucker wirkt direkt auf die Ich-Organisation. Er verstärkt dieselbe in sich. Unser Heilmittel bewirkt also das Folgende: Blei wirkt wie die Ich-Organisation, nicht wie der Astralleib, abbauend. Der Honig überträgt die abbauende Wirkung des Astralleibes auf die Ich-Organisation und der Zucker versetzt die Ich-Organisation in die Lage, ihre spezifische Aufgabe zu erfüllen. – Man kann bemerken, daß die Anfangszustände der Sklerose sich darin äußern, daß die Schlagkraft des Denkens und die exakte Herrschaft über das Gedächtnis aufhören. Wendet man unser Heilmittel schon in diesem Stadium dieser Krankheit an, so wird man die reiferen Zustände der Sklerose vermeiden können. Doch erweist es sich auch wirksam in diesen späteren Zuständen. (Die Anwendung geben wir in Aufschrift dem Präparate bei.

2. Das Migräne-Mittel «Biodoron»

Die Kopforganisation ist so beschaffen, daß der nach innen gelegene, Gräulich-weißliche Gehirnteil das physisch am weitesten vorgeschrittene Glied der menschlichen Organisation ist. Er enthält eine die übrigen Sinne zusammenfassende Sinnestätigkeit, in die das Ich und der Astralleib hineinwirken. Er nimmt Anteil an dem rhythmischen System des Organismus, in das der Astralleib und der Ätherleib hineinwirken, und er nimmt auch Anteil, aber in sehr geringem Maße, an dem Stoffwechsel-Gliedmaßensystem, in welches der physische und Ätherleib hineinwirken. Dieser Gehirnteil unterscheidet sich von dem ihn umschließenden peripherischen Gehirn, das in seiner physischen Organisation viel mehr vom Stoffwechsel-Gliedmaßensystem, etwas mehr vom rhythmischen System, aber am wenigsten vom Nerven-Sinnessystem enthält. Wird nun durch eine zurückgestoßene Tätigkeit der Ich-Organisation das zentrale Gehirn ärmer an Nerven-Sinnestätigkeit und reicher an Verdauungstätigkeit, d. h. wird es ähnlicher dem peripherischen Gehirn, als es im normalen Zustande ist, so entsteht

these processes need to remain transitory in their course. This happens by mixing in honey. Honey enables the ego organization to exert the necessary control over the astral body. Therefore it takes away the astral body's relative autonomy in sclerosis. Sugar works directly on the ego organization. It strengthens this in itself. Our medication thus brings about the following: lead works in catabolism like the ego organization, not like the astral body. Honey transfers the catabolic function from the astral body to the ego organization and sugar puts the ego organization in a position to fulfil its specific task.—One may have noticed that the initial stages of sclerosis express themselves in a loss of the efficiency of thinking and the exact control over the memory. If our medication is applied in this stage of the disease, then advanced stages of sclerosis may be prevented. It proves effective, however, in these later stages, too. (The indications are included with the preparation on the package insert.)

2. The preparation for Migraine. "Bidor"

The head organization has the property that the grayish-whitish portion of the brain, which lies more internally, is physically the most highly advanced part of the human organization. It embodies a sensory activity which combines all other senses, and into which the I and the astral body work. It participates in the rhythmic system of the organism, into which the astral body and the ether body work, and it also participates, though to a very small extent, in the metabolic-limb system, into which the physical and ether body work. This part of the brain differentiates itself from the peripheral brain, which encloses it. The peripheral brain embodies much more the metabolic-limb system in its physical organization, somewhat more the rhythmic system, but least of all the nerve-sense system. If now the central brain becomes poorer in nerve-sense activity and richer in metabolic activity because the activity of the ego

die Migräne. Ihre Heilung wird daher abhängen: 1. von einer Anregung der Nerven-Sinnestätigkeit; 2. von einer Transformation der rhythmischen Tätigkeit aus einer solchen, die dem Stoffwechsel zugeneigt ist, in eine solche, die der Atmung zugeneigt ist; 3. in einer Eindämmung der rein vitalen Stoffwechseltätigkeit, die der Regulierung durch die Ich-Organisation entbehrt. Das Erste wird erreicht durch Kieselsäure. Silicium in Verbindung mit Sauerstoff enthält diejenigen Prozesse, die gleich sind denen im Organismus beim Übergange der Atmung in die Nerven-Sinnestätigkeit. Das Zweite wird erreicht durch *Schwefel*. Er enthält denjenigen Prozeß, durch den der dem Verdauungssystem zugeneigte Rhythmus verwandelt wird in den, der der Atmung zugeneigt ist. Und das Dritte wird erreicht durch *Eisen,* welches unmittelbar nach dem Verdauungsprozeß den Stoffwechsel hinüberleitet in den des Blutrhythmus, wodurch der Stoffwechselprozeß selbst unterdrückt wird. *Eisen, Schwefel* und *Kieselsäure* in entsprechender Weise verarbeitet müssen daher ein Mittel gegen die Migräne sein. Das hat sich uns in unzähligen Fällen bestätigt.

3. Ein Mittel gegen Tracheitis und Bronchitis. Pyrit

Wir wollen nunmehr ein Mittel besprechen, das sein Dasein der Erkenntnis verdankt, die die Prozesse der Stoffe in die rechte Beziehung bringen kann zu den Prozessen des menschlichen Organismus. Man muß dabei berücksichtigen, daß ein Stoff eigentlich ein zum Stillstand gebrachter Prozeß ist, gewissermaßen ein erstarrter Prozeß. Man müßte eigentlich nicht Pyrit sagen, sondern Pyritprozeß. Dieser Prozeß, der im Mineral Pyrit wie in Erstarrung festgehalten ist, entspricht dem, was aus dem Zusammenwirken des Eisenprozesses und des Schwefelprozesses entstehen kann. Das Eisen regt, wie schon in dem vorigen Abschnitte gezeigt ist, die Blutzirkulation an, der Schwefel vermittelt die Verbindung zwischen Blutzirkulation und Atmung. Gerade da, wo Blutzirkulation und Atmung in ein Verhältnis treten, liegt der Ursprung der Tracheitis und der Bronchitis, sowie auch gewisser Formen des Stotterns. Dieser Prozeß

organization is pushed back, i.e., it becomes more like the peripheral brain than in the normal state, then migraine comes about. Its cure will therefore depend: 1. on a stimulation of nerve-sense activity; 2. on a transformation of rhythmic activity from one that inclines to metabolism, into one that inclines to breathing; 3. on a limiting of purely vital metabolic activity which lacks regulation by the ego organization. The first is achieved by *silicic acid*. Silica in combination with oxygen embodies the processes that are equivalent to those in the organism located at the transition from breathing to nerve-sense activity. The second is achieved by *sulfur*. It embodies that process by which rhythm inclined to the digestive system is transformed to one that inclines to breathing. The third is achieved through *iron*, which transfers the metabolism immediately after the digestive process to the process of the rhythm of the blood, and that suppresses the metabolic process itself. *Iron, sulfur* and *silicic acid* processed in an appropriate way must therefore be a preparation for migraine. We have seen this confirmed in countless cases.

3. A Preparation for Tracheitis and Bronchitis. Pyrite

We now want to discuss a preparation that owes its existence to insight which can connect the processes of substances in the right way to processes in the human organism. One has to keep in mind with this that a substance is in actual fact a process brought to rest, in a certain sense a frozen process. One should actually not say pyrite, but pyrite process. This process, which is captured as if frozen in the mineral pyrite, corresponds to what can come into being when the iron process and the sulfur process work together. Iron, as was shown in the previous section, stimulates the circulation of the blood; sulfur mediates the connection between blood circulation and breathing. Just there, where blood circula-tion and breathing come into relation with each other, lies the origin of tracheitis and bronchitis, as

zwischen Blutzirkulation und Atmung, der zugleich der Prozeß ist, aus dem die entsprechenden Organe im Embryonalleben gebildet werden und im weiteren Leben sich immer wieder erneuern, kann von der dem Körper zugeführten Eisenschwefelsubstanz übernommen werden, wenn er im Organismus nicht normal verläuft. Von dieser Erkenntnis ausgehend bereiten wir aus dem Pyrit ein Heilmittel gegen obige Erkrankungsform, indem wir das Mineral so zum Präparate umgestalten, daß seine Kräfte bei einer innerlichen Indikation den Weg in die erkrankten Organe finden. Man muß natürlich den Weg, den gewisse Substanzprozesse im Organismus nehmen, kennen. Der Eisenprozeß wird von dem Stoffwechsel bis in die Blutzirkulation geführt. Der Schwefelprozeß tritt von der Blutzirkulation in den Atmungsvorgang über.

4. Wirkungen von Antimon-Verbindungen

Das Antimon hat eine außerordentlich starke Verwandtschaft zu andern Körpern, z. B. zum Schwefel. Dadurch zeigt es, daß es in leichter Weise den Weg mitmachen kann, den der Schwefel im Organismus durchläuft, so z. B. den zu allen Atmungsprozessen. Eine weitere Eigenschaft des Antimons ist seine Neigung zu büschelförmiger Kristallbildung. Es zeigt dadurch, daß es leicht gewissen Kräftestrahlungen in der Erdumgebung folgt. Diese Eigenschaft tritt noch mehr hervor, wenn das Antimon dem Seigerprozeß unterworfen wird. Durch ihn wird es feinfaserig. Und noch bedeutsamer kommt das zum Vorschein, wenn das Antimon in den Verbrennungsprozeß übergeführt wird und sein weißer Rauch sich entwickelt. Dieser Rauch legt sich an kalte Körper an und bildet die charakteristischen Antimonblumen. Gerade so, wie das Antimon außer dem menschlichen Organismus den auf dasselbe wirkenden Kräften folgt, so im menschlichen Organismus den formbildenden Kräften. Man hat nun im Blute gewissermaßen den Gleichgewichtszustand zwischen formbildenden und formauflösenden Kräften. Das Antimon kann wegen seiner beschriebenen Eigenschaften die formbildenden Kräfte des menschlichen

well as of certain kinds of stuttering. When this process between blood circulation and breathing, which is at the same time the process out of which in the embryonal period the corresponding organs are formed and out of which they again and again renew themselves in the course of life, is not working normally in the organism, it can be taken over by iron-sulfur substance introduced into the body. Out of this insight we prepare a medication from pyrite for the above disease form, thereby transforming the mineral into a preparation in such a way, that, when indicated, its forces can find their way into the diseased organs. Of course, one has to know the course that certain substance processes take in the organism. The iron process is led from the metabolism right into the blood circulation. The sulfur process makes the step from the blood circulation over into the process of breathing.

4. Effects of Antimony Compounds

Antimony has an extraordinarily strong affinity with other substances, for example with sulfur. It thus shows that it can readily accompany sulfur on the course which the latter takes through the organism, e.g., into all the breathing processes. A further property of antimony is its inclination for sheaflike crystal formations. Here it shows that it readily follows certain force radiations in the earth's environment. This property comes even more to the fore when antimony is subjected to the Seiger process.[33] Through this it becomes filamentous. This manifests even more so when antimony is converted in the process of combustion to a white vapor. This vapor precipitates on cold surfaces and forms the characteristic "flowers of antimony." Just as antimony follows the forces that work upon it when outside the human organism, so within the human organism it follows the form-giving forces. Now, in the blood, one has in a certain sense a state of equilibrium between the form-giving and the form-dissolving forces. On account of its described properties,

Organismus in das Blut überführen, wenn dazu der Weg durch die Verbindung mit dem Schwefel gebahnt wird. Daher sind die Kräfte des Antimons diejenigen, welche in der Gerinnung des Blutes wirken. Geisteswissenschaftlich stellt sich die Sache so heraus, daß der astralische Leib in denjenigen Kräften, die zur Gerinnung des Blutes führen, verstärkt wird. Man muß im astralischen Leibe den Antimonkräften ähnliche Kräfte sehen, die im Organismus von innen nach außen zentrifugal wirken. Diesen antimonisierenden Kräften wirken entgegen die von außen nach innen gerichteten Kräfte, die das Blut verflüssigen und verflüssigtes Blut plastisch in den Dienst der Körperbildung stellen. In der Richtung dieser Kräfte wirken auch diejenigen des Eiweißes. Die im Eiweißprozeß enthaltenen Kräfte verhindern fortdauernd die Gerinnung des Blutes. Man nehme den Fall des Typhus; er beruht auf einem Überwiegen der albuminisierenden Kräfte. Bringt man dem Organismus in feinster Dosierung Antimon bei, so wirkt man den Typhus-bildenden Kräften entgegen. Es ist aber zu berücksichtigen, daß die Wirkung des Antimons eine ganz verschiedene ist, je nachdem, ob man es innerlich oder äußerlich anwendet. Bei einer äußerlichen Anwendung, wie Salben oder dergleichen, schwächt es die zentrifugal wirkenden Kräfte des Astralleibes, die sich z. B. in Ekzembildungen äußern; bei innerlicher Anwendung stellt es sich den zu stark zentripetal wirkenden Kräften, wie sie im Typhus zum Vorschein kommen, entgegen.

Ein wichtiges Heilmittel ist Antimon in allen Erkrankungen, in denen eine gefährliche Herabdämpfung des Bewußtseins (Somnolenz) eintritt. In diesem Falle sind die formenden zentrifugalen Kräfte des Astralleibes und damit die Gehirn- und Sinnesprozesse zum Teil ausgeschaltet. Führt man dem Organismus Antimon zu, so schafft man die fehlenden Astralkräfte künstlicherweise. Man wird immer bemerken, daß die Antimonaufnahme Gedächtnisverstärkung, Hebung der schöpferischen Kräfte der Seele, innere Geschlossenheit der Seelenverfassung

antimony can transfer the form-giving forces of the human organism to the blood, if the way is prepared for this by combining it with sulfur. The forces of antimony are therefore the very forces that work in the coagulation of the blood. To spiritual science it becomes apparent that the astral body is strengthened in those forces that lead to the coagulation of the blood. One must recognize forces in the astral body similar to those of antimony, working from within outward, centrifugally, in the human organism. These antimonizing forces oppose the forces directed from without inward, which liquefy the blood and place the liquefied blood plastically in the service of the formation of the body. Protein forces also work in the same direction. The forces embodied in the protein process continuously prevent the coagulation of the blood. Take the case of typhoid fever; it is based on a preponderance of the albuminizing forces. If antimony is administered to the organism in minutest dosage, then the forces that bring about typhoid fever are counteracted. It must, however, be taken into consideration that the function of antimony is quite different depending on whether it is administered internally or externally. Administered externally in ointments and the like, it weakens the centrifugal forces of the astral body which express themselves, for example, in the formation of eczema; administered internally it counteracts the forces which work too strongly centripetally, as they appear in typhoid fever.

Antimony is an important medicine in all illnesses in which there arises a dangerous diminution of consciousness (somnolence). The formative, centrifugal forces of the astral body, and thus the processes of the brain and senses, are partially disconnected in this case. If one introduces antimony into the organism, then the failing astral forces are created artificially. One will always notice that intake of antimony strengthens the memory, enhances the creative powers of the soul, improves the inner cohesiveness of the soul disposition. The organism is

hervorrufen. Der Organismus wird von der verstärkten Seele aus regeneriert. Das fühlte man in der älteren Medizin. Ihr war daher das Antimon ein Universalmittel. Wenn wir auch nicht auf diesem extremen Standpunkte stehen, so müssen wir doch, wie aus dem Obigen hervorgeht, in dem Antimon ein vielseitiges Heilmittel suchen.

5. Zinnober

Wir konnten in dem Zinnober ein wichtiges Heilmittel finden. Gerade an diesem Stoffe bietet sich Gelegenheit, die viel verteidigte und viel angefochtene Beziehung des Quecksilbers zum menschlichen Organismus zu studieren. Das Quecksilber ist derjenige erstarrte Prozeß, der mitten darinnen steht zwischen den Fortpflanzungsvorgängen, die innerhalb des Organismus dessen Wesen von ihm selber fast völlig absondern. Die Quecksilberkräfte haben nun die Eigentümlichkeit, diese abgesonderten Kräfte wieder zur Resorption im ganzen Organismus zu bringen. Man kann also das Quecksilber (man muß es in feinster Dosierung tun) therapeutisch überall dort anwenden, wo im Organismus sich absondernde Prozesse bilden, die wiederum in die Herrschaft des ganzen Organismus geführt werden sollen. Es sind dies alle katarrhalischen Prozesse. Sie entstehen dadurch, daß durch äußere Einwirkung irgend ein Trakt des Organismus aus der Herrschaft des ganzen Organismus herausgerissen wird. Beim Luftröhrenkatarrh und allen in der Nähe befindlichen katarrhalischen Erscheinungen ist das der Fall. Führt man dahin die Quecksilberkräfte, so wirken sie heilend. Es ist eine schon mehrfach erwähnte Eigenschaft des Schwefels, daß er sich wirksam erweist in dem Gebiete des Organismus, wo Zirkulation und Atmung aneinander grenzen, also bei allem, was von der Lunge ausgeht. Zinnober ist eine Verbindung von Quecksilber und Schwefel; es ist ein wirksames Heilmittel für alles Katarrhalische in den bezeichneten Gebieten des menschlichen Organismus.

regenerated by the strengthened soul. This was felt by earlier medical practitioners. Antimony was therefore a universal preparation for them. Even if we do not take it to such an extreme, still, as follows from the above, we must see in antimony a many-sided medication.

5. Cinnabar

We were able to identify in cinnabar an important medication. An opportunity presents itself, especially in this substance, to study the much defended and much attacked relationship of quicksilver to the human organism. Quicksilver is the frozen process that stands in the midst of reproductive processes which, within the organism, almost entirely separate the organism's being from itself. The forces of quicksilver have the peculiar property that they can bring these separated forces to resorption again into the whole organism. Quicksilver, therefore, (it must be used in minutest quantities) can be used therapeutically wherever processes of separation establish themselves in the organism, processes which need to be brought under the control of the organism as a whole again. These are all the catarrhal processes. They come into existence when one or the other tract of the organism is torn away from the control of the whole organism by some external influence. This is the case with tracheal catarrh and all other catarrhal symptoms in the proximity. If one brings mercury forces there, they have a healing effect. The characteristic property of sulfur, which has been mentioned before, is that sulfur proves its efficacy in the area of the organism where circulation and breathing border on each other, thus with everything that comes from the lung. Cinnabar is a compound of mercury and sulfur; it is an efficacious medication for all catarrhal processes in the indicated areas of the human organism.

6. Das Heuschnupfen-Mittel «Gencydo»

Beim Heuschnupfen haben wir als Krankheits-Symptome entzündliche Erscheinungen der Schleimhäute von Augen, Nase, Rachen und der oberen Luftwege, und die Anamnese bei den an Heufieber leidenden Patienten weist häufig darauf hin, daß auch in der Kindheit Krankheitsprozesse vorgelegen haben, die in das Gebiet der «exsudativen Diathese» gehören. – Wir werden somit auf den Ätherleib und das Verhalten des astralischen Leibes verwiesen. Der Ätherleib überwiegt in seinen Kräften, und der astralische Leib zieht sich zurück, hat die Tendenz, nicht richtig in den ätherischen und physischen Leib einzugreifen. Und die katarrhalischen Erscheinungen sind die Folge davon, daß in den erkrankten Partien die geordnete Einwirkung vom Astralleib – und dadurch auch der Ich-Organisation – gestört ist. Astralischer Leib und Ich-Organisation werden überempfindlich, und erklären sich auf diese Weise auch die krampfartig und anfallsweise auftretenden Reaktionen auf Sinneseindrücke wie Licht, Wärme, Kälte, Staub und ähnliches. – Der Heilungsprozeß muß also dem Astralleib entgegenkommen und ihm zum richtigen Eingreifen in den ätherischen Leib verhelfen. Dies ist möglich durch Anwenden von Fruchtsäften aus Früchten, die lederartige Schalen haben. In solchen Früchten zeigt sich schon die Anschauung, wie gestaltende, von außen nach innen wirkende Kräfte besonders stark tätig sind. Und äußerlich und innerlich angewendet erreicht man mit solchen Säften eine Anregung des Astralleibes in der Richtung nach dem Ätherleib hin; ihr Gehalt an mineralischen Bestandteilen wie z. B. Kalium, Calcium und Kieselsäure bewirkt gleichzeitig eine Unterstützung von seiten der Ich-Organisation (vergl. Kap. XVII), so daß eine wirkliche Heilung des Heufiebers erzielt wird. — Nähere Angaben über die Gebrauchsanweisung werden dem Präparat beigelegt.

6. The Preparation for Hay Fever. "Gencydo"

The pathological symptoms of hay fever are inflammatory phenomena of the mucous membranes of eyes, nose, throat and of the upper respiratory tract. And the history of the patient suffering from hay fever frequently indicates that in childhood, too, there were pathological processes which may be included in the term "exudative diathesis".[34]—Thus we are referred to the ether body and to the way the astral body functions. The forces of the ether body prevail, and the astral body withdraws, having the inclination not to take proper hold of the etheric and physical body. And the catarrhal phenomena result from the fact that in the diseased parts, the orderly influence of the astral body—and therefore also of the ego organization—is disturbed. Astral body and ego organization become hypersensitive and account in this way also for the cramplike and paroxysmal occurrence of reactions to sense impressions like light, heat, cold, dust and similar things.—A healing process must therefore come to meet the astral body and help it to intervene properly in the etheric body. This can be done with the use of juices of fruits that have a leathery rind. In such fruits it becomes visible how form-giving forces that work from without inwards, are active in a particularly strong way. And by giving the juices of such fruits externally and internally, one can stimulate the astral body to be inclined toward the ether body; the mineral content of the juices, e.g., potassium, calcium and silicic acid, at the same time brings about a support from the side of the ego organization (cf. Chapter XVII), so that a real cure of hay fever is realized.— Further indications for directions for use are enclosed with the preparation.

[Die früheren Ausgaben waren von einem Vor- und einem Nachwort aus der Hand von Frau Dr. Wegman begleitet. Sie sind hier wiedergegeben.]

VORWORT ZUR ERSTEN AUFLAGE

Der Lehrer, Führer und Freund, Rudolf Steiner, ist nicht mehr unter den Lebenden. Eine schwere Erkrankung, deren Anfang in einer physischen Erschöpfung lag, raffte ihn hinweg. Mitten aus der Arbeit mußte er sich auf das Ruhelager hinlegen, seine Kräfte, die er in so reichlichem Maße, so uneingeschränkt dem Wirken in der Anthroposophischen Gesellschaft geschenkt hatte, reichten nicht mehr hin, seine Erkrankung zu überwinden. Und alle, die ihn liebten und verehrten, mußten es mit ungeheuerlichem Schmerz erleben, daß der von so vielen geliebte Mensch, er, der so vielen Menschen hat helfen können, bei sich selber das Schicksal hat walten lassen müssen, wohlwissend, daß höhere Gewalten hier lenkten.

Die Frucht geeinter Arbeit wurde in diesem kleinen Buche niedergelegt.

Die Lehre der Anthroposophie, die gerade für die medizinische Wissenschaft eine Goldgrube der Anregungen ist, konnte ich als Arzt restlos gelten lassen und fand in ihr eine Weisheitsquelle, aus der man unermüdlich schöpfen konnte, und die viele, heute noch ungelöste Probleme der Medizin beleuchten und lösen kann. So entstand zwischen Rudolf Steiner und mir eine rege Zusammenarbeit für medizinische Erkenntnisse, die besonders in den letzten zwei Jahren sich vertiefte, so daß das gemeinschaftliche Schreiben eines Buches möglich werden und zustande kommen konnte.

Es war stets das Bestreben Rudolf Steiners – und ich brachte ihm hierin vollstes Verständnis entgegen –, das alte Mysterien-Wesen zu erneuern und in die Medizin einfließen zu lassen. Denn von altersher ist dieses Mysterien-Wesen mit der Heilkunst in engstem Zusammenhang gewesen, und wurde das Erringen geistiger Erkenntnisse mit dem Heilen in Zusammenhang gebracht. Nicht sollte in dilettantisch laienhafter Art die wissenschaftliche Medizin unterschätzt werden; diese wurde voll anerkannt. Es kam aber darauf an, zu dem Bestehenden dasjenige hinzuzufügen, was aus einer wahren Geist-Erkenntnis für das Erfassen der Krankheits- und Heilungsvorgänge erfließen kann. Selbstverständlich sollte nicht die seelisch instinktive Art der alten Mysterien wieder aufle-

[The earlier editions contained a Preface and a Postcript by Ita Wegman. They are here reproduced.]

PREFACE TO THE FIRST EDITION

Our teacher, guide and friend, Rudolf Steiner, is no longer among the living. A severe illness, beginning in physical exhaustion, tore him away. In the very midst of his work he had to lie down and rest. The forces he had given so abundantly, so unstintingly, to the work in the Anthroposophical Society no longer sufficed to overcome his illness. With untold grief and pain, all those who loved and honored him had to witness how he, who was loved by so many, who had been able to help so many others, had to allow destiny to take its appointed course when it came to himself, knowing very well that higher powers were guiding these events.

In this small book the fruits of our joint work were laid down.

As a physician, I could vouch for the teachings of anthroposophy, which are especially for medical science a veritable gold mine of inspiration. I found a fount of wisdom in it from which one can draw unremittingly, and which is able to illumine and solve many a problem in medicine that had as yet been unsolved. Thus there arose between Rudolf Steiner and myself a lively cooperation in the field of medical knowledge and research. Especially in the last two years our cooperation deepened, so that it became feasible jointly to author a book, which we then accomplished. It had always been Rudolf Steiner's endeavor—and in this I could meet him with fullest sympathy and understanding—to renew the essence of the ancient Mysteries and have it flow once more into the field of medicine. For, from time immemorial, the essence of the Mysteries has been most intimately connected to the art of healing, and attainment of spiritual knowledge and perception was brought in relation to healing. However, we did not want to underrate contemporary scientific medicine with the dilettantism of amateurs. We recognized it fully. What mattered was to complement existing science with what can flow from a true knowledge of mind and spirit toward the understanding of the processes of illness and of healing. Of course our purpose was not to

ben, sondern eine solche, die dem vollentwickelten, zum Spirituellen gehobenen, modernen Bewußtsein entspricht.

So wurden die ersten Anfänge gemacht, und hat das von mir gegründete klinisch-therapeutische Institut in Arlesheim die praktischen Unterlagen für die hier dargelegten Theorien gegeben. Und es wurde versucht, denjenigen Wege für die Heilkunst zu zeigen, die in dem hier angedeuteten Sinne nach einer Erweiterung ihrer medizinischen Erkenntnisse Verlangen tragen.

Wir hatten vor, diesem kleinen Buch noch manches aus gemeinsamer Arbeit folgen zu lassen. Leider war dies nicht mehr möglich. Doch habe ich die Absicht, aus den vielen Anregungen und Notizen, die ich besitze, noch einen zweiten, vielleicht auch einen dritten Band folgen zu lassen. – Möge aber dieser erste Band, dessen Manuskript noch drei Tage vor dem Tode Rudolf Steiners von ihm mit Freude und innerer Befriedigung korrigiert wurde, seinen Weg finden bei allen, die suchen aus den Rätseln des Lebens zum Verständnis des Lebens in seiner Herrlichkeit und Größe zu kommen.

Arlesheim-Dornach. September 1925
Dr. med. Ita Wegman

NACHWORT

Soweit liegt heute die Frucht gemeinsamer Arbeit vor und mußte hier, gewiß zu unser aller Schmerz, die Fortführung der Niederschrift ruhen, als die Erkrankung Rudolf Steiners eintrat. Es war unser Plan gewesen, in der Fortsetzung dasjenige zu behandeln, was als irdische und kosmische Kräfte in den Metallen Gold, Silber, Blei, Eisen, Kupfer, Merkur, Zinn wirkt, und auszuführen, wie dieselben in der Heilkunst zu handhaben sind. Auch sollte dargestellt werden, wie man im alten Mysterien-Wesen ein tiefes Verständnis hatte für die Beziehungen der Metalle zu den Planeten und ihre Beziehungen zu den verschiedenen Organen des menschlichen Organismus. Von diesem Wissen zu sprechen, es wieder neu zu begründen, lag die Absicht vor. – Meine Arbeit in der nächsten Zeit wird es nun sein, aus den mir gegebenen Angaben und Notizen den zweiten Teil des Buches in Bälde erscheinen zu lassen.

re-enliven the instinctive way the soul worked in the ancient Mysteries, but to bring a method of research, suited to the fully evolved modern consciousness as it rises to spiritual regions.

Thus the first beginnings of our work were made. The Clinical-Therapeutic Institute in Arlesheim, Switzerland, which I founded, has provided the practical foundation for the theories set forth in this book. And we attempted to show those, who are longing for a broadening of their medical knowledge in the sense here indicated, methods for the art of healing.

We had intended to follow this small volume up with quite a bit more out of our joint work. This, alas, was not possible anymore. However, it is still my intention to publish a second volume and possibly a third from the many notes and indications I have.[35]— As to this first volume, of which the manuscript was corrected with inner joy and satisfaction by Rudolf Steiner only three days before his death, may it find its way to all those striving to come from the riddles of life to an understanding of life in its true splendor and magnificence.

Ita Wegman, M.D.
Arlesheim/Dornach, September 1925

POSTSCRIPT

Thus far the fruit of our common work. At this point, undoubtedly to the sorrow of us all, continuation of the writing had to be suspended when Rudolf Steiner's illness set in. It had been our plan to deal in the sequel with the earthly and cosmic forces active in the metals gold, silver, lead, iron, copper, mercury, tin, and to elaborate on how they are to be used in the art of healing. It was also our intention to present how one had in the ancient Mysteries a deep understanding for the relationship of the metals to the planets and for their relationship to the different organs of the human organism. To speak of this knowledge, to lay the foundations for it again anew, was the intention.—It will be my work in the near future to publish the second part of the book from the indications and notes given to me.[36]

APPENDIX

How did the Medical Book Arise?

M. P. van Deventer

Ita Wegman had the capacity to ask Rudolf Steiner essential questions. So also once, in August 1923, at the Summer School in Penmaenmawr she asked the following question: "Could we not found a Mystery Medicine?" Rudolf Steiner answered: "That *you* are asking the question is very essential." He promised to make a beginning as soon as he returned to Dornach, and in the Fall of 1923 he began, together with her, to write the medical book.

How did they work together? If several contemporary scientists were to publish a book together, each would write his own chapter; this was not Rudolf Steiner's method of working.

In 1934 I once had the opportunity to ask Ita Wegman how this working together really went on. She described the following: Rudolf Steiner communicated to her the results of his investigations. She then had to unite her soul with these results, formulate them in her own thoughts and then write them down in her own words. Her writing then became the basis for the further work on a chapter.

How can one understand that such a co-working was a first step towards a renewal of the Mysteries?

Let us first recall what Rudolf Steiner says in the fourth lecture of *Initiate Consciousness* about the working together of teacher and student in the Mysteries of Ephesus.

It could happen that, at dusk, a student and teacher walked through the wonderful woods which surrounded the temple, and the teacher instructed the student about the activity of Kore-Persephone,—as she immerses herself by way of the eyes into the physical and etheric body—into Pluto's realm. Then, during sleep, the student could experience the deeds of Pluto and Persephone, while the teacher experienced something corresponding, that was more connected with the formative aspects of things.

When they met again at dawn, the teacher could describe, in a conversation about a plant or about a tree, how the forms of the leaves or of the trunk came about—the figurations, which are formed from above downwards. The student would possibly speak about the secrets of chlorophyll, of the plant saps, which spread out in the plant from below upwards, In this way there was a marvelous, mutually complementary exchange.

"This is why in the old days, the student learned from the teacher, the teacher from the student. For one type of revelation was dominated by the spiritual aspects and the other by soul aspects. A conversation moving between these two poles yielded out of human experiencing together in community the highest insights."

In those times this was the method of investigation. Today it is the Saturn path which Rudolf Steiner describes in the last three lectures of the same lecture course.

This path of investigation first directs the gaze upon the same objects that conventional medical science also investigates, namely the human organs. Now, however, not in order to do anatomy in the usual sense, but rather to evolve a "spiritual anatomy." The investigator first creates for himself a clear image of a human organ in order to then ascend to an imaginative comprehension of this organ, and thereby enchants—as Rudolf Steiner expresses it—the Saturn sphere into the imaginative picture. With this one achieves the general spirit-structure of the organ. Then, through a further living oneself into this spirit-structure, the Jupiter sphere is enchanted into it, and it is then revealed how the organ is an earthly image of a divine spiritual being. Thus arises a great, gigantic human being which encompasses the cosmos.

Now these perceptions are ephemeral, arising and rapidly disappearing. In order to hold on to them a cooperative working of several human beings is necessary. Rudolf Steiner used the following formulation: they must be taken hold of with those forces "that arise out of a shared, common striving of human beings...." They must be taken hold of "with forces that human beings bear within themselves from a preceding life on earth..." About the Saturn path in general he said: it is a path, "on which there must arise awareness that it finds its support, its strength, in the development of human karmic forces, not

so much to receive memories, but to hold on to them so that they can be described."

For then the Mars sphere enters into the Saturn and Jupiter spheres. "From there on things begin to speak, become manifest through inspiration. And then one comes back to the Sun with the inspired consciousness."

In the context of these comments Rudolf Steiner points several times to the medical book that he is writing together with Ita Wegman.

In this brief sketch of the Saturn path we can find the background for the cooperative work on the medical book, as it was described earlier.

What arose in Ephesus out of the illuminated sleep-consciousness, must today be investigated with day-consciousness extended by imagination and inspiration.

We see at the same time what far-reaching consequences arose out of the question for the new Mysteries: for the first time the Saturn path can be traversed, and a book comes about that—according to Rudolf Steiner—will once provide the basis for *the* medical science.

A New Mystery Book

(From Chapter II of *Medicine and Mysteries* by Walter Holtzapfel, Mercury Press 1994)

Rudolf Steiner's last book, entitled *Fundamentals of Therapy*, is the only one he co-authored. A certain karmic constellation made it possible for him to work with Dr. Ita Wegman. True enough, Rudolf Steiner had cooperated with other important physicians before. It was his expectation that after he had given a number of indications, they would contribute medical publications. He did not think this would happen in the case of Ita Wegman, who was not a person of words but of deeds. However, he was able to write the book with her.

The longer we work with it, the more we realize this is a unique publication: it provides not only information but also a specific training.

A book that reveals new possibilities to acquire medical knowledge and skills bears a professional mark. It also takes a unique position within Rudolf Steiner's entire life work; for in spite of the fact that in conversations, courses, and lectures he gave numerous indications for many professions, including medicine, he wrote a book only for physicians.

It was certainly meant to be read by the public. Everybody has access to it. However, readers will soon perceive that, in spite of the clear and refined style, they continue to come upon baffling passages. What they encounter is in fact the first aspect of training for medical work, the daily practice of which puts ever new riddles across our way, questions we cannot always solve right away. Yet by struggling with problems, the physician grows.

We can tell from the way in which the book was written that it was not only intended to teach and to pass on prescriptions but above all to provide a means of practicing medical abilities.

These thoughts of Rudolf Steiner, which were from the beginning intended to be printed as a book, are of a nature quite different from the numerous lectures and courses he gave, which were usually recorded and later printed. The words he uttered in his talks were partly shaped at that time by the inner needs of the audiences, whereas his written words were affected by anthroposophy as such. This explains that such a book contains more than the words themselves initially can convey.

Rudolf Steiner went as far as saying that there was really no need for him to give his lectures because those who read his basic books intensively enough could work out for themselves the ideas he developed in his talks.

This statement of his means that we should not only take in the ideas we read but also work on them so that something can come alive that did not exist before. Sure enough, this is asking a lot of the reader. However, the way that the book was written makes this approach possible.

This slim volume of medical indications contains more than many compendia. Our first impression is that it describes only a few case histories, especially in the area of metabolic disorders. Then we discover, however, that every chapter, sometimes even a single sentence, opens a window that allows us to perceive an aspect of medical reality.

Let us focus upon a few such core sentences and listen to their characteristic quality:

"It is of the very greatest importance for us to realize that the normal forces of thinking are refined forces of growth and formation." (*Chapter 1*)

"Wherever in the human being the spirit is to be active, there substance must withdraw from its activity." (*Chapter 1*)

"Our entire human organism is not an independent system of interacting processes." (*Chapter 7*)

"Wherever there is sugar, there is the ego organization." (*Chapter 7*)

"The essential nature of our organism lies in its activities, not its substances." (*Chapter 18*)

What sentences these are! In their succinctness they express concentrated thought that can be expanded into comprehensive overviews.

....

Rudolf Steiner emphasized that this work, published only after his death, meant the beginning of modern initiate medicine. He had for previous years been giving medical indications and detailed esoteric instructions to physicians. Why then did he speak of a beginning at this point? What he meant was medicine as such could become a path of initiation. Like the other basic books of his, this one also contains a description of the cognitive approach proper which moves through the stages of imagination, inspiration, and intuition. In the other works this description used to come toward the end of his writing and he explained why this was so. Here, however, it occurs in the first chapter. *Fundamentals of Therapy* begins where the other books leave off. Normally the organic sequence would be to describe first the cognitive path, then the process of walking it and finally the acquisition of individual inner experiences. However, illnesses such as the ones mentioned in this book, are physical images of spiritual conditions.

Through their contacts with illnesses, physicians are placed in the center of spiritual activities. They do not generally realize this fact. Once they become aware of it, however, medicine can become their path toward initiation.

This book can help in such a striving, because it is down to earth and at the same time filled with mysteries. It is of an esoteric nature, not because it is restricted to a few, but because it reveals its profound contents only to those who strive intensively. Thus it unites complete openness with effective esotericism.

In the person of Ita Wegman, Rudolf Steiner had met someone gifted with the greatest understanding for modern initiate medicine. Without her, this book would not have come about. The Clinical Institute she founded and which now bears her name provided the practical basis for her indications. Once readers deal with the ideas contained in the book, they can enter a dialogue with the two authors in which both practical and scientific problems can ever be newly formulated.

In our time a lot of people stress the fact that medical knowledge is of transitory value and has a half-life of only ten years. However, if the new results of medical research are constantly related to the structure of *Fundamentals of Therapy*, physicians can take the present knowledge into the centuries to come.

Rudolf Steiner's and Ita Wegman's work is a new mystery text in several respects. It focuses on problems the solving of which helps physicians sharpen their understanding; it contains core sentences which throw light upon vast regions of medicine; the structuring of certain chapters allows ancient mystery processes to take on new life; it enables physicians to experience and to understand the spiritual significance of what they learn from their contacts with patients; and, last but not least, it opens a door for them to enter into a dialogue with the two authors.

NOTES

1. The German *in sich* could be translated as *in itself*, referring to the thinking, or also as *in himself*, referring to the human being.

2. Published in English by Anthroposophic Press, New York and Rudolf Steiner Press, London.

3. The German word *bildsam* signifies both the possibility to form as well as to be formed.

4. The German *in ihm* could refer to *the human being*, or to *the human being as a whole*, or to *any single organ*.

5. Emil Du Bois-Reymond, physiologist in Berlin, lived from 1818-1896. The quoted passage can be found in a lecture that was published as: "Über die Grenzen des Naturerkennens. Ein Vortrag in der zweiten öffentlichen Sitzung der 45. Versammlung deutscher Naturforscher und Ärzte zu Leipzig am 14. August 1872" (Beyond the boundaries of knowledge of nature. A lecture at the second public meeting of the 45th congress of German scientists and physicians in Leipzig on August 14, 1872), Leipzig 1872, page 25-27.

6. At the time of the writing of this book the vegetative nervous system was known as the sympathetic nervous system.

7. See note 4.

8. The German *ohne diese* could refer to *the strengthening* or to *the ego organization*.

9. In the Seiger process antimony ore with less than 90% Sb_2S_3 is heated to 600° C (the melting point of antimonite is at 546° C) in order to rid it of its impurities (quartz, calcite, barytes and deads). In the process the antimonite is melted out from the ore, which has been reduced to 1-4 cm small pieces. It drops from the deads like sealing-wax on a sloping base and is collected in containers. This kind of antimony sulfide was formerly called crude antimony.

One can further roast the crude antimony and treat it with reducing agents to get to pure antimony, the so-called *Regulus*. When the solidified antimony, the solidified *Regulus*, is cooled down under specific conditions, then the surface shows a fern-like crystalline structure, the so-called antimony star.

10. Rudolf Steiner has spoken about the foundation of curative eurythmy in a course, held from April 12-18, 1921. It is published in English under the title *Curative Eurythmy* by Rudolf Steiner Press, London 1983.

11. In addition to many brief introductions, two eurythmy courses were held by Rudolf Steiner. They were published in English under the titles *Eurythmy as Visible Speech,* Rudolf Steiner Press, London 1984; and *Eurythmy as Visible Music,* Rudolf Steiner Press, London 1977; the last book was also published in a new translation as *Eurythmy as Visible Singing,* Anderida Music Trust in cooperation with Robinswood Press, Stourbridge, England 1996.

12. The Clinical-Therapeutic Institute in Arlesheim, Switzerland, is now also called the Ita Wegman Clinic.

13. In addition to the Clinical-Therapeutic Institute in Arlesheim, Switzerland (see note 13), there was one in Stuttgart, Germany, which is now also a county hospital: "The Filder Clinic."

15. Also described in Hilma Walter: *Abnormitäten der geistig-seelischen Entwicklung*, case history 44. Natura Verlag, Arlesheim, Switzerland, 1987. English translation in preparation by Mercury Press.

15. Plumbum D10

17. Also described in Hilma Walter: *Abnormitäten der geistig-seelischen Entwicklung*, case history 88. Natura Verlag, Arlesheim, Switzerland, 1987.

17. Levico D4 or D5

18. Phosphorus D4

19. Also described in Hilma Walter: *Die Metalle*, case history 61. Natura Verlag, Arlesheim, Switzerland, 1966. English translation in preparation by Mercury Press.

20. At the time that this book was written the expression *catarrh* was used when swelling and exudate of the mucous membranes were present. Now we mostly use the expression "cold" for this, or we give the symptoms the name of an "-itis". What used to be called catarrh of the

sinuses, for instance, we now call sinusitis. The difference is that the word *catarrh* describes symptoms, and the expressions *cold* and *-itis* point to a presupposed viral or bacterial cause of the disease. Therefore the use of the word catarrh has been kept in the translation.

21. Honeyclover essence

22. Melilotus 3 parts with burdock root 4 parts

23. Kalium sulfate D5/Kalium carbonate D5/Teucrium scordium D5

24. Also described in Hilma Walter: *Abnormitäten der geistig-seelischen Entwicklung*, case history 98. Natura Verlag, Arlesheim, Switzerland, 1987; and *Die Pflanzenwelt*, case histories 155, 156, (mother and aunt respectively), Natura Verlag, Arlesheim, Switzerland, 1971. (English translation by Mercury Press pending.)

25. Therapeutic eurythmy exercises recommended by Rudolf Steiner were: SMA, LMI, TMU

27. See Hilma Walter's case history for details: three days baths with Solidago, four days Stellaria backrubs.

27 Stannum D5 p.o. every third day.

28 Papaver somniferum D10

29 Also described in Hilma Walter: *Die Metalle*, case history 60. Natura Verlag, Arlesheim, Switzerland, 1966.

30 Cuprum D3

31 Pancreas D6 s.c. injections.

32 Argentum D30

33. For the liquation of antimonite ore see note 10.

34. *Exudative diathesis* is a term that was common usage in the time this book was written and signifies the body's readiness to create exudates.

35. See note 1.

36. Only the present volume was published.